Peace and Prosperity through World Trade

T0328790

The International Chamber of Commerce (ICC) was created in 1919 by business leaders who described themselves as 'merchants of peace' and whose motto was 'world peace through world trade'. Since then a number of initiatives, including the founding of the World Trade Organization (WTO) in 1995, have provided the proper regulatory conditions for a dramatic increase in world trade. This has generated unprecedented growth and allowed many countries to enjoy great gains in wealth and welfare. Yet despite these gains we are still far from achieving the ICC's goal of world peace through world trade. This book provides a broad overview of the forces that shape international trade and global interdependence, showing business leaders and entrepreneurs how we can address the shortcomings of the multilateral trading system. Most importantly, it shows how we can turn international trade into one of the key global instruments to achieve peace and prosperity in the twenty-first century.

FABRICE LEHMANN is Research Associate and Chief Editor with the Evian Group at IMD, Lausanne. In this capacity, he has drafted numerous reports for a global audience on the ongoing Doha Round of trade negotiations at the WTO, as well as the United Nations Framework Convention on Climate Change (UNFCCC) negotiations, with special attention to the linkages between these negotiations.

JEAN-PIERRE LEHMANN is Professor of International Political Economy and Founding Director of the Evian Group at IMD, Lausanne. Following an academic and consulting career primarily in Asia and Europe, he founded the Evian Group in 1995 and joined IMD in 1997. He frequently participates in global policy forums and is a compulsive writer of articles and briefs on numerous issues related to international economic and political affairs and global governance.

Peace and Prosperity through World Trade

FABRICE LEHMANN
JEAN-PIERRE LEHMANN

CAMBRIDGE
UNIVERSITY PRESS

CAMBRIDGE UNIVERSITY PRESS
Cambridge, New York, Melbourne, Madrid, Cape Town,
Singapore, São Paulo, Delhi, Tokyo, Mexico City

Cambridge University Press
The Edinburgh Building, Cambridge CB2 8RU, UK

Published in the United States of America by
Cambridge University Press, New York

www.cambridge.org
Information on this title: www.cambridge.org/9780521169004

© The Evian Group 2010

First published 2010

A catalogue record for this publication is available from the British Library

Library of Congress cataloguing in publication data
Peace and prosperity through world trade / [edited by] Fabrice Lehmann,
   Jean-Pierre Lehmann.
      p. cm.
   Includes bibliographical references and index.
   ISBN 978-1-107-00042-1 (hardback) – ISBN 978-0-521-16900-4 (pbk.)
   1. International trade.   2. International relations.   3. Peace.
   4. Economic development.   I. Lehmann, Fabrice.   II. Lehmann,
   Jean-Pierre, 1945–
   HF1379.P43 2010
   382–dc22
   2010033022

ISBN 978-1-107-00042-1 Hardback
ISBN 978-0-521-16900-4 Paperback

INTERNATIONAL CHAMBER OF COMMERCE

This volume was commissioned by the ICC Research Foundation to mark the ninetieth anniversary in 2009 of the founding of the ICC.

Contents

Notes on contributors   *page* xii

Foreword   xvii
PETER D. SUTHERLAND

Preface: the ICC vision   xxi
VICTOR FUNG

Historical overview and dynamics   xxvii
JEAN-PIERRE LEHMANN

Editorial note   xxxiii

A   Global systemic transformations   1

Editorial introduction   3

A1   Trade in the new Asian hemisphere   5
      KISHORE MAHBUBANI

A2   US allegiance to the multilateral trading system:
      from ambivalence to shared leadership   9
      JAMES BACCHUS

A3   Trade for development: the case of China   13
      GANG FAN

A4   Trade in the USA–China relationship   17
      EDWARD GRESSER

A5   Unravelling India and strengthening external
      engagement for sustainable growth   22
      RAJU KANORIA

A6   Japan's contribution to an open trading system   27
      SHUJIRO URATA

A7   Rebalancing Korean trade policy: from bilateral
      to multilateral free trade   32
      SOOGIL YOUNG

A8   Vietnam: a rising Asian tiger?   36
      NATASHA HANSHAW

A9   The European compact on trade still stands   41
      FREDRIK ERIXON

A10   Synergies with the Russian Federation   45
      FABRICE LEHMANN

A11   Reasons for an optimistic future view of trade
      and Latin America   51
      FÉLIX PEÑA

A12   Is the Brazilian giant finally awakening?   55
      UMBERTO CELLI

A13   The Arab region and the GCC in tomorrow's trade   59
      ABDULAZIZ SAGER

A14   Growing African trade amid global economic turmoil   64
      MILLS SOKO

B   Governance of global trade   69

      Editorial introduction   71

B1   Securing the global trade regime: the demand
      for global governance   73
      RICHARD HIGGOTT

B2   The trade regime and the future of the WTO   78
      PATRICK MESSERLIN

B3   WTO reform: the time to start is now   83
      URI DADUSH

B4   'Murky protectionism' and the WTO   89
      SIMON EVENETT

B5   Preferential trade agreements: imagining a world
      with less discrimination   93
      ELISA GAMBERONI AND RICHARD NEWFARMER

B6   The G-20 after the Great Recession: rebalancing trade   101
BRUCE STOKES

B7   The missing piece: global imbalances and the
exchange rate regime   105
PAOLA SUBACCHI

B8   Trading knowledge fairly: intellectual property rules
for global prosperity and environmental sustainability   109
CAROLYN DEERE-BIRKBECK

B9   Trade and subsidies: undermining the trading system
with public funds   114
MARK HALLE

B10   Trading labour: a dilemma for migration regimes   119
PRADEEP S. MEHTA

C   Poverty and global inequities   123

Editorial introduction   125

C1   Trade and poverty: an old debate rekindled   127
CARLOS A. PRIMO BRAGA

C2   Trade policy as an instrument of social justice   133
VEENA JHA

C3   Trade, employment and global responsibilities   138
MARION JANSEN

C4   Misconceptions about the WTO, trade,
development and aid   144
FAIZEL ISMAIL

C5   Two hundred years after Jefferson   149
IQBAL QUADIR

C6   Trade, coercive forces and national governance   153
FRANKLIN CUDJOE

C7   Gender equality in trade   158
HAIFA FAHOUM AL KAYLANI

C8   Trading health for comfort   164
BRIGHT B. SIMONS

C9   Unlocking entrepreneurial potential   168
      KAREN WILSON

C10   Trade and security: a vital link to sustainable
      development in a troubled world   175
      TALAAT ABDEL-MALEK

      D   The long view on interlocking crises   181

      Editorial introduction   183

D1   Trade and sustainable development: the ends
      must shape the means   185
      RICARDO MELÉNDEZ-ORTIZ

D2   Trade and climate change: the linkage   191
      DOAA ABDEL-MOTAAL

D3   Destructive trade winds: trade, consumption
      and resource constraints   195
      CHANDRAN NAIR

D4   Trade and energy: a new clean energy deal   201
      ALEXANDER VAN DE PUTTE

D5   Agriculture and international trade   207
      MANZOOR AHMAD

D6   Water scarcity: how trade can make a difference   211
      HERBERT OBERHÄNSLI

D7   Water resources: a national security issue for the
      Middle East   216
      NIDAL SALIM AND NINA NINKOVIC

D8   Trade, technology transfer and institutional catch-up   222
      MARC LAPERROUZA

D9   A frail reed: the geopolitics of climate change   227
      CHO-OON KHONG

      E   Global business responsibilities   233

      Editorial introduction   235

E1   Responsible leadership   237
      JOHN WELLS

E2   For great leadership   242
     SURENDRA MUNSHI

E3   A lesson on trade, regulation and competition policy?   245
     ARTHUR E. APPLETON

E4   International trade and business ethics   249
     STEWART HAMILTON

E5   Who's driving twenty-first century innovation?
     Who should?   253
     BILL FISCHER

E6   Responsible sourcing   259
     MARTIN WASSELL

E7   Trade, international capital flows and
     risk management   264
     THIERRY MALLERET

E8   Trade, corporate strategies and development   268
     MICHAEL GARRETT

E9   How can trade lead to inclusive growth?   273
     RAVI CHAUDHRY

E10 Trade and human rights: friends or foes?   279
     CÉLINE CHARVÉRIAT AND ROMAIN BENICCHIO

E11 Trade: the spirit and rule of law   284
     VALÉRIE ENGAMMARE

Conclusion: the imperative of inclusive global growth   289
VICTOR FUNG

Index   293

Contributors

Editors

FABRICE LEHMANN is Research Associate and Editor with the Evian Group at IMD, Switzerland.

JEAN-PIERRE LEHMANN is Professor of International Political Economy at IMD and Founding Director of the Evian Group, Switzerland.

Contributors

VICTOR FUNG is Emeritus Chairman of the International Chamber of Commerce (ICC), Chairman of the Board of Trustees of the ICC Research Foundation and Chairman of the Li & Fung Group of companies. He is also co-Chairman of the Evian Group.

PETER D. SUTHERLAND was the founding Director-General of the WTO, Chairman of the London School of Economics, Chairman of the Advisory Council of the ICC Research Foundation and Chairman of Goldman Sachs International.

Illustrator

FRANÇOIS OLISLAEGER works regularly with the French press, including *Le Monde*, *Libération* and *Les Inrockuptibles*, and is the author of cartoon albums published by Denoël and Hachette.

Authors

TALAAT ABDEL-MALEK is Professor of Economics at the American University in Cairo and Economic Adviser to the Minister of International Cooperation, Egypt.

DOAA ABDEL-MOTAAL is Counsellor on agricultural and environmental issues in the Cabinet of WTO Director-General, Geneva.

MANZOOR AHMAD served as Director of the FAO Liaison Office with the United Nations, Geneva, and previously served as Pakistan's Ambassador and Permanent Representative to the WTO.

HAIFA FAHOUM AL KAYLANI is founder and Chairperson, Arab International Women's Forum, London.

ARTHUR E. APPLETON is a Partner in the Geneva office of Appleton Luff – International Lawyers, and teaches at the World Trade Institute, University of Bern.

JAMES BACCHUS is a former Chairman of the Appellate Body of the WTO and a former Member of the Congress of the United States.

ROMAIN BENICCHIO works for Oxfam International as a policy and media advisor working on trade, access to medicines and climate change.

CARLOS A. PRIMO BRAGA is Director, Economic Policy and Debt Department, the World Bank.

UMBERTO CELLI is Professor of International Trade Law at the University of São Paulo, Brazil.

CÉLINE CHARVÉRIAT is Deputy Advocacy and Campaigns Director of Oxfam International.

RAVI CHAUDHRY is the Founder Chairman of CeNext Consulting Group, based in New Delhi, and was previously CEO/Chairman of five companies in the Tata Group.

FRANKLIN CUDJOE is Founding Director of IMANI Center for Policy & Education, a Ghanaian think tank.

URI DADUSH is Senior Associate and Director at the Carnegie Endowment's new International Economics Program, Washington.

CAROLYN DEERE-BIRKBECK is Director of the Global Trade Governance Project at the University of Oxford's Global Economic Governance Programme.

VALÉRIE ENGAMARRE is Advisor at the international economic law section of the Swiss State Secretariat for Economic Affairs and was Associate Fellow at the Evian Group.

FREDRIK ERIXON is a Director and co-founder of the European Centre for International Political Economy (ECIPE), Brussels.

SIMON EVENETT is Professor of International Trade and Economic Development at the University of St Gallen, Switzerland.

BILL FISCHER is Professor of Technology and Management at IMD, Switzerland.

GANG FAN is Professor of Economics at Peking University's HSBC Business School and Director of National Economic Research Institute, China Reform Foundation.

ELISA GAMBERONI is an Economist with the World Bank.

MICHAEL GARRETT is Co-chairman of the Evian Group and was previously Executive Vice President of Nestlé Group responsible for Asia, Africa, Middle East and Oceania.

EDWARD GRESSER is Director of the Trade and Global Markets Project at the Democratic Leadership Council, United States.

MARK HALLE is Executive Director of the International Institute for Sustainable Development, Geneva.

STEWART HAMILTON is Professor of Accounting and Finance at IMD, Switzerland, and Dean of Finance and Administration.

NATASHA HANSHAW works as a consultant on USAID projects in economic governance, San Diego.

RICHARD HIGGOTT is Professor of International Political Economy and Pro Vice Chancellor at the University of Warwick.

FAIZEL ISMAIL is the Head of the South African Delegation to the WTO in Geneva.

MARION JANSEN is a Senior Specialist on trade and employment in the Employment Sector of the International Labour Office, Switzerland.

VEENA JHA is a visiting professorial Fellow at the University of Warwick and a Research Fellow at IDRC, Canada.

RAJU KANORIA is Chairman and Managing Director of Kanoria Chemicals & Industries Limited and immediate past President of ICC India.

CHO-OON KHONG is Chief Political Analyst in the Global Business Environment team, Shell International.

MARC LAPERROUZA is Senior Advisor to the Evian Group and Senior Research Associate, Swiss Federal Institute of Technology.

KISHORE MAHBUBANI is Dean of the Lee Kuan Yew School of Public Policy, National University of Singapore.

THIERRY MALLERET is a Senior Partner and Head of Research and Networks at IJ Partners, an investment company based in Geneva.

PRADEEP S. MEHTA is the Secretary General of CUTS International, India.

RICARDO MELÉNDEZ-ORTIZ is the co-founder and Chief Executive of the International Centre for Trade and Sustainable Development (ICTSD), Switzerland.

PATRICK MESSERLIN is Professor of Economics and Director of Groupe d'Economie Mondiale at Sciences Po (GEM), Paris.

SURENDRA MUNSHI is a Fellow of the Bertelsmann Stiftung and retired Professor of Sociology at the Indian Institute of Management Calcutta, India.

CHANDRAN NAIR is founder and Chief Executive of the Global Institute For Tomorrow (GIFT), an independent social venture think tank based in Hong Kong.

RICHARD NEWFARMER is the World Bank Special Representative to the WTO and United Nations.

NINA NINKOVIC is from the Geneva School of Diplomacy and International Relations, University Institute, Switzerland.

HERBERT OBERHÄNSLI is Assistant Vice President/Head Economics and International Relations Nestlé SA and Assistant for Economic Affairs to the Chairman of Nestlé Group.

FÉLIX PEÑA is Director of the Institute of International Trade of the Standard Bank Foundation and of the Jean Monet Module and

Interdisciplinary Center of International Studies at Tres de Febrero National University, Argentina.

IQBAL QUADIR is the founder and Director of the Legatum Center for Development and Entrepreneurship at MIT and the founder of Grameenphone in Bangladesh.

ABDULAZIZ SAGER is Chairman and founder of the Gulf Research Center, Dubai.

NIDAL SALIM is Director and founder of Global Institute for Water Environment and Health (GIWEH), Geneva, and has worked as a Director at the Palestinian Water Authority.

BRIGHT B. SIMONS is an entrepreneur and Director at the Ghanaian think tank IMANI Centre for Policy & Education.

MILLS SOKO is an Associate Professor at the University of Cape Town's Graduate School of Business, and the Founding Director of Mthente Research and Consulting Services, South Africa.

BRUCE STOKES is the international economics columnist for the *National Journal* and a Transatlantic Fellow at the German Marshall Fund, United States.

PAOLA SUBACCHI is Director of International Economic Research at Chatham House (Royal Institute of International Affairs), London.

SHUJIRO URATA is Professor of Economics at Waseda University in Tokyo.

ALEXANDER VAN DE PUTTE is Senior Director and Head of Scenario Processes & Applications at PFC Energy International, United States.

MARTIN WASSELL is First Director of the ICC, having previously served as Economic Director.

JOHN WELLS served as President of IMD, Switzerland.

KAREN WILSON is founder, GV Partners and Senior Fellow at the Kauffman Foundation, United States.

SOOGIL YOUNG is President of the National Strategy Institute (NSI) in Korea.

Foreword

PETER D. SUTHERLAND

This thought-provoking collection of essays, looking at the prospects and challenges for the next decade, could hardly be more timely. As 2009 drew to a close, the scale of the collapse in world trade in that year was alarming.

It is rare for the value of global trade to decline at all. Yet in the first half of 2009, it was a third lower than in the same period the previous year. There has been nothing like this since the Great Depression of the 1930s, when the downward spiral of trade contributed to the political instability of that decade.

Historical parallels are not exact, and there are features of the modern global economy which help explain the sensitivity of international trade to recession. However, it is important not to forget the inevitable links between what happens in the economic and political spheres. This is after all what motivates the mission of the ICC to act as the 'merchant of peace through world trade'.

There are two characteristics of the world economy of today which have made the recent collapse in trade flows so severe.

The first is the way supply chains in many sectors now operate across national borders. Not only high-technology products such as mobile phones but even shoes and clothing are manufactured in a global network. The consequent trade in intermediate goods used to make final products means that a drop in consumer demand translates into a much bigger decline in world trade flows compared with the past.

The second feature is the increased synchronization of major economies, compared with previous recessions. The decline in trade in each country has amplified the declines elsewhere.

These features do mean that trade should bounce back quickly once the economic recovery is under way. But this is not something to be complacent about. A resumption of healthy trade growth, with its beneficial impact on growth, jobs and incomes, is at risk from protectionism.

This is where the interplay with politics is likely to be decisive. On the one hand, the extensive interconnectedness of the world economy makes it unlikely that there will be anything like a repetition of the catastrophe of the 1930s. It is hard to believe that even the most populist government would want to destroy the supply chains which have helped their own businesses become more productive and given consumers everywhere wider choice and lower prices.

On the other hand, the severity of the recession resulting from the financial crisis has tempted many governments to announce measures which are either directly protectionist or indirectly so. From the 'Buy American' provisions in the US fiscal stimulus package to the tariff increases implemented or announced by several countries, these have taken a range of shapes. Unfortunately, the effects are the same. The growing number of measures – especially those introduced by major trading countries such as the USA – will make it harder for trade volumes to recover quickly.

So there is a clear challenge of political leadership in the next decade. It is vital for politicians and business executives alike to avoid the illusory attractions of flag-waving, which only ever delivers short-term benefits to a minority of firms and workers.

There is also a challenge for business leadership. One of the consequences of the financial crisis and recession is widespread scepticism about the benefits of markets and globalization. The fact that much of what has been said and written in this vein is either exaggerated or plain incoherent is no excuse for ignoring the need to ensure that the benefits of trade are widely shared. Business leaders must engage in trying to find growth paths which are sustainable – environmentally, politically and socially. This debate began well before the recent crisis, and many businesses have been actively engaged in it; but the need to tackle the difficult issues it raises is acute.

All of these subjects, from the global balance of economic power to appropriate governance structures for world trade, from environmental sustainability to social inclusivity, are addressed in the contributions in this volume. The contributors offer stimulating and sometimes provocative views about what the next decade will bring. As we move towards the hundredth anniversary of the ICC in 2019, we should remember that business is one of the most influential forces for change in the world, a responsibility to be taken more seriously then ever in the light of the recent challenges.

Preface: the ICC vision

VICTOR FUNG

In 1919, in the wake of World War I, a group of business leaders from Belgium, Italy, France, the UK and the USA, met in Atlantic City, New Jersey, to found the International Chamber of Commerce (ICC). They identified themselves as 'merchants of peace' and adopted the motto 'world peace through world trade'. The following year, under the aegis of the French statesman and entrepreneur Etienne Clémentel, the ICC established its headquarters in Paris, where it has remained ever since. The ICC mission from its inception was to champion an open global economy as a force for economic growth, job creation and prosperity. These three elements, reasonably distributed, are the fundamental ingredients for peace.

In the tenth year of the ICC, in 1929, the Great Depression occurred and in the twentieth year, 1939, World War II broke out. In the intervening decade the global economy contracted dramatically as countries engaged in trade wars and unemployment soared. Though the causes of World War II are obviously multiple and complex, there can be no doubt that the breakdown of trade and the surging protectionism that ensued were important causal factors.

On the thirtieth anniversary of the ICC, in 1949, the world economy seemed to be back on track. Following the first round in Geneva in 1947 that formally established the GATT (General Agreement for Tariffs and Trade), a second round was launched in the French city of Annecy, which proceeded to expand membership and reduce tariffs. The ICC vision was re-enforced by the establishment of a rules-based multilateral trading regime, to which it has remained completely committed throughout the ensuing decades.

One of the most remarkable achievements of the post World War II world has been the exponential increase in trade. This not only brought great prosperity to the 'familiar' actors in world trade – North America, Western Europe, Japan, Australia and New Zealand – but also in the course of the 1970s there emerged the 'newly industrializing-economies'

(Hong Kong, Korea, Singapore and Taiwan), whose industrialization was driven considerably by trade.

These forty years witnessed numerous violations of key GATT principles – mainly that of non-discrimination – and the application of new forms of protectionism. For example, in the mid/late 1980s the USA and the EU imposed on Japan 'voluntary export restraints' (VERs) in various sectors including automobiles and semiconductors.

Fundamentally, however, the system worked and many parts of the world that included GATT members prospered.

In 1989, the seventieth anniversary of the ICC, the destruction of the Berlin Wall heralded the emergence of an open global market economy that seemed indeed to correspond perfectly to the ICC founding vision of 'world peace through world trade'. The Cold War ended and markets opened virtually everywhere. With the conclusion of the Uruguay Round in 1994 the World Trade Organization (WTO) was formerly established on 1 January 1995. In the ensuing decade-and-a-half, the membership of the WTO has expanded enormously, notably with the accession of China in 2001, with the result that today only a very small minority of countries are neither members nor countries seeking accession. On that basis the World Trade Organization is truly the *World* Trade Organization. Furthermore, in addition to the traditional GATT negotiating function, the WTO has a Dispute Settlement Unit that has significantly increased its aura and its clout as not only a rules-making body, but also a rules-enforcing body. In the course of the decade 1989 to 1999 it seemed as though globalization had embarked on an 'irreversible' course.

1999–2009: a decade of high growth and lost opportunities

In the ninetieth year of the founding of ICC, 2009, talk of globalization being 'irreversible' had ceased, while the term 'de-globalization' increasingly became current in describing possible future scenarios.

In fact, it has been a paradoxical period. On the one hand, until the global recession of 2008–2009, the world economy and especially world trade experienced exponential growth, while the membership of the WTO continued to increase, with new members such as not only China, but also Vietnam, Saudi Arabia and Ukraine. On the other hand, the world trade policy process and agenda have badly stalled. The attempt to launch a new Round in Seattle in 1999 ended in an unqualified fiasco. A Round was launched in Doha two years later, in December 2001, though the impetus for this came mainly from the initial aftershocks of the 9/11 cataclysm. At the following WTO ministerial meeting, in Cancún in 2003, it was clear that there were deep entrenched problems of multilateral trade policy immobilism.

It is not the purpose here to analyse the causes for the paralysis in the Doha Round talks that have seen several years of procrastination and repeated breakdowns. There are clearly, however, four major elements that are actively playing an influentially negative role.

The first is that this period has witnessed unprecedented change in the nature and structure of the global economy. The major dynamic has been the tremendous surge of the emerging economies in the global market. There has been a clear problem on the part especially of the established global powers – the EU, USA and Japan – to adjust to this new world; but problems of adjustments also apply to some of the major emerging economies.

The second is that the problem of adjustment has been compounded by an absence of vision and direction on the part of the political leaders. It has been repeatedly and rightly said that the Doha Round is unlikely to be concluded without political leadership. With the last WTO ministerial meeting (at the time of writing) having been held in Geneva in November 2009, it is clear that political leadership remains conspicuous by its absence.

The third is that there is an element of institutional sclerosis. The WTO is badly in need of reform, especially with respect to the decision-making process. There would appear, however, to be a Catch-22 situation in that without reform the WTO Doha Round may be impeded from reaching conclusion, yet conclusion of the Doha Round may be needed to bring about reform.

The fourth is the most fundamental and the most elusive. What is notably lacking in the international community today is trust. It was repeatedly said that if the global community could not cooperate on the trade agenda – which is relatively straightforward – it seemed improbable that it would succeed in cooperating on far more complex challenges, notably climate change. The outcome of the Copenhagen Climate Change Conference in December 2009 has unfortunately proved this assumption to be correct.

The decade that seemed to be marked by unprecedented growth and optimism came to an end with the worst economic crisis the world has seen since the 1930s. Instead of creating wealth, the decade ended with its significant destruction.

From the trade perspective, while it is highly disappointing that the trade policy agenda remains mired in paralysis, the great relief is surely the fact that contrary to justified apprehensions the world did not fall into the 1930s trap of an outbreak of protectionism and trade wars. The very existence of the WTO must account in a significant way for the absence of this negative outcome – for the fact that the protectionist dog did not bark.

Going forward to 2019 – the ICC's hundredth anniversary

If the Great Recession of 2008–2009 failed to result in trade wars and surges of protectionism, it would be prematurely dangerous to claim victory and especially to fall into a complacency trap. The world trade system enters the second decade of the twenty-first century in a turbulent and fragile state. Protestations from global government leaders to the contrary notwithstanding, there are good reasons to suspect that 2010 will not see the conclusion of the Doha Round. Trade tensions between China and the USA are pretty much bound to intensify. It is of course in the interests of both nations and of the global trading system generally that these tensions should be contained and indeed resolved. The absence of a strong multilateral framework, indeed the weakness of the WTO, in that context, as in many others, must be matters of concern.

The multilateral trading system is further undermined by the growth, proliferation and intensification of PTAs (preferential trade agreements). As the multilateral system appears bogged down, nations and indeed whole regions have moved to substitute it with a plethora of bilateral trade arrangements. Initially it was hoped by some policy makers that this would have the effect of bringing about 'competitive liberalization' and thus provide ultimately momentum to the multilateral agenda. This assumption has proved woefully wrong.

The ICC vision remains constant in seeking to bring about economic growth, job creation, prosperity, and hence peace, through an open global market economy based on a multilateral trading regime. This was the vision in 1919 and it is the hope that it will reflect global reality when the ICC celebrates its hundredth anniversary in 2019. In addition the ICC vision has come to encompass the other key issue of the twenty-first century, the climate change agenda. A robust rules-based open global trading system will definitely be a critical constructive force in ensuring greater global sustainability.

To achieve this vision, the global agenda for the next decade must address the four impediments I noted above. First, economies, both industrialized and emerging, must adjust to the new realities of the twenty-first century world economy. Second, political leadership and political will must be brought to bear on the trading agenda. Third, there is an imperative of institutional reform in the WTO to make the process more responsive to current transformations and challenges. Fourth, we need to restore trust.

It is a very challenging agenda. But what are the alternatives? In achieving this vision and meeting this challenging agenda for the next decade, the business community, through the ICC, must play an active and constructive role.

Historical overview and dynamics

JEAN-PIERRE LEHMANN

To Europeans the dawn of the twentieth century was seen as a period of great progress and great prospect; as the 'golden age' of globalization. The mood is captured in the famous phrase by Sir Norman Angell in his best-selling book, *The Great Illusion*, published in 1910: 'international finance is now so interdependent and tied to trade and industry, that political and military power can in reality do nothing'.

The great illusion was shattered four years later as Europe and the world entered a protracted period of seemingly endemic wars and revolutions that lasted well into the twentieth century, finally coming to an end with the destruction of the Berlin Wall and the subsequent collapse of the Soviet Empire.

By the beginning of the twenty-first century Europe achieved a level of peace and prosperity that could have been dreamed of in 1900, but would have appeared totally unfathomable a decade-and-a-half later and for the ensuing decades. Imagine being told in 1975, for example, that in thirty years Estonia would be a member of the European Community. Unimaginable!

Yet it did come to pass that by the end of the turbulent twentieth century, the vision of the founders of the International Chamber of Commerce (ICC), 'world peace through world trade', had finally been translated into reality for Europe. For the rest of the world, though prospects are encouraging, the jury of history remains out.

While perspectives in Europe at the dawn of the twentieth century may have been brimming with enthusiastic self-confidence, it has to be said that perspectives from China – and indeed most parts of the non-European world – were rather different. In 1900 China was in the throes of a major upheaval – known as the Boxer Uprising – which involved both civil strife and foreign invasion. This conformed to a pattern set some six decades earlier with the outbreak of the first of two Opium Wars and that was sustained until the middle of the twentieth century.

It was the opium trade that 'opened' China, brought it into the Western imperial sphere and proceeded both to impoverish and inflict huge physical damage on the country. This is not to say that trade was entirely responsible for China's demise, but it would have been difficult in 1900 – or indeed in 1919 when the ICC was founded and China was still being exploited by multiple foreign powers, including its neighbour, Japan – to convince the Chinese that trade is a win–win proposition, let alone that world trade engenders world peace!

The point to emphasize is that trade per se is neutral, neither good, nor bad, and, as history shows, as often engendering war as engendering peace. What matters is what is traded and how trade is conducted. Clearly trading in people – the slave trade – through plunder is both morally wrong and both cause and consequence of warfare. There are many examples that can be cited well into the twenty-first century: the drug trade in Colombia, the diamond trade in Africa, the arms trade in the Middle East and elsewhere are among some of the most egregious, but by no means exceptional, ones of trade contributing to human misery.

The 'sutra' of how trade should be properly conducted comes from the famous words of Cordell Hull enunciated in 1937 – at the height of the pre-war trade wars: 'I have never faltered, and I will never falter, in my belief that enduring peace and the welfare of nations are indissolubly connected with friendliness, fairness, equality and the maximum practicable degree of freedom in international trade.'

So freedom, yes, but not without friendliness, fairness and equality. These fundamental ingredients have much improved in the last several decades since the founding of the GATT in 1947; but they are still not conspicuous by their presence in 2010. To cite one very accusatory figure – taken from the 'Trade Fact of the Week' of 14 October 2009 by Edward Gresser, one of the authors of this volume – the tariff rates imposed by the USA on imports from three of the world's poorest countries, Cambodia, Bangladesh and Pakistan, are respectively 16.7%, 15.3% and 9.9%, while the tariff rates imposed on the UK and France, two of the world's richest countries, are 0.6% and 0.8%. The USA earns twice as much revenue from tariffs imposed on Bangladesh than it does from the UK – US$392 million versus US$180 million – on a value of less than 10 per cent of imports – US$2.56 billion for Bangladesh versus US$30 billion for the UK. This could hardly be described as friendly, fair, or equal. Such data demonstrates how much further we need to go to meet Cordell Hull's strictures.

Cordell Hull was a major architect of the post-war global multilateral trade system. As he rightly pointed out at the time: 'a revival of world trade [is] an essential element in the maintenance of world peace. By this I do not mean, of course, that flourishing international commerce is of itself a guaranty of peaceful international relations. But I do mean that without prosperous trade among nations any foundation for enduring peace becomes precarious and is ultimately destroyed.'

One of the great innovations of post-war institution building was to establish rules for the conduct of international trade; hence reference is made to the rules-based multilateral trading system. The rules and the adoption of the principle of non-discrimination are meant to try to ensure that the evil practices of trade will not be resorted to and that so far as possible the aim will be to achieve 'friendliness, fairness and equality'. Fair trade, therefore, must take precedence over free trade.

The system that was established by the GATT in 1947, by the successive rounds of trade liberalization and by the founding of the WTO in 1995, has provided the proper regulatory conditions for a dramatic increase in world trade, which, in turn, has generated unprecedented growth and allowed many economies, such as Turkey, Hong Kong, Korea, Taiwan, Chile, the Association of Southeast Asian Nations (ASEAN) countries, and more recently China, Mexico and Brazil, that have participated in global trade, to enjoy great gains in wealth and welfare. However, we have clearly not yet arrived at the 'world peace through world trade' destination. The long-term paralysis of the Doha Development Agenda and the unwillingness of the rich countries to level the trade playing field demonstrate how seemingly insuperable obstacles remain.

As we enter the second decade of the twenty-first century, with virtually all the countries of the world having joined the global market – in stark contrast to the situation that prevailed throughout much of the second half of the last century – and having acceded to the WTO, it is an appropriate time for reflection on the dynamics and nature of trade per se and the prospects for the future. How will historians write about this period in coming decades? Are we moving closer to the vision of world peace through world trade? Or are we making a U-turn?

Trade is an intrinsic part of humanity's DNA. It is as natural an instinct as, say, courtship. Throughout history and in all societies whenever attempts have been made by states to prevent trade, means were found to circumvent the interdictions. For example, when the imperial power in Beijing sought to ban trade during the Ming and again under the Qing dynasties, the rapid result was the emigration of Chinese traders to continue their activities in surrounding countries – which is the origin of the large numbers of 'Overseas Chinese' to be found in Southeast Asia. During the reign of Mao Zedong, trade was banned. As soon as Deng Xiaoping lifted the lid, trade boomed and Chinese traders, from major corporations to the street hawker, rapidly expanded worldwide.

The Arabs, the Persians, the Mongols, the Indians, as well as the Europeans, have all been great traders at one time or another. Indeed the global Indian diaspora is another testimony of what happens when home conditions on trade become constraining – those who can just leave to pursue trade elsewhere. South Asia has the dubious distinction of being the region with the lowest share of intra-regional trade (about 8 per cent). The official figures reflect the restrictive trade policies between the countries of SAARC (South Asian Association for Regional Cooperation), though the 'real' figures would have to include the considerable amount of smuggling that occurs across borders or through third countries, such as Dubai.

While efforts need to be committed to providing the proper framework for the global governance of trade, the obligation of individual countries is to set the rules to ensure that trade is properly conducted, but also to provide the proper incentives and the necessary infrastructure for traders to trade. The fact that today, for example, Africa is far less engaged in the global market than many other regions of the world – notably Asia – does not mean that trade is not in the African DNA. The shortest of visits to any African country will confirm that Africans are actively engaged in trade in whatever manner they can. In light, however, of poor infrastructure and a generally highly constraining domestic regulatory environment, this results in both limited trade and much of it conducted in the 'informal sector'. While recognizing that there have been abuses and that elements of the trade regime are grossly unfair to Africa – cotton stands out as a flagrant example – the proposition, nevertheless, in contrast to what is advanced by many in the anti-globalization community, is not that trade is bad for Africa, but that African states have generally been bad at trade.

The dream articulated by the founders of the ICC in 1919 – 'world peace through world trade' – degenerated within two decades into a nightmare. The trade wars of the 1930s preceded and constituted a critical cause in the full-scale fighting war that subsequently broke out. The great contrast between the first half of the twentieth century and the second half was the exponential expansion of world trade and the many benefits it has bestowed on the planet.

This has emphatically been the case in East Asia. In the period following World War II until the mid/late 1970s, East Asia was engaged in multiple wars, revolutions, conflicts and tensions. It is an incontrovertible fact that trade has greatly contributed not only to reducing poverty on an unprecedented scale, but also to peace. Trade between Taiwan and the People's Republic of China, as one key example, is incontestably an important reason why there has not been conflict between the two. Or one thinks of Southeast Asia, where the war in Vietnam has become a distant memory; and the opening up of the country to trade has witnessed the return of the boat people! Indeed Southeast Asia, which was mired in bloodshed and seemed destined to be the hotspot of the Cold War, has been transformed from a battlefield to a marketplace.

But it would be a very grave mistake to believe that global trade can be sustained on autopilot or that it will necessarily maintain a forward momentum. The 2008–2009 global financial crisis posed an immense danger to trade with justified fear of the resurgence of protectionism. At the time of writing, fortunately, this has not happened. But we must not be complacent. We live in a fragile world. We also live in a rapidly changing world. The systemic shifts in global economic power and the emergence of new major global actors, China in particular, and new forces, notably climate change, pose new and actually quite daunting challenges.

There is a need to adapt to the new actors and the new forces. The trade regime built on the embers of World War II was put together by Western architects and, consequently, aimed at serving Western interests. With Japan as an appendage, it was primarily in fact a North Atlantic framework that brilliantly succeeded in enhancing peace and prosperity to the North Atlantic. In the twenty-first century it will be necessary to ensure that the 'global South' is well accommodated in the trade structure.

This must be the agenda for policy makers and policy thinkers. But it must also be on the agenda of business leaders. In setting out the motto of 'world peace through world trade', the founders of the ICC did not, obviously, consider that this was a fait accompli. It was the articulation of an aspiration. Global business leaders must seek to ensure that when the ICC comes to celebrate its centenary, in 2019, that robust and dynamically adaptive trade policies and trade activities will have contributed significantly to overcoming the daunting challenges the next decade faces and to ensuring that the dream is significantly closer to reality.

Editorial note

The articles compiled in this publication are voluntarily eclectic in subject, opinion and geographical focus. They represent the views of a multiple range of experts with contrasting backgrounds originating from all corners of the world. The authors have also been drawn from different generations. They describe a patchwork of forces that drive the multilateral rules-based trading system in the early twenty-first century as well as propose avenues to the understanding of future patterns of international trade. These narratives aim to shed light on the complex nature of global interdependence and to encourage readers to seek further knowledge on issues pertaining to international trade and to its broader implications related to peace and prosperity.

Under the broad heading 'Peace and Prosperity through Global Trade', authors were asked to provide an opinionated article on specific topics outlining their vision of the immediate future with an emphasis on poverty reduction, social justice and environmental sustainability. The areas of focus vary greatly from one article to the next. The 2008–2009 global economic crisis in which the articles were drafted and compiled has also had an incidence on analysis and recommendations. The articles have been grouped into five chapters for the sake of clarity but many of the issues are deeply intertwined.

While of diverse opinions, the authors share an active commitment to address the shortcomings of the multilateral trading system and turn it into one of the key global instruments to achieve peace and prosperity. The Evian Group is fond of quoting the fourteenth-century scholar Ibn Khaldun: 'Through foreign trade, people's satisfaction, merchants' profits and countries' wealth are all increased.' By foreign trade Khaldun meant not only the exchange of goods, but also the exchange of ideas. We hope to have succeeded in the latter.

Global systemic transformations

Editorial introduction

Global systemic transformations

The articles in this opening chapter assess the shift in global economic equilibrium from Western hegemony to Asian resurgence through different country and regional perspectives. It is probable that historians will see the 2008–2009 financial crisis as hugely significant in the relative redistribution of geopolitical and economic power. The robustness of the multilateral trading system over the next decade will partly depend on how we manage this transition. Established powers will need to accommodate newcomers whereas emerging powers will need to assume responsibilities to govern the international system.

Seven of the fourteen articles focus on Asia although we return in detail to other regions of the world in subsequent chapters of the book. As all of the articles demonstrate, the global scene is one of intense systemic shifts. The global trade chessboard is undergoing considerable transformations: new actors are emerging in more prominent roles and new trade and investment channels are being explored.

The first four articles chart the re-emergence of Asia, with an emphasis on China, look at dynamics within the United States, and offer an assessment of the benefits and interests of the USA–China trade relationship. We then turn to India's domestic reform path. Japan, Korea and Vietnam, countries that have all relied on the expansion of exports for development, are the subject of the following three contributions. Europe, a leading trading bloc and a unique model of integration, is then discussed. This is followed by an analysis of internal dynamics in the Russian Federation. The final four articles outline the trajectories and prospects of Latin America, the Arab region and Africa as the global landscape transforms.

A1 | *Trade in the new Asian hemisphere*

KISHORE MAHBUBANI*

For over two thousand years, the rise of new great powers has been accompanied by rising tension and conflict. Today, we are witnessing the greatest shifts of power with the rise of China, India and other Asian powers. Yet, instead of seeing rising geopolitical conflict and tension, we are seeing a remarkable degree of geopolitical calm in Asia.

Why are we witnessing this strange phenomenon? We can find many complex explanations. But one key explanation will be trade. The creation of the 1945 open liberal international trading order, first under the auspices of the GATT and later under the WTO, is one key reason for the geopolitical calm.

To understand the impact of this 1945 liberal trading order, look at the history of Germany and Japan in the twentieth century when they emerged not once, but twice, as great powers. The first time they emerged before World War II. Then the only means to acquire great power status were by conquering and colonizing as they were the only secure ways of obtaining natural resources and commodities. This explains why Japan overran most of Southeast Asia, one of the most resource-rich regions in the world. However, when Germany and Japan re-emerged as great powers after World War II, they did so peacefully. Why? Simple. They could go around the world and buy any commodities they needed. In return, they could export their products to any corner of the world. It is not surprising therefore that Germany and Japan emerged as two of the leading exporters in the world. The average annual rate of growth of Japanese exports was 15.9% from 1950–1960, 17.5% from 1960–1970 and 20.8% from 1970–1980. In

---

* Kishore Mahbubani is Dean of the Lee Kuan Yew School of Public Policy, National University of Singapore and has recently published *The New Asian Hemisphere: the Irresistible Shift of Global Power to the East.*

the same periods, German exports grew at 16.6%, 11.4% and 19.1% respectively. The key point to note here is that exports do not just produce wealth. They also generate peace.

Exports also explain why China is similarly engaged in a 'peaceful rise'. For many years, Chinese exports were dwarfed by German and Japanese exports. From 1950–1980, China's share of world exports remained consistently less than 1%. On the other hand, Japanese exports, which accounted for only 1.3% of the total exports in the world, grew to 3.1% by 1960 and 6.1% by 1970. Similarly, Germany's share in world exports, which was 4.2% in 1950, grew to 7.4% by 1960 and 9.1% by 1970. But more recently, Chinese exports have grown much faster. Total Chinese exports grew from US$9.8 billion in 1978 to US$438 billion in 2003. China's share of world exports rose phenomenally, at more than four times from 1.8% to 7.5%. As long as China could grow successfully through exports, there was no reason for it to emerge as a militaristic power, like the Soviet Union (which incidentally exported very little). Indeed China learned a very powerful lesson from the collapse of the Soviet Union: that it was better to emerge as an economic power rather than a military power.

The great historical irony here is that China's peaceful rise may have been generated by several Western powers who were not aware that they had 'caused' it. When China applied to join the GATT/ WTO in 1986, the Western states decided to set a very high bar for its entry. They forced China to open up many of its economic sectors and to abandon its protection of state-owned enterprises. Most observers expected China to baulk at these stiff conditions and walk away from joining the WTO. Russia's unwillingness to accept similar conditions illustrates well the traditional reluctance of great powers to make painful compromises to gain entry into a multilateral organization.

It was therefore a great surprise in 2001 when China willingly accepted the stiff conditions for entry into the WTO, which included judicial review, uniform administration and transparency, product specific safeguards, non-tariff measures and anti-dumping and tariff rate quota administration. It also undertook extensive reform of agriculture, industrial subsidies, technical barriers to trade, trading rights and trade in services. The tough, shrewd and astute prime minister of China, then Zhu Rongji, wisely calculated that the more China was forced to liberalize by the WTO, the more it would benefit in the long run as these processes of opening up would naturally make the Chinese economy more competitive.

This is exactly what has happened. Both America and Europe used to provide the workshops in the world. Today, the most competitive manufacturing industries in the world are found in China and East Asia. Accepting the rules of WTO has been hugely beneficial to China.

The success of East Asia has led to a change in mindset in India also. For decades, the Mumbai Industrialists Club fought against tariff reduction and trade liberalization because they were convinced that Indian industries would be 'raped' and 'destroyed' by Western multinational corporations (MNCs). Today, amazingly, the same Mumbai Industrialists Club is in favour of rapidly opening up the Indian economy because Indian entrepreneurs believe that Indian companies can compete against the best companies in the world.

This new openness to trade also explains why the fastest-growing trade flows in the world are in Asia. A recent Asian Development Bank (ADB) study has found that the value of total merchandise trade between East Asia and South Asia increased eightfold to about US$140 billion between 1990 and 2007. It also notes that there are around twenty cross-regional free trade agreements (FTAs) at different stages of implementation in Asia. These have significantly improved economic welfare. Take the case of China. At the end of the Cold War, China's trade with Japan totalled just US$16 billion; with South Korea, US$3.8 billion, and with India, US$260 million. In 2005, the trade with Japan had hit a whopping US$213.3 billion; with South Korea, US$111 billion, and with India, US$20 billion. Having spent fifty years after World War II as the arena for the world's biggest wars, Asia is now contributing more to the increase in global prosperity than any other region.

What is truly remarkable is how fast trade is growing between Asian powers who are potentially rivals and competitors. Take the case of China and India. While individually, trade in each country is growing at 20–25% a year, trade between the two countries is growing at the rate of 50% a year. Trade between the two countries increased from around US$300 million in 1992 to about US$2 billion in 1997 to US$12 billion in 2004, and crossed the US$50 billion mark in 2008. Similarly, trade between China and Japan has grown significantly. From 1990 to 2007, total bilateral trade between Japan and China increased from US$18.2 billion to US$236.7 billion.

This remarkable growth in Asian trade provides a powerful leading indicator of how and why the twenty-first century will become the Asian century. Trade also explains why these great shifts of power are happening peacefully in Asia.

The moral of this story is a simple one. Trade is too important a subject to be left to traders or trade policy makers. Since the benefits are enormous, trade should always become the first priority of global leaders whenever they meet. And they should work relentlessly towards reducing all trade barriers and ending all trade-distorting subsidies.

A2 US allegiance to the multilateral trading system: from ambivalence to shared leadership

JAMES BACCHUS[*]

Trying to discern the shape and the substance of the international trade policy of the United States of America can be almost as difficult as trying to discern the meaning of the 'covered agreements' of the World Trade Organization.

Both seem ever in need of clarification.

The USA is the largest trading nation in the world. No other country has a greater volume of imports and exports. Therefore, no other country has as great an interest as the USA in increasing the flow of trade, or as great an interest in ensuring the continued flow of trade by upholding the rules for trade on which it and other countries have agreed.

Yet the USA has seemed increasingly reluctant, in recent years, to do all that needs to be done to remove the remaining barriers to trade, and to uphold the international rule of law in trade.

Why is this?

Why is it that the USA, which did so much through long decades to establish the multilateral trading system under the auspices of the WTO, now seems so ambivalent about that system, and so hesitant to help provide the leadership it so much needs?

Part of the answer lies in the changed nature of the world economy as we waken to the realization that a new century has brought a new world. The USA remains the world's leading trading nation, to be sure. But other nations have recently emerged as 'major players' in the global economy and, as a result, in the trading system. The USA has

---

[*] James Bacchus is a former Chairman of the Appellate Body of the WTO, a former Member of the Congress of the United States, and a former international trade negotiator for the United States. He is one of two chairs of the global practice group of the global law firm Greenberg Traurig, and a member of the Commission on Trade and Investment Policy of the ICC.

9

not yet learned the subtle skills of shared leadership in a new world in which US leadership is not automatic.

Part of the answer lies, too, in the passion with which many in the USA cling to traditional notions of sovereignty. Unlike, say, Europeans, Americans are unaccustomed to being second-guessed by 'foreigners', in international tribunals and otherwise. They overlook the important fact that the USA itself is a 'common market' of individual commercial states united by the US Constitution. The USA has not yet fully comprehended that, just as Americans can be most effective when they act nationally as one, in a globalized world, national sovereignty often can only be effective through the exercise of shared sovereignty internationally.

Part of it, too, can be found in the way many Americans cling – often unconsciously – to the illusion that America's trade and other economic challenges can be overcome through purely American solutions to what are, by definition, international trade issues. It might be assumed that recent events would have shattered this illusion. Most of the rest of the world has wakened to the fact that global economic concerns are precisely that – global. The USA is – as we Americans say – 'talking the talk'; but politically, and psychologically, it is not yet 'walking the walk'.

Then, too, there is the tendency of those in positions of leadership in the USA to favour short-term over long-term interests in the pursuit of trade policy. For members of the US House of Representatives in particular, there is always another election just around the corner of the next trade vote. (Nothing else can explain, for example, the short-sighted recalcitrance of the USA in the seemingly endless series of 'zeroing' cases in WTO dispute settlement relating to the application of anti-dumping remedies. This is especially so at a time when, increasingly, the majority of such remedies are being applied by other countries against US exports. On this issue especially, the USA seems unable to look to its long-term interests.)

In its inability to look to the long term, American policy makers are, of course, no different from policy makers of other WTO members. Short-sightedness can be found everywhere within the world trading system nowadays. But, because of the key role of the USA in the system, its short-sightedness exacts a higher price for the USA and for all other WTO members.

Not to be forgotten, there are as well the pressing demands of domestic politics. Trade politics, like all politics, is local. And, locally, within the USA, the forces that oppose trade, though still outnumbered nationally, are deeply entrenched politically in pivotal electoral states and in crucial senior posts in the Congress (and especially in the House of Representatives).

These political pressures are intensified by calls for protection of domestic workers and industries that increase exponentially during a time of economic crisis. And protectionist pressures, for any politician who must face the voters, are hard to resist. The foreign traders who favour free trade do not vote in his district.

All of this makes it difficult for the earnest and well-intentioned new President of the United States, Barack Obama, to do what he seems personally inclined to do – support trade and support the world trading system. Now that he is President, Obama has, not surprisingly, put behind him the occasional campaign rhetoric that seemed at times to cast doubt on his devotion to trade. He seems increasingly desirous of moving forward on trade – if he can only get the members of his own political party, especially in the House, to go along with him.

Somehow, he must find a way to do so.

Adam Smith taught us that an international division of labour increases 'the wealth of nations'. Smith's follower, David Ricardo, taught us that the wealth of nations will be maximized if all nations pursue their comparative advantage in the global marketplace. The USA, for the most part, has learned these economic lessons through the generations. But Americans need to be reminded from time to time of the truth of these fundamentals of the global economy. At this time, it falls to Barack Obama to remind them.

President Obama seeks recovery from the current historic economic crisis (2008–2009). Economic recovery will not be achieved for the USA if Americans are denied the improved productivity and the higher standard of living that results from trade. The important reforms advocated by President Obama – in healthcare, in climate change, and in much more – will not work if trade is not part of America's overall economic plan.

Trade means broader consumer choices and lower consumer prices. Initiative, incentive, innovation and efficiency are inspired by the additional competition provided by trade. Without these gains from trade, Americans will fall behind others globally, no matter what may be done domestically to hasten America's recovery.

Only President Obama can lead America on this issue because only he speaks for all Americans. Only he can rise above the parochialism that threatens to lock America into autarchy and protectionism. The overriding national interest of the USA is in lowering barriers to trade, upholding the rules of trade, and agreeing with other nations on the additional rules needed to guide and expand and spread the bountiful benefits of trade. Only the President can speak *for* the national interest in securing the gains from trade.

And only the President can speak *to* the nation. Only he can inspire the Congress and the American people to lead the world forward toward freer and expanding world trade in a more open world economy.

As he has done so well on so many other issues, President Obama must explain clearly to the American people how much they have gained, and continue to gain every day, from trade. He must do domestically all that is needed to restore the confidence of Americans that they can gain much more from freer trade. Most of all, to secure these additional gains, he must propose and pursue a trade agenda that will begin by concluding the WTO's Doha Development Round of global trade negotiations, and will continue by articulating and pursuing with other WTO members a contemporary trade agenda that will meet the new commercial challenges of the twenty-first century.

He must begin now.

A3 | Trade for development: the case of China

GANG FAN[*]

Thirty years ago, China was virtually absent from international trade. Thirty years later, a rare yet broad consensus around the world, one shared by both Americans and Chinese, is that 'China depends too much on exports'. Indeed, exports are now almost 70% over the GDP (not of the GDP, please note)! And during this thirty-year period, China has enjoyed an average annual growth rate of about 9.6%.

China does have a problem of 'too much trade, too little consumption'. Household consumption only accounts for about 35% of GDP, versus 51% of GDP held as national savings in 2007. There are various factors, including certain institutional deficiencies, which have kept household disposable income low as a proportion of national income. These factors have resulted in a relatively narrow domestic consumer goods market. But even were we to assume China's domestic consumer market to be normal (in terms of the common standard of East Asian economies at similar stages of development), say up to 60 per cent of GDP consumed by the household and government sectors (a proxy to the situation in China during much of the 1980s and 1990s), Chinese purchasing power for consumption would still be very small given the fact that China's per capita income is today still less than US$3,000. And companies, either local or multinational, would still try to export as much as possible because external markets, especially markets in developed countries, are far bigger with considerably more purchasing power. The most illuminating answer I heard when I asked some owners and CEOs of manufacturing companies in coastal regions why they wanted to export rather than sell to the domestic market came in its simplest form from the mouth of a shoemaker: 'they pay higher prices!' We all know that this shoemaker

* Gang Fan is Professor of Economics at Peking University's HSBC Business School and Director of the National Economic Research Institute, China Reform Foundation.

may only earn a fraction of the full price of world-brand shoes, but the net revenue he receives may still be higher than what he can secure in the domestic market.

Of course, not all people understand this straightforward logic. I was once challenged at an international conference by a European economics professor on China's growth model: why should you export? You can grow with your own market! Yes, of course we can grow with our domestic market. But the question is, how fast? At the same rate as European countries, the United States or Japan? Even if a little faster, we may yet never attain economic development that actually means 'convergence' and 'catching up', not simply meagre 'growth'. If a poor country's growth rate is solely dependent on the expansion of its own purchasing power and domestic market, it may never narrow the gap with developed countries (and/or existing multi-nationals). It is international trade that enables developing countries to start utilizing their only productive factor, low-cost labour, in sufficient magnitude to earn more income (because of 'higher prices'!), so that these countries can start breaking the vicious cycle of poverty, accumulate savings and buy better technologies (or, in other words, purchase intellectual property rights from developed countries). The so-called 'export-oriented growth model' is a good and inevitable growth model for a poor country; this is of little wonder in modern times when the per capita income gap between advanced and backward countries has inflated by 200–300 times. Only those economies that have succeeded in their export strategies can truly be developing!

One of the unique features of China is not only the liberalization of trade, but also the open policy towards foreign direct investment (FDI). Foreign companies invest in China, manufacture in China and choose to export a great deal of their products to home or foreign markets; at least in the early stages of development, as China's domestic market is still constrained by low income. In recent years, almost 60 per cent of made-in-China exported goods came from foreign or joint-venture manufacturers. This has helped further speed up China's growth through both trade and investment channels. Problems? Yes! Such a 'dual-opening development model' has naturally resulted in the current and capital account 'twin surplus'. When FDI inflows finance a vast amount of productive equipment and technologies, and at the same time foreign companies export, the country in this situation is more likely to avert trade deficits; the latter an habitual situation for many developing economies in development history. This has also contributed to the accumulation of foreign exchange reserves with potentially contingent financial risks. China has to take action and adjust in order to minimize the negative effects of this 'twin surplus'. Nevertheless, this does not mean that China's exports are excessive or that China should stop pursuing exports as an essential growth engine. It may simply imply that China's savings are too high and household consumption too low. The conclusion to be drawn is that China needs to make changes in its economic institutions in order to improve its economic structure.

Looking ahead, China will continue to depend on the international market as much as in the past. In the course of thirty years of high growth rates, China has successfully reallocated about 200–250 million farmers to non-farming sectors. That is remarkable! In spite of this, today 35 per cent of all Chinese labourers still remain farmers, earning about 50 per cent of non-farming basic wages, whose main sources of income derive from agriculture. This means China may need to reallocate another 200 million of its labour force from agriculture to non-farming sectors before it completes its first stage of industrialization, or before China reaches the equilibrium at which agricultural wages are equal to that of blue-collar workers in other industries. What should China do to create such a huge number of jobs? China should do everything: from investing in infrastructure and urbanization to increasing household consumption; from continuing to strive for 'high-tech' industries to maintaining its competitiveness in basic labour-intensive, low-end manufacturing activities; from encouraging manufacturing to diversifying in services; and from enlarging the domestic market to further expanding international trade! Nothing less. Every job connected to trade is precious for a country like China. This has most recently been apparent through the effects of the global financial crisis and trade slump, which sent about 20 million migrants working in coastal non-farming companies back to their home villages: an employment effect that further reinforces China's fundamental interest in sustaining globalization while fighting trade protectionism.

And this is only a part of the global story. India may in due course need more jobs in manufacturing trade sectors if growth is to progressively spread to its low-income rural population. And many other countries will be in a similar position if they are to break the vicious cycle of poverty and embark on a development path. The challenge for the international community is enormous: can we maintain growth in international trade so as to include in prosperity an increasing number of individuals in poor countries, or should they be left in poverty forever?

Trade is indeed about development!

A4 | Trade in the USA–China relationship

EDWARD GRESSER[*]

'Trade provided the reason for the first interaction between American citizens and Chinese subjects in the late 18th century,' the State Department's historical office reminds us. Recalling the New York-to-Canton voyage of the optimistically named *Empress of China* – it ferried over 39 tons of ginseng, and carried back a cargo of porcelain, silk and tea – the Department goes on to remind us that trade 'accounts for the majority of contacts between citizens of the two nations today'.

Few of us need the reminder. In fact, to many trade *is* America's contemporary relationship with China.

In 2008, the container ships which are the *Empress*' great-great-great-grandchildren unloaded 8 million containers of goods at American docks, weighing in at a combined total of 70 million tons and valued at over US$340 billion. They carried a third of Americans' silks, a fifth of our tea and half our porcelain – along with 17 million tons of shrimp, 70 million electronic calculators, 340 million pairs of sunglasses, 50 million kilos of soap, 37 million video players, nine-tenths of the toys under American Christmas trees and all the souvenir baseball caps sold by Major League Baseball.

The flow of goods the other way is a good deal smaller: US$80 billion, plus another US$20 billion in services. But even this places China above Japan and Germany as the third-ranking buyer of American farm products, commercial services and factory goods.

The streams of goods, and the rivers of capital that go alongside them – trade finance, patent royalties, Treasury securities – provide

* Edward Gresser is Director of the Trade and Global Markets Project at the Democratic Leadership Council. Author of the 2007 book *Freedom From Want: American Liberalism and the Global Economy,* he earlier served as Policy Advisor for the US Trade Representative, and Policy Director for US Senator Max Baucus (D-MT).

a set of issues ample enough to occupy even governments as large and complex as those of America and China. But of course neither trade alone, nor economics generally, are the whole of this relationship. And to the extent trade can help support and stabilize the broad range of Sino–American interactions, it is a very good thing.

The modern era of Sino–American interactions, of course, did not begin with trade but with security and strategy. Nixon's opening to China in 1971 created an alliance of convenience between two radically different states, each worried about the common threat of the Soviet Union. That alliance disappeared, in retrospect naturally, at the end of the Cold War. And to the extent that security and strategy remain the foundations of relationships between great powers, the foundation of Sino–American ties today is always fragile.

The United States and China, two giant powers with vastly divergent political systems and global interests, face no common enemy. They are linked by no alliance or treaty but the UN Charter and the series of understandings spelled out in the cryptic communiqués of 1972, 1979 and 1982. They must cope with the 'frozen conflicts' in Korea and the Taiwan Strait as well as their own bilateral relations. This is the type of relationship that posed, to the gloomier Great Minds of the past, classic questions of the origin of conflict and the maintenance of peace.

The subtle political mind of Thucydides saw the rise of a new power and the disturbance of an old as the origin of the Peloponnesian War, in terms some modern determinists apply to Sino–American relations:

The real cause of the war was the one most formally kept out of sight. The growth of the power of Athens, and the alarm which this inspired in Sparta, made war inevitable.

The melancholy reflections of poet Qu Yuan, a century later on the other edge of Eurasia, pondered the relationships among unlike powers and personalities and offered little more hope than the Greek:

Eagles do not flock together like birds of lesser wing;
thus it has been since ancient times.
How is the round to fit with the square?
How can different ways of life be reconciled?

Twenty-five centuries later, the two quotations remain relevant. The facts of politics and strategy, lying quietly but unchangingly at the heart of the Sino–American relationship, could easily create a polarized relationship in which two wary governments define their interest as the checking and undermining of the other's power. In such circumstances, capable leaders, experts and diplomats in both countries should no doubt be able to avert any direct confrontation. But they might find it difficult to build the trust necessary for other big questions:

- How to work together on economic matters, in particular ensuring recovery from financial crisis and concluding the WTO's Doha Round.
- How to manage security problems such as the Iranian nuclear programme and North Korean political transition.
- How to support the Asia-Pacific's poorest countries, to address global warming, to control flows of the fissionable material used in nuclear weapons and the software that guides missiles.

For the past fifteen years or so, trade has usually been among the areas of common interest that have eased the relationship's political challenges and made collaboration on these big questions easier. Using the high diplomacy of WTO accession and the day-to-day hopes of workers, shoppers and businesses, the two governments have encouraged rapid growth in people-to-people ties along with the constant and growing exchanges of goods, services, scientific research and finance. Trade now provides the livelihoods of tens of millions of young Chinese workers and encourages China's industrial development, while American airplane factories, soybean farms and semiconductor fabs sell as much to China as to Europe.

But trade has also often been a cause for stress. The last decade's rapid expansion of trade left the flow of goods lopsided, and also created alarm over product safety in the American public as industrial expansion outpaced the development of China's regulatory state. If America's public concludes that the economic relationship is one-sided and detrimental to American industry, or that Chinese regulators are recklessly indifferent about the safety of the shrimp, soap and medicine on American tables and in bathrooms and medicine cabinets, trade can be a corrosive as well as a stabilizing element of the relationship.

China's government and America's new leaders will need to stabilize and rebalance the trade relationship in the next few years through their Strategic and Economic Dialogue, even as they continue – rightly – to see it as one of their principal areas of shared benefit and common interest. Trade will never be the whole of America's relationship with China, as it was in the eighteenth century. But assuming no unexpected political upheavals, it is very likely to hold its position at the centre of contemporary Sino–American ties, and as the single issue which most frequently brings Americans and Chinese together. Managed well, it will remain a stabilizing element in a relationship at the heart of the world's hopes for shared prosperity and durable peace.

A5 | Unravelling India and strengthening external engagement for sustainable growth

RAJU KANORIA[*]

Trade is the natural enemy of all violent passions. Trade loves moderation, delights in compromise, and is most careful to avoid anger. It is patient, supple, and insinuating, only resorting to extreme measures in cases of absolute necessity. Trade makes men independent of one another and gives them a high idea of their personal importance: it leads them to want to manage their own affairs and teaches them to succeed therein. Hence it makes them inclined to liberty but disinclined to revolution.

Alexis de Tocqueville (1805–1859)

Trade in India was important well before the Colonial period. India's external trade made a significant contribution to the world economy. An extensive internal trade network also evolved from the large size of the country.

Any analysis of India's trade must keep in perspective the large volume of trade that happens within it. India's engagement with the rest of the world is limited because of the large domestic market, which is complex owing to the typicality of the interplay between constituent states and regions.

By the year AD 1000, the estimated share of India in the world economy was over 30%, the largest in the world. This share reduced to about 25% by the year 1500.

During the Colonial period, by the end of the eighteenth century, the Indian economy witnessed large-scale exploitation of domestic

---

[*] Raju Kanoria is Chairman and Managing Director of Kanoria Chemicals & Industries Limited and immediate past President of ICC India. He chairs the Commission on International Trade and Investment Policy of the ICC, Paris. He has headed several Joint Business Councils, including India–Australia, India–New Zealand and India–Netherlands. He has been a part of the official Indian government delegations for the WTO Inter Ministerial Meetings.

resources. It became a captive supplier of raw materials. Investments in the economy fell sharply thus severely dampening growth. A study by Cambridge University historian Angus Maddison showed that India's share of world income fell from 22.6% in 1700 to 3.8% in 1952.

British systems became ingrained during two centuries of Colonial rule. The legal and political structures developed in a way that 'a few could control the destiny of many'. Political power vested with the bureaucracy, which became the most powerful institution in the governance of the country.

After independence India adopted a socialistic model of self-reliance. The task of national reconstruction fell on the government of independent India. With a fragmented and weak private sector, the role of government was not limited to social development and redistribution of income, but extended to manufacturing and the provision of basic services to citizens. In trying to become self-reliant, the country surrounded itself with barriers, particularly in the areas of industrial licensing, tariffs and controls. This prevented integration into the world economy and abetted the governance practices of 'a few managing the rest'.

This restrictive economic environment remained in place for the next four decades. India became relatively isolated from the rest of the world. It was not until the mid-1980s when Rajiv Gandhi was the prime minister that the seeds of reform and liberalization were sown. Rajiv Gandhi had the opportunity and the mandate of the people to usher in contemporary economic principles of free enterprise and even to undertake constitutional amendments if necessary. His background and sudden entry into politics constrained him from taking major decisions and then, in 1991, his life was cut short. I believe that with him India would have reformed much earlier.

It was in the early 1990s that the process of economic reforms, liberalization and structural adjustments was initiated in the wake of an unprecedented balance of payments crisis. The process began with a stutter, under compulsion and lacked a holistic approach. *The Economist* magazine editorial in May 2001 commented that: 'India's variety and vagueness conspire to frustrate anyone who tries to be objective in charting the effects of economic reforms over the past decade. The place is all subplots and no plot.'

Another factor that prevented the reforms process from gathering steam was the emergence of coalition governments represented by both national and regional political parties. With specific reference to the Indian polity based on democratic governance and a multi-party political structure, several areas of governance have languished because of short-term measures. Policies sometimes are not issue-based but are a result of reactive thinking influenced by factors that make political parties popular and help them stay in power. Populist rhetoric and political exigencies have overshadowed hard economic reality.

A fundamental distortion in delivery of good governance is often due to populist policies devoid of socioeconomic imperatives. Even partisan ideologies are sometimes sacrificed to stay popular. In the words of Lee Kuan Yew, prime minister of Singapore from 1959 to 1990, 'I do not believe that popular government means you have to be popular when you govern.'

In 1991, the choice of a non-political financial technocrat to spearhead the reforms process was one of the best political decisions taken. Under Dr Manmohan Singh's deft leadership coupled with his deep understanding of the subject, some semblance of direction was imparted to the liberalization and globalization process.

After two decades of economic reforms, India can look back to commendable achievements in unshackling the economy: dismantling of barriers, globally benchmarked tariff reductions, de-licensing industry, removal of restrictions in trade and investment, and so on. Indian industry has been supportive of these measures and has responded by enhancing efficiency and productivity.

The journey is still incomplete. Share of manufacturing in India's GDP is only 20 per cent. India needs to take several measures and internal reforms to boost trade by developing a robust manufacturing sector. These measures include infrastructure creation, simplification in fiscal structures, and development of social infrastructure, particularly education and health.

I believe that an important factor for India in the future is to become a truly homogenous entity. Historically, the country has been a federation of provinces, states and regions, bifurcated on cultural, ethnic and linguistic barriers. This has meant federalism with a multi-government, multi-policy system. What we need is an Indian Economic Union with seamless movement of goods and services. The impact on transaction costs would be tremendous.

Interstate differences prevent a common approach. More specifically, interstate movement of goods and services, legislative issues in setting up and operating industrial enterprises, documentation requirements of various governmental and municipal authorities and lack of 'co-operative competition' among states, are issues that prevent India becoming a single 'common market'.

The future course of India's development would depend on the ability to build systems that retain its diverse sociocultural fabric and yet ensure a cohesive and integrated nation. I believe that the citizens of India have the ability to shift away from parochial sectorism.

The contentious issue of agriculture should be kept in perspective. The past rounds of discussion at the WTO repeatedly brought this issue to the fore. About 65 per cent of India's population depends directly on agriculture. One needs to be conscious of this aspect while making an effort at evolving a rules-based multilateral trading system. It is also true that agriculture in developing countries could languish without a competitive environment. This is being denied through the persistence of trade-distorting and price-distorting subsidies.

In India, policy makers still appear to be in a state of denial. Penchant for popularity often obfuscates real needs. Unless corrected such a stance could create problems and even jeopardize food security, throwing trade into a downward spiral. In 1991, India was forced by external pressures to liberalize the industrial economy. A similar internal pressure is required that forces the government to aggressively initiate an agriculture-driven domestic reform programme. Such a transformation is necessary to unravel the true economic potential of the country and to ensure that the food needs of a still rising population are met.

The seamless global movement of goods and services as well as financial capital is today more or less a way of life. The world has, however, failed to develop a system to absorb the movement of human capital which will become critical to true globalization. The systems needed for such a change to happen are amorphous, subjective and based on the tenets of tolerance and understanding. Countries need to move away from nationalism and inculcate these values. Education systems need a transformation to create a positive alignment with shifts in global demographic patterns and prepare the 'global citizen' to face this reality.

In addition the developed countries need to move away from old beliefs and recognize the demographic and economic power of Asia. The current global power structure is a relic from the post-World War II era. The ICC and businesses must act together to evolve a contemporary and realistic model over the next decade.

A6 | Japan's contribution to an open trading system

SHUJIRO URATA*

Trade and high living standards

The quality of Japanese people's lives would be significantly lower without international trade. Poorly endowed with natural resources, Japan depends on foreign countries for the supply of natural resources and the products using natural resources such as food. In terms of calorie intake, Japan's dependence on foreign supply for its food consumption is higher than 60 per cent. Japan's dependence on foreign supply for oil, which is essential for leading a modern life as it is a main source of heating and air-conditioning as well as a major input for the production of vital goods such as drugs and foods, is as high as 99 per cent.

These statistics indicate the crucial importance of international trade for Japanese people to enjoy their high standard of living. Imagine the deterioration in the quality of life of the Japanese if foreign supply of vital imports were cut. The prices of food, oil and oil-related products would soar, and the budget of Japanese citizens for the purchase of other products would be significantly reduced, thereby lowering their living standard. It should be emphasized that the limitation of import opportunities would particularly hurt the poor, as their share of income for purchasing essential products is high. This point is especially relevant during a period of recession and when a widening income gap between rich and poor becomes an important social problem.

* Shujiro Urata is Professor of Economics at Waseda University in Tokyo. He was formerly a Research Associate at the Brookings Institution and an Economist at the World Bank. He is co-author of *Measuring the Costs of Protection in Japan* (1995), with Hiroki Kawai and Yoko Sazanami. He has also published a number of books on international economic issues in Japanese and English.

Trade and rapid economic development

International trade played an important role in Japan's rapid economic development following the Meiji Restoration in the mid-
nineteenth century, when opportunities for trade were unleashed as
the Japanese government abandoned the isolation policy which had
lasted more than two centuries. Taking advantage of newly arisen
export opportunities, outward-minded Japanese companies, such
as trading companies, succeeded in exporting competitive Japanese
products. Successful exporting companies obtained foreign exchange
with which they could import advanced technologies, capital goods
and natural resources, enabling them to improve their competitiveness, thus resulting in further export expansion.

Rapid export expansion helped bring about rapid economic
development for Japan, as export expansion led to output expansion. With rapid economic development and resultant changes
in quantity as well as quality of labour and capital, the product
composition of Japan's exports changed dramatically. Natural
resource-based primary products such as silk yarn and copper ore
held dominant shares in Japan's exports in the nineteenth century,
but the share of manufactured products began to increase notably
in the twentieth century. The composition of manufactured exports
changed drastically from light manufacturers such as textile products to heavy and chemical products. At present, machinery products such as automobiles and electronic products dominate Japan's
exports. These successive transformations in export composition
were accompanied by concomitant changes in production structures, enabling the Japanese economy to climb the different stages
of economic development.

Although the combative and innovative spirit of Japanese companies has led the rapid expansion of exports, one should not forget
the important contributions made by public and semi-public institutions such as the chamber of commerce in various export promo-
tional activities. These include the quality control of export products
and disseminating information on export markets. Quality control
was of particular importance as the image foreign consumers held of
cheap and low-quality Japanese products had to be changed in order
to expand exports.

Importance of maintaining an open global trading system

This brief account of the important role trade has played for Japan denotes the need for maintaining an open global trading system not only for Japan, but also for other countries to achieve higher living standards and economic growth. An open trading environment enables countries to use available resources efficiently by shifting these resources from non-competitive to competitive sectors. Such a shift is a major source of economic dynamism, promoting economic growth.

The Doha Development Agenda (DDA) under negotiation at the World Trade Organization (WTO) is at a stalemate largely because of the controversy surrounding agricultural liberalization between developed and developing countries. Although Japan is not at the centre of the controversy in the DDA, it has long adopted protectionist agricultural policies, particularly in the rice market. Japan could contribute to re-igniting and concluding the DDA by demonstrating a courageous shift towards liberalization in agriculture. Having discussed the possible contribution of a change in Japan's agricultural trade policy for sustaining an open global trading system, I emphasize that liberalizing agriculture is in Japan's own interest.

Although Japan's agriculture sector produces only 1 per cent of its GDP and employs only 2 per cent of its labour force, it has extensive linkages with other sectors such as fertilizer and machinery through input–output relations as well as with the construction sector through projects such as irrigation and road construction. Because of its extensive inter-sectoral linkages, the protection of agriculture has led to an inefficient use of resources not only in agriculture but also in other sectors. Indeed, agricultural protection may be viewed as a symbol of the declining dynamism of the Japanese economy. In addition, agricultural protection worsens the living standard of Japanese people, especially the poor, as it raises the price of essential products such as food.

Liberalization of agriculture is difficult mainly because of the existence of many opposing interest groups, who benefit from protection at the expense of consumers and competitive exporters. However, agricultural liberalization can be carried through by formulating and implementing appropriate policies, which include gradual liberalization, temporary safeguard measures, compensation for negatively affected workers, and domestic structural reform. Strong political will and leadership are of the essence in engineering agricultural liberalization.

Regional economic integration in East Asia

The number of free trade agreements (FTAs) has increased rapidly in recent decades, partly due to the stalemate in multilateral trade negotiations. FTAs presumably stimulate the economic growth of FTA members by increasing their reciprocal trade. But FTAs may have negative impacts on non-members as they are discriminated against. In recognizing this problem, while integrating the fact that FTAs are probably here to stay, it is important to make FTAs as non-discriminatory as possible. This may be done by establishing FTAs with a large membership and with substantial liberalization coverage. Furthermore, FTAs could contribute to the construction of a free and open economic environment if they include liberalization in foreign direct investment and foreign workers, neither of which are sufficiently covered in the WTO framework.

Another feature that needs to be included in FTAs is trade facilitation. As tariff protection has come down significantly as a result of successive multilateral negotiations and unilateral liberalization, non-tariff barriers, including behind-the-border measures such as non-compatible technical standards, have become serious trade barriers. Dealing with non-tariff measures through trade facilitation would contribute significantly to the expansion of trade.

In the case of FTAs in East Asia, where wide development gaps exist among signatory countries, the effective implementation of economic assistance programmes through FTAs to deal with the problems of negatively impacted individuals or communities from trade liberalization by FTAs could promote trade liberalization and also cultivate a sense of community among FTA members. Such an effect is important for achieving economic growth as it leads to social and political stability. Economic assistance under the guise of human resource development and infrastructure building contributes to economic development of developing FTA member countries.

Being located in the vicinity of developing Asia, a region with huge growth potential but suffering from a shortage of human resources and the underdevelopment of infrastructure, Japan has attempted to pursue strategies aimed at establishing a comprehensive FTA in East

Asia. This strategy includes not only trade and investment liberalization and facilitation, but also economic cooperation/assistance with the objective of attaining economic growth both for East Asia and Japan. Despite this ambition, Japan has not been able to pursue its regional FTA policy mainly because of the difficulties posed by agriculture liberalization. Japan has to liberalize its agricultural policy if it intends to pursue a regional and global trade policy that benefits not only Japan, but also the rest of the world.

A7 | Rebalancing Korean trade policy: from bilateral to multilateral free trade

SOOGIL YOUNG[*]

Korea's successful experience with export-led industrialization strategies is shared by all East Asian economies. An essential ingredient or 'enabler' in this so-called East Asian miracle is the open multilateral trading regime. For this reason, although 'new regionalism' was surfacing in the form of bilateral or regional free trade agreements (FTAs) in other regions of the world, the East Asian economies steadfastly adhered to multilateralism by refusing to pursue regional or bilateral FTAs during the 1990s.

Yet, alerted by the Asian financial crisis of 1997–1998 to failings in the global economic order, as well as by the growing evidence that further multilateral trade liberalization after the Uruguay Round on both the WTO and APEC (Asia-Pacific Economic Cooperation) track was not likely in the foreseeable future, East Asian countries began to shift from multilateralism to regionalism, especially to bilateral FTAs, by the end of the decade. In a belated domino-effect-type reaction to the proliferation of FTAs elsewhere in the world, they thus began to pursue bilateral FTAs individually, competing to a certain extent with one another. Among them, Korea has probably been the first and the most aggressive pursuer of such bilateralism.

Korea began to pursue bilateral FTAs in the wake of the Asian financial crisis and launched the negotiation of its first FTA in 1999. This was the Korea–Chile FTA which was signed in 2003. Emboldened by

---

* Dr Soogil Young is President of the National Strategy Institute (NSI) in Korea, concurrently serving as Chairman of the Korea National Committee for Pacific Economic Cooperation (KOPEC) and on Korea's Presidential Committee on Green Growth. Dr Young has served as President of the Korea Institute for International Economic Policy (KIEP) and as Korea's Ambassador to the OECD. He launched the Pacific Trade Policy Forum in the 1980s and the PECC Finance Forum in the 2000s as the founding Coordinator for each.

this experience, the Korean government formally announced in that same year its new trade policy strategy of forming a global network of bilateral FTAs and began to push many FTAs simultaneously.

As a result, by August 2009, Korea had brought into effect FTAs with Singapore, the EFTA (European Free Trade Association) and ASEAN, thereby raising the number of FTA partner countries to fifteen. It has also signed, and will soon bring into effect, an FTA with the United States and a Comprehensive Economic Partnership Agreement (CEPA) with India. Korea has also concluded negotiation of an FTA with the EU. In addition, Korea has already launched the negotiation of FTAs along multiple variants with the Gulf Cooperation Council, Peru, Australia, New Zealand, Canada and Mexico. Korea is preparing to begin the negotiation of bilateral agreements with Turkey and Colombia in 2010, while seriously studying the feasibility of an FTA with China. Furthermore, it is quite likely that the negotiation of a Korea–Japan FTA, which was halted by Korea in late 2005 on the grounds that Japan did not seem to be ready to offer substantial opening of its domestic market, will be resumed in the near future. Mercosur, Russia, the South African Customs Union (SACU) and Israel are also under consideration as possible future FTA partners.

Trade policy dynamics in Korea indicate that, barring a dramatic breakthrough in the Doha Round, all of the afore-mentioned FTAs that are not yet in force or under negotiation will have been negotiated and enacted by around 2020. It therefore appears that in the 2020s and beyond, Korea will be conducting 'free trade' with seventy or so countries, covering most of Korea's international trade and investment. The expected benefit is that most Korean goods and services will have secured unimpeded access to all major, or significant, markets around the world. With the opening of many domestic goods and services markets to suppliers and investors originating from all those countries, Korean producers will be exposed to relentless pressure for international competition and thus the imperative to strive for efficiency and innovation. The high-quality FTAs, which the Korean government has negotiated with the USA and the EU, will help Korea 'upgrade' its various domestic regulations and institutions to global best standards. And all these anticipated changes induced by the FTAs are expected to help attract FDI into Korea, including into high value-added services, enhancing Korea's economic growth potential. In this way, it is hoped that Korea's global network of FTAs will help the country maintain its export-led industrialization and further facilitate the transition to a knowledge-intensive, service-oriented advanced economy.

This is the vision of Korea as a 'free-trading' country in the 2020s which arises from the country's current trade policy strategy: one that aims to make Korea the 'hub of free trade and investment' by creating a Korea-centred global network of FTAs with all significant partner countries. The expectation is that, when it is fully realized, Korea will be able to reap trade and investment gains from the removal of barriers at home and abroad on the bilateral basis, as well as efficiency gains from opening the domestic economy to foreign competition.

As a means of achieving those gains, however, Korea's 'FTA hub strategy' is an expedient approach to free trade relative to multilateral free trade. It consists of bilateral deals in which the free trade arrangement is negotiated with one partner country at a time (or a few at most) in those goods and services whose opening to foreign competition is politically difficult and may be bypassed. Accordingly, the FTA hub approach to free trade and investment can work faster than the multilateral free trade approach in bringing gains in trade and investment. Furthermore, it allows complete free trade and investment in the sectors covered by the FTA, although on a bilateral basis only. A further advantage of the FTA hub strategy is that Korea can compete with all other countries in terms of scope and speed in the pursuit of 'free trade'. It seems that, with its current roadmap for the negotiation of twenty-one or so FTAs, the Korean government is engaged in this competition, and doing very well at that.

But as an expedient approach, Korea's FTA hub strategy is also a second-best approach to multilateral liberalization and suffers from a few major problems. These problems arise from the fact that FTAs, given the very nature of bilateral arrangements, do not provide for genuine 'free' trade but rather 'preferential' trade, and that Korea's 'free trade' in the 2020s will be regulated by at least twenty-one different bilateral preferential agreements.

First, expected benefits from the various FTAs will be undermined by the trade and investment distortions that are created by a maze of mutually conflicting rules and exceptions, including rules of origin. Second, the afore-mentioned benefits will be further undermined, and distortions further aggravated, by the proliferation of FTAs which other countries, both in and out of East Asia, will have pursued in manners parallel to Korea's. In particular, many of Korea's trade gains due to the trade diversion effect of its own FTAs will be offset by trade losses attendant to the trade diversion effects of the FTAs to which Korea is not a party.

The third problem with Korea's FTA hub strategy is that Korea's FTAs will come into coexistence with many other FTAs to which Korea is not a party. All of these FTAs, Korean or not, will constitute a global 'noodle bowl' (Bhagwati's spaghetti bowl) of hundreds of FTAs with myriad country-pair-wise sector-specific rules and exceptions governing global trade and investment. By focusing on an aggressive FTA hub strategy, Korea is in fact contributing to the acceleration of this global trend towards FTAs, exacerbating the 'noodle bowl' phenomenon, by encouraging other countries to pursue FTAs of their own. In the meantime, the Korean government does not seem very intent on making a serious effort to contribute to the revival and success of the Doha Round of multilateral trade liberalization. Quite to the contrary, an FTA between any pair of countries acts on the multilateral trading system like the strike of an axe on the stem of a giant tree. A few cuts may not fell the tree but a thousand cuts will. When the current FTA race reaches a certain stage, the global trading system will become so fragmented that the costs of trade distortions will outweigh the benefits of trade creation due to the FTAs.

The trade policy challenge for Korea is to rebalance its current strategy and approach. This should start with a renewed recognition that global and multilateral free trade is its ultimate trade policy goal. As a significant trade middle power, as well as a newly industrialized dynamic economy, Korea has the necessary clout with which it can exercise influence and leadership in helping to organize and steer international efforts towards this goal. This rebalancing will specifically require making efforts to ensure that its many FTAs, as well as those of other countries, will serve as building blocks towards that goal. If its trade policy authorities are ambitious enough, Korea could lead the way towards global free trade by leveraging on its many FTAs coupled with creative international cooperation.

A8 | *Vietnam: a rising Asian tiger?*

NATASHA HANSHAW[*]

Since the start of economic reform or 'doi moi' in 1986, Vietnam has been on a steady path of integration into the international economy, entering the World Trade Organization (WTO) in January 2007. From 1989, Vietnam recorded remarkable economic growth that averaged 7.4% annually, bringing the poverty rate – those living on less than US$1 a day – down from more than 60% to less than 15% by the end of 2008. This remarkable record of growth and poverty reduction is bringing Vietnam into the ranks of middle-income countries, with a gross national income (GNI) per capita of just over US$1,000.[1] Today Vietnam is one of the world's largest exporters of rice, coffee beans and cashew nuts. Further, A. T. Kearney's Global Services Location Index, a ranking of the most attractive countries for outsourcing, includes Vietnam in its top ten in 2009.

Economic reforms promoting private business and foreign investment have been key components of this growth, first initiating large corporate investment inflows in the mid 1990s from companies such as Canon, Nike and 3M. The 2000 Enterprise Law, which facilitated business registration, marshalled billions of dollars of investment capital and millions of jobs into the growing private sector. In 2007, entry into the WTO precipitated a surge of capital inflows that accounted for a striking 30 per cent of Vietnam's gross domestic product (GDP).[2]

---

[*] Natasha Hanshaw has worked and travelled extensively in Vietnam. She has conducted research and analysis for private sector and economic development projects funded by the EU, USAID and the World Bank, in Southeast Asia. She is a former Research Associate at the Evian Group and currently works as a consultant on USAID projects in economic governance.

[1] According to International Monetary Fund (IMF) income classifications based on gross national income (GNI) per capita, as of July 2009.

[2] See further Jonathan Pincus and Vu Thanh Tu Anh, 'Vietnam Feels The Heat', *Far Eastern Economic Review*, May 2008.

Vietnam was unprepared for the inflow of capital that followed WTO entry, a monetary shock that financed aggressive and unchecked lending by banks, and sparked a real-estate bubble with property prices and shares doubling or tripling within a year. This monetary shock was compounded by Vietnam's expansionary fiscal policy, in particular in public investments, where public sector investment as a share of GDP exceeded 20 per cent in 2007. That year, Vietnam experienced its fastest growth since 1996 with 8.5 per cent growth in GDP.

This growth halted abruptly in 2008, when the HCMC stock market fell 57 per cent from its peak a year earlier, and the first-quarter trade deficit was four times higher than the first quarter in 2007.[3] Vietnam's economic instability deepened as rising global commodities prices contributed to inflation and the global financial crisis impacted Vietnam's exports, exacerbating the trade deficit.

Responding to the economic crisis, the government implemented a huge stimulus package in early 2009 (at a cost equivalent to 10 per cent of GDP) and a second smaller stimulus beginning in 2010. Yet as Vietnam works to restore economic stability, it faces inflationary pressures, a weak banking system, fiscal deficit, inefficient state enterprise sector, and widespread corruption that risk the successful implementation of the government's stimulus packages and undermine future stability.[4] Successfully navigating these risks will be crucial to the effectiveness of the stimulus packages throughout the economy, in particular in maintaining employment levels and job creation to absorb the approximate 1.5 million new entrants into the workforce every year.

Two decades of growth are colliding with infrastructure stretched beyond capacity, misallocation of public investments, a floundering education system, and growing inequality. The Communist Party's legitimacy and popular support have been built on its economic and social accomplishments over the last two decades. Maintaining political legitimacy domestically and foreign investor confidence is increasingly contingent upon the government's ability to address these

---

[3] *Ibid.*
[4] See further Martha Ann Overland, 'Corruption Undermines Vietnam's Stimulus Package', *Time Magazine*, 23 February 2009.

economic challenges and structural capacity constraints, and will require overcoming political constraints that tie the hands of policy makers in a patronage-laced political system. It remains to be seen whether the current leadership has enough flexibility and foresight to put forward a stronger leadership at the National Party Congress in 2011 that will be able to implement a tough reform agenda.

These challenges and capacity constraints risk Vietnam's ability to attract foreign investors and stall the competitiveness of Vietnam's domestic enterprises, both for those competing against cheaper imports as well as those exporting to new markets abroad. Exporting products still requires many more signatures and takes far longer than the average Asia-Pacific economy.[5] Regulatory and administrative barriers still hamper foreign business entry and widespread corruption remains rampant.[6] The government aims to improve transparency and with it reduce corruption, rein in red tape, and improve the overall administrative environment for businesses through the Administrative Procedures Simplification Project (Project 30), the success of which will play out over the next few years.

To attract more foreign investors and to become a major logistics and transportation hub the government must combat the misallocation of public investment. For example, investment in a slew of deep-sea ports in the central region is diverting infrastructure investment away from the HCMC, Ba Ria Vung Tau, Binh Duong and Dong Nai provinces that together account for over 30 per cent of the country's GDP, and are stretched far beyond capacity. This misallocation of huge public investments is one of the most visible problems indicative of the patronage schemes that are undercutting the imperative for programmatic structural investment planning.

Vietnam possesses a young, literate (over 90 per cent) and increasingly urban population. Yet there is an acute underinvestment in the country's higher education system. The high level of literacy is not being translated into high levels of skilled workers, which is creating a barrier to innovation and investment from foreign companies higher

---

[5] In 2006, Vietnam required 12 signatures compared to 6.2 on average in other APEC economies, and 35 days to export compared to 18.15. 'Trading Across Borders', *Doing Business in 2006*.
[6] Vietnam was ranked 121 out of 160 countries in Transparency International's Corruption Perception Index in 2008.

up the production value chain. Investing in higher education could be achieved by redirecting public investment towards its ambitious, young workforce rather than towards import-intensive projects that contribute heavily to the current account deficit.

On the back of its phenomenal growth, Vietnam has already realized the United Nation's Millennium Development Goals (MDGs) in poverty eradication, gender equality and combating malaria. Unlike China, Vietnam has been remarkably successful in its poverty reduction and in containing the inequality concomitant with rapid urbanization, making it somewhat of a 'poster child' of development. However, a gulf is growing between those benefiting from the open economy as they move into the middle class and those who remain trapped in poverty. For example, far fewer ethnic minority children are enrolled in primary school. The government must continue to ensure that its poverty reduction programme, Programme 135, which targets poverty among ethnic minority groups, continues to deliver tangible improvements to community infrastructure, access to markets and access to social services.

Vietnam is on target to achieve almost all the MDG goals by 2015, except in environmental sustainability. It is unclear whether it will be able to reverse the loss of its closed-canopy forest and biodiversity, or halve the share of those without drinking water or basic sanitation. Vietnam is already paying for poisoned rivers, as serious health problems and economic fallout from environmental degradation become growing concerns. In addition, as a coastal country, rising sea levels from climate change over the next few years are expected to severely impact the southern coastal provinces and the Mekong Delta, home to agriculture hubs and industrial zones. If the country is to avoid future economic and social fallout, the government must undertake a systematic effort to implement and enforce a sustainable development agenda.

Vietnam's leaders have a way of finding pragmatic solutions and among Vietnam experts optimism prevails that the country's leadership will find its way through the current bumpy road of reform and economic instability. As an emerging middle-income country, Vietnam needs to go beyond 'development at any cost' to focus on transparent processes and the quality of growth. The country's leaders and its young, ambitious population are in a hurry to surpass their neighbours in becoming a modern and prosperous nation. This goal is attainable by improving transparency and accountability in the public investment approval process, improving regulation of the financial and banking system, long-term strategic investment in the young and highly literate population, improving infrastructure to global trade networks, and a sustainable approach toward its rich endowment of natural resources.

A9 | *The European compact on trade still stands*

FREDRIK ERIXON[*]

Few continents can testify to the benefits of free trade and the perils of protectionism as much as Europe. It has been the continent of wars and bloodsheds, of blockades and iron curtains. It has been the cradle of Marxism and mercantilism, of Luddites and colonial looters. But it has also been the home for a compact of trade – before and after the World Wars. Tutored by great trade economists such as Adam Smith and David Ricardo, Europe started the wave of trade and economic reforms that facilitated industrialization and globalization in the nineteenth century. Guided by recent lessons of competitive economic nationalism, post-war leaders in Europe restored the continent by following the dictum of the late French economist Frédéric Bastiat: if goods don't cross borders, armies will.

In both these European epochs, free trade was part of the quest for civilization. Europe's own internal search for peace and prosperity, which led up to what is today the European Union, also gave Europe foreign clout – projectionary power as well as hard economic power – of a kind that noxious mercantilism or raw colonial exploitation never could deliver. Paradoxically, when Europe has liberalized internally, it has become an economic power externally; but when Europe has attempted to use its foreign economic power for non-liberal purposes, it has grown weak.

The European compact on trade still stands. Trade is and will remain the backbone of European cooperation. Europe has grown to be the biggest trading bloc in the world, and European producers and consumers have fared well in the age of globalization. European

* Fredrik Erixon is a Director and co-founder of the European Centre for
  International Political Economy (ECIPE), a world economy think tank based
  in Brussels. He is the author of several books and papers about international
  and European political economy. He is an advisor to several governments,
  and prior to founding ECIPE he was an academic economist and worked for
  JP Morgan and Timbro, a Swedish think tank.

multinationals have successfully entered new markets and made use of sourcing opportunities. Declining real prices of many consumer goods has boosted European purchasing power. Real hourly earnings in Europe would have been around 20 per cent lower if globalization had frozen at its level in 1970.

Yet the European compact on trade is fraying at the edges. There is an increasing belief that open trade does not benefit Europe as much as it has done in the past. The rising economic powers in the Far East are often viewed as threats to European prosperity. Behind this view lurks what Paul Krugman has called 'pop internationalism' and David Henderson, 'DIYE' ('do-it-yourself-economics'): the false notion that other countries' wealth comes at your expense.

But Europe's increasing anxiety over trade and globalization also rests on genuine domestic economic problems and a disbelief in Europe's industry-led model for trade and growth. There are three pressing problems.

First, structural change in the West European economies has been far too slow. Growth in output and employment in service-based and innovative sectors has not been high enough to foster a smooth transit from an industry-based economy to a knowledge-based one. Global trade speeds up structural change, and is a vector for dissemination of technology, the greatest factor behind structural change. But policies in Europe have made this change more difficult and governments have been unwilling to pursue substantial economic reforms. It is a testimony of European reform inertia that agricultural subsidies occupy almost 50 per cent of the EU's budget at a time when the hallmark programme for the EU has been to make Europe the most competitive economy in the world. A few years ago, France shielded its yoghurt-producing firms from the embrace of globalization, calling it a strategic sector. To pursue what Patrick Messerlin has called the 'strategic yoghurt policy' at a time of rapid economic change in the world is nothing but absurd.

Second, inflexibilities in European labour markets are particularly worrying for Europe's ability to reap the full benefits of trade and foster smooth structural change. Admittedly, structural labour market change is more difficult today than in the past fifty years. Europe has moved from an intra-sectoral model for change to an inter-sectoral model. When an industrial worker became unemployed a few decades ago because of trade or technological change, he or she could often find a new job in another industrial firm. It did not require massive re-education to become employable in another industrial sector; on-the-job training often sufficed. Today, however, it often requires a new set of skills for an industrial worker, unemployed by global competition, to get a new job. Investment in education is often necessary.

Friends of inflexible and highly regulated labour markets assert that restrictions on companies' freedom to fire people will make them more prone to invest in staff training and education, making the workforce more competitive and adaptive to structural change. This assertion is partly true: some, but not all, highly regulated labour markets in Europe make more investments in staff education than some, but not all, lightly regulated labour markets. But this assertion does not distinguish between different sorts of education: much of the company-based investment in staff education makes the staff more competitive in the sector where they are active, but does not make the staff more employable in other sectors.

The assertion also hides the more troubling aspects of inflexible labour markets. Of particular interest from the viewpoint of structural change is the preference for unemployment over nominal decreases for structurally uncompetitive wages and the unwillingness to switch jobs. The effect is high unemployment, high thresholds to enter the labour market and disincentives for labour market mobility. This is troubling from a trade perspective. Trade and foreign competition often get blamed for job losses and unemployment.

Third, Europe has been unwilling to open up for trade sectors where they are globally competitive and could increase output and employment through trade. Healthcare is an example. While big parts of industrial production in one way or the other will move to low-cost countries, Europe has strong comparative advantages in healthcare. There are enormous export opportunities – to countries inside and outside Europe. There are also considerable savings to be made for cash-strapped healthcare systems if they made greater use of trade. But European healthcare systems do not seize upon these opportunities. In fact, most European governments are unwilling to reform their healthcare systems to make them more susceptible to trade. Again, reform inertia prohibits Europe from reaping the full benefits from trade.

Europe's position in global trade moves bottom-up: when Europe liberalizes internally it becomes competitive externally. That's a big part of the story of European post-war economic success. But its future ability to grow its economy as much through trade as it has done in the past will hinge upon its willingness to reform its economy. Europe is not about to turn to protectionism or a 'fortress Europe'. Such a move would almost be impossible – and it would seriously contract European economies. Nor is Europe's role as a leading trading bloc in the world disputed. It will remain at the top for the foreseeable future. But for a continent whose economies have been as dependent on increasing trade as Europe, past achievements are not enough. New reforms must be pursued to keep this growth vehicle on track. The European compact for trade is now fraying at the edges. It needs to be rebuilt. As W. B. Yeats put it in *The Second Coming*: things fall apart; the centre cannot hold.

A10 | Synergies with the Russian Federation

FABRICE LEHMANN[*]

The Russian trajectory of the past twenty years has been a mercurial blend of the extraordinary and the dreary. It has carried little synchronicity with the triumphalist political and intellectual hubris in Western quarters which greeted the disintegration of the Soviet Union.

Few had foreseen the speed with which the policies introduced by a reformist General Secretary would unravel the contradictions of Soviet developmentalism and snowball into outright collapse. Yet the vocal foreign experts and principal architects of post-Soviet Russian economic policy deceived themselves into believing that the core of a disintegrating Empire – comprising a military-industrial rustbelt, a demoralized workforce, a dispersed population, a rising wave of nationalist and ethnic sentiment, serious environmental damage, collapsing state structures and a lingering concern over territorial integrity – would morph into a democratically sanctioned liberal market economy.

The immediate demonstration of this euphoric lack of humility was the reckless imposition of an economic model based on radical liberalization and privatization whose defining virtues were velocity and conceptual intransigence – a form of therapy no Western society had been subject to. The culminating point at the time of writing is a Russian development model characterized by highly unequal standards of living and a strong statist form of corporatism articulated along opaque verticals of power referred to as sovereign democracy.

Without drawing hasty conclusions on causality, it has been argued by Russian social analysts that the country has, since the late 1980s, been in a state of almost perpetual crisis – the latest cycle being the sharp swing in household fortunes from energy and credit-fuelled

* Fabrice Lehmann is Research Associate and Editor with the Evian Group at IMD. He has worked, studied and travelled extensively in Russia.

consumption to contraction associated with the 2008–2009 global economic downturn – and it is in this context that Russia's involvement in the global polity should be understood. Twenty years after the fall of the Iron Curtain, Russia is still struggling to determine its precise place in an increasingly interdependent and multipolar world.

Two evocative statistics can help procure a sense of the vagaries that Russia's population has been whisked through over the past generation when their nation experienced an economic collapse with few – if any – comparisons in contemporary world economic history. The first is that life expectancy at birth has yet to return to 1989 levels: it stood at 66 in 2006 compared to 69 in 1990. The second is that according to the All-Russia Institute for Public Opinion, 38 per cent of Russian citizens do not trust their judicial system and 46 per cent do not trust their law-enforcement agencies. Social and economic indicators have improved since the chaos of the 1990s during which the state came precariously close to losing its monopoly on violence, although this has been achieved at a debilitating political and institutional cost. The public spirit and trust central to the good operation of a just economy dissolved.

There are two further variables to take into account when assessing Russia's socioeconomic landscape. The first is that Russian society is fragmented by chronology. Pensioners were essentially disenfranchised from the transition process through the lifting of price controls, hyperinflation, stripping of state assets and the 1998 currency crisis when Russia defaulted on its domestic debt.[1]

At the other extreme, a young and predominantly urban population is materializing for whom the anarchy of those same years holds decreasing sway. There is considerable disagreement as to the fragility or cohesion in terms of basic values of this social group, but, as noted by the *Financial Times*, 'with the same fervour that orthodox Marxist-Leninists once placed their hopes in the proletariat, a new generation of political scientists believes the emerging middle class to be the engine of history'.[2]

---

[1] The restoration of certain unpalatable historical truisms is partly related to this.
[2] 'The Middle Class: New Consumers Present a Conundrum', *Financial Times*, 14 April 2009.

The second variable is geography. Population and resources are very unevenly distributed across Russia's landmass, with capital essentially concentrated in a few urban centres and resource-rich regions. Even within these comparative pockets of wealth, one only needs to stray a few kilometres from the gravitational core to be confronted with parlous living conditions.

The processes through which post-Soviet elites have surfaced are extremely shady and convoluted. The rise and gradual taming of the self-styled tycoons known as the oligarchs has been well documented. Neither is the mounting importance of the security apparatus and newly coalesced Nomenklatura open to conjecture. The fabric through which much of this has occurred is a feature that continues to strike many Western observers of contemporary Russian society – the ad hoc nature of changes in legislation and its selective application, perverse corruption permeating daily transactions, and informal mechanisms from the securing of property rights to the procurement of resident permits or the acquisition of licences.

The second phase of asset and industrial consolidation that started with the 1998 rouble collapse and accelerated during Vladimir Putin's first presidential term has gradually led to a convergence of state and business interests aptly described as 'a symbiosis rooted in the neo-patrimonial form assumed by capitalism in Russia'.[3] Although by no means exclusive to Russia, the state has gradually been captured by business interests for whom bureaucratic positions are an investment and an asset.

One of the questions to arise from the 2008 financial crisis is whether it will bring about further changes in business-political structures as it is far from clear where the dominant forces of power will reside, nor the extent to which market forces will be allowed to operate, nor how enterprises under stress or that are recognized to be of strategic significance will be channelled and supported.

This brings us to international trade and multilateralism. The Russian Federation is at present the only major economy not to partake in the principles of the rules-based multilateral trading system. The Kremlin expects – at least officially – to complete the labyrinthine

[3] Tony Wood, 'Contours of the Putin Era', *New Left Review*, March–April 2007.

sixteen-year accession process to the WTO by 2011 or 2012. It appears to be a sufficiently important policy objective in Moscow – albeit erratic and subject to fluctuating influences – for one to wonder what is driving this issue. Twenty-first century globalization poses some tough questions to a bureaucratic state traditionally guided by mercantilist or geopolitical considerations.

President Medvedev's advisors seem to have reached the conclusion that while their nation is well positioned in the global scramble for energy resources, Russia will not be modernized on the back of oil, gas and metals. Two-thirds of Russian export revenue is presently derived from energy, which has often been used to exact Russia's influence in regional and global affairs.

Thanks to this rent the Central Bank has accumulated the third-largest pool of foreign exchange reserves in the world. Yet infrastructure suffers from underinvestment, educational levels have dropped, public health services are extremely precarious, universities are underfunded, and a grass-root entrepreneurial body has largely failed to materialize. At the same time, Russia has been unable to produce a regional integration model of any durable allure.

Interests within the state believe that if Russian businesses are to produce innovative goods that compete in the global market, changes in tax laws, property rights and customs regulations are necessary to encourage investment, as well as attract risk capital to supplement government funds in research and scientific priorities. In essence, sophisticate and diversify a primitive market economy for which WTO accession acts as a lever. As ever, whether these efforts actually trickle down and benefit Russia's populace at large remains to be seen.

We conclude with an open question on a subject often coated in polite resignation. Russia is the world's fourth-largest emitter of greenhouse gases while the near entirety of the former Soviet space suffers from acute environmental problems. Given Russia's varied topography and the many climatic zones it covers, predicting with any certainty the overall impact of global warming on domestic agriculture or its productive base is impossible. Yet the increased variability of weather patterns will without doubt be disruptive to urban and rural populations within its borders and immediate vicinity.

A lot of ink is spilt on Russian pipeline diplomacy, geostrategic dynamics in the Arctic region, NATO expansion and its future role in energy security, population imbalances in the Russian Far East, dispersed nationalities and demographic decline, frictions over Crimea and conflict in the Caucasus, human rights and freedom of press, interference in domestic prerogatives or the manner of Russia's influence over weak states in its near abroad.

Surely there exist channels for regional cooperation on environmental disruption of shared concern which could qualitatively improve the nature of these dialogues and are worthy of greater effort and investigation. In the tender words of Osip Mandelstam after a bout of depression in the late 1920s: 'And I could have whistled through life like a startling, / eating nut pies ... / But clearly there's no chance of that.'

A11 Reasons for an optimistic future view of trade and Latin America

FÉLIX PEÑA[*]

There are several good reasons to hold an optimistic view about Latin America (LA) in world trade during the next ten years. These reasons are related to the region's learning process over the last decades, some significant cultural changes and the impact of new international realities. As a result, some LA nations are becoming more assertive, pragmatic and optimistic. This new attitude also accounts for the internationalization of many regional firms, including the growing number of small and medium enterprises (SMEs) that are integrating transnational production networks.

The trend towards improvements will continue despite occasional ups and downs. This is not to underestimate the huge and familiar challenges that remain to be overcome over the next years, including those related to the region's pattern of foreign trade.

It is precisely with those challenges in mind that it may seem convenient, before continuing, to raise a word of caution. Everyone knows that in a world of deep systemic changes, forecasting can be dangerous. Mindful of the views on LA that predominate in many quarters, it has always been safer to predict negative, if not catastrophic, scenarios. But today it appears that some factors enable one to risk a more positive forecast concerning the future contribution of the region to global trade and governance.

To begin with the bad news, let me briefly make reference to the well-known inventory of reasons to be sceptical about the future trade and investment performance of LA. The following are some of

* Félix Peña is Director of the Institute of International Trade of the Standard Bank Foundation and of the Jean Monet Module and Interdisciplinary Center of International Studies at Tres de Febrero National University (UNTREF), Argentina. He is also member of the Executive Committee of the Argentine Council for International Relations (CARI), President of the Academic Council of Export-Ar Foundation and member of the Evian Group Brains Trust.

the factors, among others, that could feed into a pessimistic view: the extent of poverty and huge social inequalities; poor institutional quality and weak capacity to assure the rule of law; political instability with a continued recurrence of unsustainable populist approaches; absence of a sufficient number of firms capable of competing in fair conditions in national and global markets; low levels of innovation and investment in science and technology; and finally the potential political impact of organized crime and narcotraffic networks. These factors still prevail in many appraisals of the future of LA in world trade, even when compounded with positive structural factors such as natural resources, for example.

Let us now move to the good news, exploring the resilience of these factors. Before doing so, I must recall that they are not necessarily always valid for all LA countries. The region is sufficiently large and diverse to preclude any approach without differentiations. With this in mind, my argument is that factors which justify a more optimistic forecast about the future of LA in world trade are not necessarily evident in all of its countries. Today they are mostly visible in some key countries. And it is precisely those countries that appear to have a strong potential to spread their eventual successes to the rest of LA.

One of the most illustrative, albeit not exclusive, examples is Brazil. Deep changes are transforming the largest country in the region in what could eventually become a driving force towards a more positive future for the rest of LA in world trade. This does not imply that Brazil alone could lead the region – especially South America – to a different pattern of economic and political development. On the contrary, building a regional space that is functional to a scenario in which peace, political stability and sustainable development prevails will require cooperation between several countries, including third nations with strong interests in LA. But it does mean that the consolidation of its recent institutional and economic performance could stimulate, and also amplify, similar processes in other key countries. Working together, Brazil, Argentina, Chile and Uruguay in the south, as well as Mexico in the north, for example, now seem to be in a better condition to take on the role of a core group of rationality, democracy, economic modernization and social cohesion. In so doing, they could have a strong and positive impact on the rest of the region, including those countries which encounter greater difficulties in overcoming certain social conflicts with deep roots in their national history.

Let me now move to what I consider to be the main reasons for an optimistic view about the future of LA in world trade.

The first is that several countries of the region seem to have learned a lot from their past experiences. This learning process is more evident in a number of aspects. One is the recognition of the importance of fiscal discipline and macroeconomic stability to assure development goals. The second is that institutional quality is now considered to be crucial for productive transformation and social cohesion. And the third is the clear understanding that, within the present international system, the destiny of every country should be shaped through the deeper and stronger participation of all society.

A second major reason to be optimistic is the existence of strong signals pointing to a cultural change taking hold in some LA countries concerning their future. These signals are related to the greater value attached to long-term goals and more pragmatic strategies. It implies owning a sense of where each country is willing to go, of what it can realistically achieve, and especially of what are the required steps to advance in the chosen direction. Here, differences among LA countries are more evident. Unresolved structural problems, including those related to the active participation of all social sectors in the nation-building process, explain some of these differences. Some countries are as yet in the transition toward more integrated societies. It is possible to observe in these cases greater political instabilities, as well as proposals for more radical economic and social policies. As a result, their future prospects could eventually become uncertain and controversial.

And finally, the third main reason is related to the impact of deep changes that are transforming the global landscape. Today, LA countries have more options in terms of foreign markets and external sources for investments and technologies. Diversification is increasing the scope of action for LA countries' external relations and for the internationalization of their firms. They also discern greater value in their potential contribution to solving some critical issues on the global agenda. Energy, food security, water and climate change are some of the central issues on which LA countries will have something (or eventually a lot) to say in the next ten years.

The fulfilment of optimistic scenarios for LA trade and development will require strengthening regional cooperation through patterns of collective leadership and a wide range of effective heterodox methodologies, including multiple speed and variable geometry agreements. Mercosur and other formal integration processes could yet play a positive role. But they will require the adaptation of their main instruments and working methodologies to the new regional and global trade and investment realities.

It will also require the drawing of multiple strategic alliances with countries from other regions with common interests, as well as the active participation of the region in future multilateral global trade negotiations. Without doubt, a strong WTO will continue in the future to be one of the key elements of LA's strategy for expanding its participation in world trade. And a stronger LA will also imply a positive contribution to a more effective and development-oriented multilateral global trade system.

A12 | Is the Brazilian giant finally awakening?

UMBERTO CELLI[*]

Over recent years, Brazil has emerged on the international scene as one of the world's fastest-growing emerging economies and markets alongside Russia, India and China, all of which compose a grouping labelled the 'BRICs' by the international financial institution Goldman Sachs in an influential 2003 report.

After the end of the military government in 1985, it took almost a decade of civilian leadership and a series of crises for the country to eventually find a path to economic stability in a politically plural, open and more competitive environment. Strategic reforms, initiated in 1994, have brought about a positive combination of mature democracy, strong and consolidated democratic and republican institutions, with price stability and a diversified economy.

More recently, global growth and income distribution programmes, such as *Bolsa Família*, have contributed to a decrease in the country's notorious levels of inequality (millions of poor people became consumers for the first time) and to the expansion of the middle class. The country's agricultural sector, which until not long ago was often associated with slavery and the abuse of workers' rights, has also undergone outstanding improvements. Owing to the rapid development of the sugar ethanol industry, Brazilian agriculture is now a symbol of the country's emergence as a social innovator on the world stage.

A large stock of harvested and unused fertile land, a hospitable climate and abundant water have made it possible for Brazil to become a leader in global agricultural commodities markets, with the expansion of its food exports likely to continue given the competitive cost of these commodities. This global prominence in agriculture, combined with a diversified industrial sector, a competitive mining industry and the imminence of becoming an important oil exporter (the so-called

---

[*] Umberto Celli is Professor of International Trade Law at the University of São Paulo, Brazil.

55

Pré-Sal Exploitation Programme recently announced by the government), have transformed Brazil into a major player in the realms of international trade and foreign investment; a fact to which the central and leadership role it exercises in the WTO bears testimony.

After having emerged in the mid-1990s from decades of economic volatility Brazil demonstrated resilience to the 2008–2009 global crisis, which erupted shortly after the restructuring of its banking system. The banking system and capital markets alike are subject to stricter rules than in many other jurisdictions, including in developed countries. While a number of developed countries use guidelines laid down by the Bank for International Settlements (BIS) in Basel, under which banks should hold assets equal to at least 8% of their lending, the minimum requirement under Brazilian regulations is 11%, although the average level is in practice closer to 18%.

When the financial crisis hit the country, the government was immediately able to adopt countermeasures in response: US$50 billion was released by the Central Bank to provide relief to liquidity-starved banks; an additional US$50 billion was provided to the Brazilian Development Bank (BNDES), the government's development bank, in order to finance investment and working capital for businesses; and cuts in sales taxes on motor vehicles, construction materials and household electrical goods were enacted. The effectiveness of these measures allowed Brazil to surface from the crisis faster than expected and strengthened the confidence of foreign investors (GDP is expected to grow by at least 6% in 2010).

Despite the sizeable progress achieved on many fronts, the country is confronted with no less considerable challenges, which makes one wonder whether its present trajectory of economic growth and development is in fact sustainable. On the political front, old and deleterious habits, such as the reproachable behaviour of a number of Brazil's political leaders (the Senate has been the focus of numerous scandals), are difficult to reconcile with one's expectations of a modern economy and society. Public sector corruption is still an endemic problem. On the commercial side, the expansion of trade (domestic and foreign) is limited by the lack of adequate infrastructure, particularly roads, to transport goods. Although the government has been massively investing in logistics, the country still lags behind many other emerging countries. With respect to fiscal and tax policies, a number of measures are still necessary for the government to enhance the productivity and competitiveness of domestic companies. These include the long-awaited tax reform, which should at the very least involve a reduction of the numerous federal taxes levied cumulatively on the productive chain, and the reduction of the huge tax burden caused by inefficiencies in public spending. The productivity and competitiveness of Brazil's economy would also certainly improve if the enormous spreads in the banking industry and the towering interest rate (one of the world's highest) were brought down.

Access to foreign markets is another key element for the sustainable development of Brazil. Brazil's share in international trade (slightly over 1 per cent) is not commensurate with its GDP (among the world's ten largest), geographical expanse and population size (190 million). A pragmatic international trade policy should play a crucial role in enabling the country to gain access to foreign markets. As one of the key actors in the WTO (Brazil is no longer a mere importer of rules, but an important conceiver of norms in the functioning of the international system), Brazil should not abandon its efforts and hopes to close the Doha Round of trade negotiations as soon as possible. The deal on the negotiating table on NAMA (Non-Agriculture Market Access) and Agriculture, interrupted in 2008, is essentially favourable to the country. Reinforcement of the multilateral trade system continues to be the most efficient way for the country to tackle the current trend of protectionism and gain access to new markets. This does not mean that Brazil should overlook the general tendency of major global players towards implementing regional and bilateral agreements.

The country and its partners in Mercosur (the South American customs union formed by Brazil, Argentina, Uruguay and Paraguay – with Venezuela's accession process under way) should be prepared to initiate, deepen or resume trade negotiations with important economic trading blocs such as the European Communities, or emerging economies such as India. A difficulty arises in that Mercosur is a customs union (albeit incomplete), which prevents its members from individually negotiating or signing trade agreements. Over the last years, Mercosur has experienced a stagnant regional integration process, one marked by trade conflicts as well as diverging trade and economic policy views and interests often difficult to reconcile. Unless its members manage to overcome these difficulties, which at this stage seems to be unlikely, the idea that Mercosur should confine itself to being a free trade area rather than a customs union, thus allowing each member to negotiate trade agreements individually, should not be ruled out.

As in the other 'BRICs' countries, a significant economic and social transformation has unquestionably occurred in Brazil over recent years. Certain imperatives, such as the adoption and the enactment of a more consistent project to improve education at all levels, a more effective policy on the distribution of income (one of world's most unequal), and urban and social interventions to reduce poverty and violence, especially in the big cities, are suggestive of the tough challenges that still lie ahead. In any event, it would not be imprudent to assert that the Latin American giant is finally and irreversibly awaking.

A13 | The Arab region and the GCC in tomorrow's trade

ABDULAZIZ SAGER[*]

The Arab countries are heavily dependent on international trade for their prosperity – in fact the region is characterized by very high levels of openness to international trade, and has therefore a clear and very keen interest in the continuation of the process of progressive liberalization of global exchanges.

The image of the Arab economies as being closed and inclined to protectionism reflects old nationalist rhetoric and import-substitution policies, but is by now totally non-representative of reality.

The Arab country with the lowest openness to international trade (measured as imports + exports/GDP) is Sudan, where the openness indicator takes a value of 43. In comparison, the USA has a degree of openness of 27 and Japan of 31: even Sudan is more open than either of the two. All other Arab economies have greater openness, topped by the United Arab Emirates with a very high level of 159.

The stereotype according to which the Arab economies are relatively closed and protectionist dates back to the period of Arab nationalism, when it was felt that pursuing regional integration between the Arab countries would open the door to industrialization and reduce dependence on the outside world. It would also open the door to political unification and the rebirth of the Arab nation.

But the Arab region is not the same as Germany in the nineteenth century. The Arab region is structurally extroverted, because it is huge by geographical extension and sparsely populated – two features that discourage the intensification of intra-regional trade. The distance

---

[*] Abdulaziz Sager is Chairman and founder of the Gulf Research Center. He is also President of Sager Group Holding and a member of the Makkah Province Council. In addition, he serves as a member on the advisory board of the Arab Thought Foundation, Geneva Centre for the Democratic Control of Armed Forces (DCAF) and on the advisory group for the 4th Arab Human Development Report for the United Nations Development Programme (UNDP).

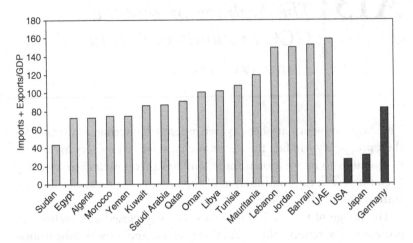

Figure A13.1: Arab economies' degree of openness
Source: Based on data from WTO.

between Rabat and Dubai is about 6,000 kilometres, and in between there is mostly empty desert. In contrast, the distance between Rabat and Madrid is barely 800 kilometres: how can we be surprised that Morocco's, or Tunisia's, trading relations are primarily with Europe?

Not only is the Arab region geographically vast and underpopulated, but the state of modern communication infrastructure is frequently not up to standard. With the exception of the Gulf countries – where large sums have been devoted to establishing a road network which was totally non-existent in the past, and where projects are being pursued to create rail links at least along major traffic corridors – the quality of road and rail connections rapidly declines as soon as the immediate surroundings of the capital city are left behind. Moving merchandise from one Arab state to the next is not an easy task, and it is made even more difficult by frequent unfriendly political relations and the complexity of customs procedures. Long-distance, maritime-based trade is often easier than short-haul land-based exchanges.

Furthermore, the Arab countries are still primarily exporters of raw materials, and mostly competitors rather than complementary. True, some Arab countries have no oil or gas at all, and they will tend to specialize in providing goods and services to neighbouring Arab countries (examples are Lebanon or Jordan), but in the vast majority of cases the competitive aspect prevails over complementarities.

Such structural factors – compounded by multiple conflicts frequently opposing neighbouring Arab countries – result in a region that is the most extroverted in the world. Africa is the only region to have a lower share of intra-regional trade than the Middle East.

Furthermore, a historic shift has progressively taken place in the relative economic weight of individual Arab countries. In the past, the political, cultural and also economic centre of the region used to be the population-rich countries of the Levant and Egypt. Today, the countries of the Gulf Cooperation Council account for 60 per cent of the GDP of the Arab region – and Saudi Arabia accounts for 60 per cent of the GDP of the GCC. The GCC countries are even more closely integrated in the globalization process than the rest of the region.

Shifting relativities will become an even more important factor in the coming years. The Mediterranean policy of the European Union has essentially failed to create an area of closer economic integration between the Union and its Mediterranean partners, which included some, but not all, Arab countries. With the possible exception of Morocco and Tunisia, access to the European internal market has offered limited benefits for the region's economic development. Even in the case of Morocco, as in that of Jordan, economic integration with the United States has proven as important and dynamic, if not more, as with the European Union.

However, the situation might change as the process of industrialization of the Gulf countries continues at a rapid pace. Further economic diversification in the GCC countries may offer more important opportunities for expanding intra-regional economic relations. Although the GCC economies will remain widely open to imports from all over, the Arab neighbours will also be able to benefit from the success of the GCC.

The GCC is thus increasingly turning into the dynamic heart of the region, and its future trade developments will characterize the entire region. Initially, the GCC countries had been hesitant to acquire membership and engage in the WTO process, but this phase belongs to the past. Although the practical implementation of the GCC customs union still faces challenges, and Gulf countries find it difficult to present a unified position to the outside world, progress is constantly being made.

The GCC economies can build and consolidate a competitive advantage based on their potential for transforming hydrocarbons and engaging in carbon capture and sequestration, rather than being confined to exporting crude oil exclusively. A specialization in petroleum derivatives may seem relatively narrow, but considering the extraordinary number of different uses of petrochemical products it is not. In any case, the GCC countries are bound to remain highly specialized in their export trade, simply because their resource endowment is so peculiar.

The specialization pattern dictates that trade between the GCC and the rest of Asia will intensify in the coming decades. The complementarities are here very evident, and even protectionist policies would not be sufficient to alter what is a strong structural trend. In addition, the Asian markets are growing rapidly, while the European market is stagnating at best; Asia therefore offers the best opportunities for accommodating the rapid growth of GCC petrochemical exports.

Carbon capture and sequestration (CCS) may also become an important source of competitive specialization, if indeed the international community is to be serious in tackling the danger of climate change and the need to reduce carbon emissions. The GCC countries in fact enjoy ideal conditions to engage in CCS – as well as in exploiting some renewable sources, notably solar – and this may be a further reason to support a pattern of relative specialization in energy-intensive production processes.

The GCC countries are also eager to expand trade with Africa. This is motivated in part by concerns related to food security and in part by the perception that Africa offers some very promising growth opportunities in the coming decades, which the GCC business community is keen to exploit.

This means that, contrary to the historical pattern, which sees emerging countries as being primarily interested in developing trade with the main OECD economies, the GCC countries are and will increasingly be a dynamic factor in 'South–South' trade and investment links. In this context, economic relations within the Arab region itself will also find an opportunity for expansion, reducing the extreme level of extroversion that characterizes the region still today.

The process of trade liberalization and globalization, which has on many occasions been accused of fostering a 'hub and spokes' model of international economic relations, may thus evolve in an entirely different direction. As the OECD economies are trapped in a crisis unlikely to be resolved quickly, they are bound to stagnate, if not decline, for some time, and then experience a difficult recovery, amid inflation fears and the need to contain public debt. In contrast, the positive interaction of the GCC countries with Asia on one side and Africa on the other holds the promise of creating a novel development dynamic.

So, paradoxically, while the industrial economies are increasingly tempted to fall back on good old protectionist practices, the Arab region may be expected to continue in the path of liberalization, following the steps of the GCC.

A14 | *Growing African trade amid global economic turmoil*

MILLS SOKO[*]

For Africa, the 1990s heralded a crucial break from the grim 'lost decade' of the 1980s. In recent years, the African continent has undergone a remarkable political and economic transformation. Even though the continent is still faced with governance and development challenges, it is a far better place today than it was twenty years ago.

For one thing, Africa is by and large more politically stable today. Several civil wars, such as those in Angola, Rwanda, Sierra Leone and Mozambique, have ended and the number of inter-state conflicts has declined. Many African countries, including Liberia and Tanzania, have made appreciable progress in terms of improving governance and combating corruption. Other countries, such as Algeria, Niger and Sierra Leone, have shown marked improvements in strengthening the rule of law and in promoting government accountability.

The increasingly stable political environment across the African continent has coincided with an improving business climate. Over the past few years, a number of African states have implemented business-friendly reforms. In 2008, four African states – Botswana, Burkina Faso, Egypt and Senegal – were identified by the World Bank as among the top ten business regulation reformers in the world. These success stories have been emulated elsewhere on the continent. For example, until recently Rwanda had no commercial courts. This meant that disputes had to be resolved through the normal judicial system and the courts had to contend with a seven-year backlog of 3,000 cases. Thanks to a US$5 m project funded by the Investment Climate Facility, the government has been able to set up commercial courts and the backlog has been slashed by 70 per cent.

---

[*] Dr Mills Soko is an Associate Professor at the University of Cape Town's Graduate School of Business, and the Founding Director of Mthente Research and Consulting Services, South Africa.

Against the backdrop of growing political stability and business-oriented economic policies Africa has chalked up impressive growth. Between 2001 and 2008, growth in national economic output on the continent averaged 5.9% annually, the strongest consistent performance since the early 1970s. In 2007, Sub-Saharan Africa's exports accounted for 3% of world trade, from 2% in the late 1990s. Coupled with this improved – albeit worryingly sluggish by world standards – trade performance has been growing flows of foreign investment into the continent; foreign investment stocks grew from US$202 billion in 2003 to US$393 billion in 2007.

Undoubtedly, Africa's phenomenal growth has been powered by a commodity super cycle, driven primarily by Chinese and Indian demand. Commodity revenues grew from US$363 billion in 2007 to US$460 billion in 2009. Between 2002 and 2008, commodity prices rose by an enormous 200% and African exports by 260%.

This hard-earned economic progress, however, has been undermined by the 2008–2009 global financial crisis that originated in the United States. Although the crisis was not of Africa's making, the region has not been spared its deleterious effects, with national economic output growth for the continent projected to decline to 2.0% in 2009 and 3.9% in 2010.

The crisis, epitomized by a precipitous decline in global growth, has reduced demand for African commodity exports, the chief source of export receipts for most African nations. The fall in export revenues has, in turn, diminished government revenues, thereby aggravating the already precarious fiscal situation in many African countries. The global credit crunch has also led to a slump in private investment flows and bank financing, reflected in reduced foreign direct investment, migrant remittances and trade finance. Moreover, shrinking private capital flows have had damaging effects on African countries that are currently financing huge current account deficits, such as South Africa, Uganda and Tanzania.

Even though the global economic recession did not emanate from Africa, African countries cannot bury their heads in the sand. To be sure, the financial crisis provides African countries with a golden opportunity to consolidate the economic and political reforms they initiated in the 1990s. As Mozambique's President Armando Guebuza noted: 'The current global economic crisis is yet another and louder call for our countries in Africa to improve the competitiveness of their economies, institutions and policies. More importantly, it provides the stimulus for us to strengthen our resolve and quicken our pace in doing so.'

Concerted actions and responses are required to mitigate the effects of the crisis, safeguard the economic gains made, and pursue the long-term goals of global competitiveness, economic prosperity and social development. In the short term, African governments – at least those with the capacity to do so – should implement appropriate fiscal and monetary responses to cushion the impact of the crisis on their economies.

In the long term, African nations must enhance their global competitiveness and secure economic prosperity, while maintaining macroeconomic, political, social and environmental stability. This means, first, prioritizing agriculture, the bedrock of African economies and the key to the continent's economic revitalization. Besides making up 35% of Africa's economic output, it accounts for 70% of the region's employment and 40% of its exports. Developing the agricultural sector is crucial to securing food self-sufficiency, expanding economic opportunities for growth and driving industrialization across Africa.

It also means diversifying Africa's production and exports. Barring a few countries such as South Africa, Morocco and Mauritius – which have a diversified export base – African foreign trade is based on one or two traditional commodities, predominantly oil and agricultural exports. Diversifying the continent's exports is vital to bolstering its trade performance and protecting its economies against external shocks.

Moreover, to become internationally competitive African states must shore up regional integration and expand intra-regional trade. Intra-regional trade constitutes 10% of the continent's trade flows. This pales into insignificance when compared with the 75% trade that takes place among European Union member states, and the 50% trade that occurs within the East Asian and North American regional blocs. Likewise, expanding trade with other developing countries in the context of South–South cooperation is essential to African nations' efforts to diversify their export markets and lessen their dependency on developed country markets.

Furthermore, African countries must strengthen their markets and institutions, and invest in infrastructure, education and health. They must also lower the still high cost of doing business. Even though the business climate in Africa has improved considerably over the past few years, the costs of doing business on the continent remain the highest in the world. Many African entrepreneurs are hampered by weak financial systems, insufficient transport and communications infrastructure, erratic power supply, a lack of protection for property rights and the absence of dispute settlement mechanisms for private parties. Infrastructure deficiencies reduce the productivity of African firms by 40 per cent, according to the World Bank.

International policies are as crucial as domestic policies in tackling Africa's trade challenges. In particular, broadening access for African agricultural exports is vital to promoting the continent's trade. High agricultural subsidies in the developed countries impair African economies. These trade barriers must be eliminated if African trade is to be rejuvenated. In addition, the international community needs to accord special attention to Africa's least developed countries, whose ability to participate effectively in global trade has been hindered by capacity constraints. Improved technical assistance, coupled with suitable compensation and adjustment programmes, could enable these countries to better assess their economic interests, manage their trade obligations and enhance their participation in world commerce.

Africa has made substantial strides in positioning itself as an attractive investment and business destination. If African countries are to attain economic prosperity, however, they must continue to promote political and economic stability, uphold good governance, build markets and institutions, strengthen productive capacity, diversify exports, increase intra-regional commerce, invest in infrastructure and skills, and secure a favourable external trade environment for their exports. Realizing these goals will require strong political will and a genuine desire on the part of governments and the private sector to work together to forge domestic consensus on the primacy of economic reform, high growth rates and policies that alleviate poverty and social inequality.

Governance of global trade

Editorial introduction

Governance of global trade

The focus of this chapter is on the institutions and rules that govern world trade. The World Trade Organization (WTO) has been locked in a protracted negotiation process ever since 2001, when the Doha Development Agenda was launched. Hence the following articles offer different analyses and recommendations for the improved governance of international trade. Governments around the world recurrently face pressures to withdraw from the multilateral rules-based trading system designed on the legitimacy of a set of principles and norms that have allowed global trade to liberalize and flourish. At the heart of these GATT principles lies non-discrimination.

The opening article contends that the failure to conclude the WTO negotiations exposes serious flaws in the architecture of trade governance and global economic governance more generally. The following two contributions propose a set of reforms to render the WTO more effective and adapted to the structures of the world political economy. This is then complemented by an approach to opposing protectionism in the coming decades and an analysis of the ways in which regional agreements can be pushed towards convergence with multilateral principles.

The build-up and sustainability of global imbalances is the subject of the next two articles, both of which underline the importance of international policy coordination to deal with tensions and cascading effects. We then turn our attention to three trade-related issues often surrounded in controversy: the rules and enforcement of intellectual property rights, current patterns of subsidy use, and the institutional linkages between trade and migration in a world undergoing substantial spatial transformations.

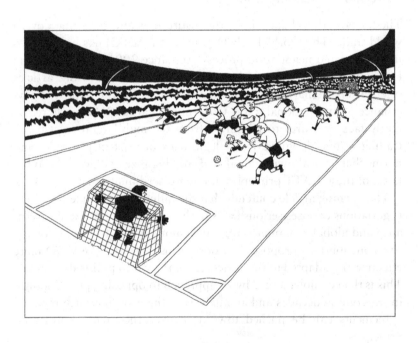

B1 | *Securing the global trade regime: the demand for global governance*

RICHARD HIGGOTT[*]

The world lacks systematic global economic policy coordination from its existing institutions. More specifically, the governance of global trade and the stability of the international trade regime have clearly been affected by the fallout from the wider economic turmoil of 2008–2009. The multilateral trade system is threatened by the perception that globalization has been tarnished by speculative investment and other excesses in financial markets seeking larger profits at the expense of sound business practice. Growing public anger about bad practice in the financial sector since 2007 spilled over into a growing demand for protectionism. This connection might be irrational, but it is all too easily made. Indeed, it is part of a disturbing trend towards rising economic nationalism. Unfairly, the WTO often carries the criticism for excesses in other sections of the global economy, especially the financial sector.

Not only is the future collective management of the global economy crucial to the environment in which trade governance exists, but the architecture of the trade regime will need to accommodate the new stresses placed upon it by questions of sustainability and economic development emanating from the financial crises and the protective sentiments and practices that have ensued. The WTO cannot nor should it try to address all these issues. However, it is apparent that in an increasingly interdependent world, trade policy makers can ignore neither the context in which they operate nor the need to contribute to the resolution of other challenges.

But these challenges raise major questions of institutional policy coherence, or what we increasingly call 'global governance'. It is in

* Richard Higgott is Professor of International Political Economy and Pro Vice Chancellor at the University of Warwick. Since 1995 he has been Editor of *The Pacific Review*. His latest work, with Shaun Breslin, is *Essays in the International Relations of the Asia Pacific* (four volumes, Sage, 2010).

this context that the WTO finds itself in a malaise not of its own making. The difficulties with concluding the Doha Development Round not only demonstrate the difficulties of conducting multilateral trade negotiations in the twenty-first century but also expose serious fault lines in the contemporary architecture of trade governance and global economic governance more generally. Even so, the WTO remains central to our hopes for a more coherent system of global governance. For all the pressures, it remains the most functional global institution. But any discussion about how to improve its effectiveness and efficiency as an agenda-setting and decision-making body must address the 'legitimacy question' and the 'consensus problem'.

The WTO will also need to address the changing power balance occasioned by the rise of new actors such as India and China. Any readjustment in power relations will inevitably be accompanied by a messy transition from one equilibrium to another. A further challenge to the WTO is the extent to which the issues of fairness, justice and democratic accountability are addressed. This goes to the heart of the debate about global governance. The WTO gathers regular and fierce criticism from NGOs and numerous developing country governments, dissatisfied with what they see as the qualified legitimacy present in its negotiating and decision-making processes. This criticism is invariably overstated, often misplaced and fails to understand the complexity of the 'legitimacy question' in global governance in general and for international organizations in particular.

The WTO is clearly ahead of other international organizations in this regard and especially the international financial institutions (IFIs) in the current crisis. Indeed, the WTO displays many attributes of a democratic club. Its rules provide for consensus decision making and the results of negotiations are applied on a most-favoured nation (MFN) basis, thus ensuring that all members enjoy the same benefits. It is responsive to its members. Notwithstanding obvious asymmetries of expertise and power within the membership, the weakest WTO members gain from being part of a rules-based organization. But growing frustration with the multilateral regime has seen policy makers turn to other vehicles for reform – notably bilateral and regional agreements. The largest trading nations have so far desisted from negotiating preferential trade agreements (PTAs) among themselves. But if the WTO membership is seriously to address challenges to the coherence and stability of the trading system, the largest trading nations in the system should show leadership. They should foreswear establishing PTAs among themselves.

The amorphous concept of global governance takes on a more concrete form at a time of crisis such as the one the world has recently experienced (2008–2009). Only a new regulatory regime will assure the newly influential state actors, especially the BRICs, that a balance can be restored between the benefits and risks of globalization. We have known for several decades that key policy areas (trade, climate change, infectious diseases, food and water supply) reflect an increasing global *interdependence* as opposed to national *independence*. But it has taken the financial crises of the early twenty-first century to expose the limitations in our abilities to manage the risks attendant on interdependence via collective action problem solving. The 'underdevelopment' of the global polity, less visible in normal times, is only too easy to see in times of crisis. There is growing disconnect between the globalization of risk and the lack of globalization of responsibilities. A lesson of the early twenty-first century is that this cannot be left simply to market forces.

Pointing to these problems, and their potential consequences, is not to suggest that the essence of a system of global economic governance is absent. There are some foundations on which to build. Indeed, we have a set of rules, principles and processes that underpin the multilateral trade system and that can address other challenges. Under stress they may be, but the principles and rules underwritten by the WTO have not been disavowed. Key players may play fast and loose with them at times but they do not question their normative importance for the system, and if the economic crises of the early twenty-first century have revealed anything, it is that rules matter.

The challenge for global governance is to recognize that while it is made up of its parts it is also more than the sum of its parts. The regulation of the financial system and the governance of the trade regime require different policy responses; but to solve the problems in one domain we also need to solve them in the other. Trade liberalization may well continue; indeed, unilateral trade liberalization has been strong over the last two decades, but the process has slowed and pressures for rollback have been growing in the current economic downturn.

For many supporters of the WTO, factors other than trade liberalization are important, especially its role as the guardian of the principles and rules of global trade. The global community needs to reaffirm these principles, the importance of which, especially with regards to the value of multilateralism and institutions as venues and vehicles for global policy making, are becoming 'unlearned' by some major players at exactly the time, ironically, that they are becoming more appreciated by many smaller players. These principles need reaffirmation and coordination across policy areas. We need what Pascal Lamy calls a 'triangle of coherence' with the joining-up of the three major sets of actors and activity present in global economic decision making.

Down one side of the triangle is to be found enhanced political leadership and policy direction via emerging G-20 and/or other relevant (G-'N') processes; down the second side we find the rules, norms and the provision of action-oriented technical expertise provided via the international organization (IMF, World Bank, WTO, specialist organizations, emerging regulatory networks). The third side would provide enhanced venues for accountability and representation, and hence legitimacy, beyond the territorial state. We might call this the political leg. But, if we accept Hannah Arendt's definition of power as 'the ability to act in concert', then this leg is largely powerless and, as a consequence, an impediment to the development of Lamy's 'triangle'.

This third leg may have been less important in the early stages of globalization, when global policy issues were less connected. In the area of trade for example, prior to the creation of the WTO, legitimacy was provided by the accountability of trade ministers to their domestic parliaments. But in the contemporary era, where thick and complex policy interconnections at the global level have become the norm, an absence of intermediate politicians speaking directly to domestic constituencies is a factor in the 'democratic deficit' of international organizations. International organizations are staffed by technicians and public servants, not politicians who intermediate between domestic publics and policy makers. This deficit will continue to prove difficult to fix.

The legitimacy of multilateralism, to the extent that it exists, is embedded in shared norms (usually of elites, rather than wider national publics) and is underwritten by judicial instruments (such as the ICC or the dispute settlement mechanism of the WTO). However, in the absence of a global polity or 'global agora', achieving enhanced policy coordination will continue to prove difficult. The primary process of legitimation remains largely state-based. A task for scholars, practitioners (both public and private) as well as interested sectors of global civil society, is to design politico-institutional structures that will enhance the legitimacy of the international organizations.

B2 | *The trade regime and the future of the WTO*

The year 2009 and early 2010 offer a fascinating paradox. Following the autumn 2008 financial collapse, the world trade regime has displayed remarkable resilience to the severe world economic crisis with so far little evidence of a rise in protection, contrary to prevalent claims. Meanwhile, the obstacles to conclude the Doha Round remain intact. Such a contrast between the resilience of the trade regime and the inertia at the WTO suggests an ongoing systemic shift in the future role of the WTO.

Domestic politics and the WTO Rounds

An initial explanation to the Doha Round inertia – that there are many more WTO members – is not convincing. The Doha negotiations are still largely limited to a few countries, a dozen if the EU is counted as a single entity.

As so often in international trade, more convincing reasons can be found in domestic factors. An increasing number of WTO members are democracies. Many constitutions impede deep trade liberalization. In the United States, for example, the constitution gives a lot of weight to agricultural lobbies in the Senate, and the president has only eight years (with three intervening electoral campaigns) to launch and conclude multilateral trade negotiations.

Moreover, since the late 1980s, all the industrial democracies have experienced increasingly thin governing majorities (regardless of which party ends up governing). Thin majorities offer small and strong vested interests a power out of proportion with their real importance, suffocating the wide support for freer trade among consumers and business.

*Patrick Messerlin is Professor of Economics and Director of Groupe d'Economie Mondiale at Sciences Po (GEM), Paris.

These constraints are with us for a long time. They require changes in the WTO, which was conceived in a different world – before the erosion of governing majorities and before new trade topics began to bite deep.

The WTO as a rule maker

Key WTO rules are non-discrimination (most-favoured nation and national treatment) and 'bound' commitments (that is, commitments, such as bound tariffs in goods, which cannot be reneged on by a WTO member without paying compensation to the other members, at the risk of retaliatory measures).

In today's open world, these rules are more essential than ever because they deliver certainty and undistorted competition. The recent global crisis, for example, underlines the value of binding: we would be more at ease if all WTO members had bound their tariffs at their applied level, imposed disciplines on export subsidies or taxes similar to those on tariffs, and introduced a ratchet provision in their commitments in services.

That said, such strong rules cannot realistically be imposed on all the domains covered by the WTO with the same robustness; for instance on goods that have been liberalized for half a century and on services which are at an early stage of market opening. The WTO as a rule maker thus needs flexibility, a feature hindered by the Single Undertaking principle (under which every WTO member should sign all the agreements negotiated during a round).

The WTO as a negotiating machinery

The WTO is also a negotiating machinery on market access in goods and services. But there is a systemic shift in the relative importance of these two exercises, with major consequences for the WTO's role in the future.

In the goods sector, WTO Rounds are on the decline because the thirty-five odd countries that represent over 90 per cent of world trade and GDP apply mostly small to moderate tariffs. What remains to be done is thus eliminating the remaining high tariffs and binding more firmly and systematically the others.

This objective can be achieved with an appropriate balance between an efficient liberalization formula (the 'Swiss' formula) and a set of exceptions accommodating political constraints. Such a mix should be handled with care. During the Doha Round, developed countries have tabled excessive requests on cuts in industrial tariffs by developing countries, thereby fuelling requests for so many exceptions that the outcome of the Round could be insignificant.

In sharp contrast, the negotiating agenda in services offers vast opportunities to firms and huge gains to consumers for many decades to come – they cover 70 per cent of world GDP. But opening services markets requires trust between partners because it consists of a dynamic and long process of regulatory reforms, often hard to anticipate when negotiating the initial agreements.

Such trust cannot be delivered by the WTO because the regulatory reform capacities of its members are too heterogeneous. This renders agreements in services among a narrower group of countries more attractive. Such plurilateral agreements could be negotiated within the WTO, but they could also be initiated outside it and then repatriated under the WTO rules of non-discriminatory bindings. The WTO as a negotiating machinery becomes less pre-eminent, but, as a rule maker, it remains the ultimate anchor.

The systemic shift between goods and services has a final consequence. It makes shorter but more frequent rounds attractive. Such rounds (framed by appropriate plurilaterals in services, and each applying a 'careful' use of the Swiss formula combined with few exceptions) appear more promising than a few 'ambitious' rounds difficult to start and to conclude, and which are ultimately deceptive.

The Single Undertaking and preferential trade agreements

The WTO as a negotiating machinery is also hindered by the Single Undertaking which has induced many WTO members to form coalitions pre-empting commitments – the 'small and vulnerable economies', the 'cotton producers', the 'recently acceding members', etc. The WTO has consequently become a forum that is increasingly fragmented, irrational, chaotic and ultimately unjust.

As a result, the Single Undertaking should only be made enforceable at distant periods in time, and not on a permanent basis (indeed, its introduction under the Uruguay Round was 'ratcheting' the first fifty years of the GATT). Amid two enforcements, negotiating WTO members should be allowed to 'discriminate positively'; that is, to open their markets by participating in plurilateral agreements without waiting for an agreement between all members.

Such a reinterpretation would rebalance the relations between the WTO and preferential trade agreements (PTAs). A more flexible WTO negotiating process focused on high protection in goods and services via shorter and more frequent rounds would cut the ground under the PTAs by eliminating their core *raison d'être*, substantial trade preferences.

Such a reform would also help maintain a balance between negotiation and litigation in the WTO, thereby reducing the risks of an overburdened and over-stretched WTO dispute settlement mechanism.

Future key challenges: climate change and water

During the last decades, trade negotiators have looked to 'new frontiers': investment protection, competition policy or government procurement. The WTO has no comparative advantage in these issues. By contrast, a focus on market access deals with huge potential as unexploited sources of economic gains (particularly in services) deserves its full attention.

Maintaining the WTO focus on market access would also allow the institution to confront the two major challenges in the decades to come – climate change and water. Today, these issues are widely perceived as antagonistic to the world trade regime at large, hence to the WTO.

This is a major mistake. Climate change and water availability will require more – *not less* – trade, particularly in agricultural goods and services. The half-dozen available models on the impact of climate change differ in almost all their results except one: the key way to soften the hard-to-forecast adjustments required by climate change is to facilitate trade among countries.

Similarly, water resources are very unevenly distributed among countries or regions. If water is a 'local' good, agricultural trade is the highly desirable link between such a local good (and the derived farm products) and widely dispersed food consumers.

In short, cuts in tariffs and in other trade barriers take a new *raison d'être*. They become available tools for the fight against climate-driven hunger and water-driven conflicts.

Of course, climate and water management require proactive domestic policies, which include taxes on CO_2 emissions, investment policies providing an appropriate mix of crops, etc. But the range of such proactive policies is broad. A key role or function of the WTO in the future will be to help choose the best proactive policies – those with minimal negative impact on trade flows since trade will be so vital for world prosperity and peace.

B3 | WTO *reform: the time to start is now*

URI DADUSH*

The WTO is an essential plank of globalization. Imperfect and incomplete as WTO disciplines are, they provide a degree of predictability and stability to trade relations, the value of which has been brought home yet again by the 2008–2009 financial crisis. In a world of sluggish growth and burgeoning protectionist pressures, the importance of rules increases and the need to tighten them becomes more urgent.

The need for reform

However, to a worrying degree, the WTO is today living off the gains of its predecessor, the GATT system. In crucial aspects of its traditional mission, namely reducing actual and bound (i.e. maximum allowable) tariffs, the institution has become increasingly ineffectual. No new trade liberalization in goods and no new lowering of bound tariffs have been agreed under multilateral negotiations since the Uruguay Round concluded in 1994.

In newer areas, such as cutting agricultural subsidies and opening up the markets for services trade, the WTO has so far failed to deliver

* Uri Dadush is Senior Associate and Director at Carnegie's new International Economics Program. His work currently focuses on trends in the global economy and the global financial crisis. Dadush previously served as the World Bank's Director of International Trade for six years and before that as Director of Economic Policy for three years. He has also served concurrently as the Director of the Bank's World Economy Group over the last eleven years, leading the preparation of the Bank's flagship reports on the international economy over that period.

The author is grateful to Shimelse Ali and Lauren Falcao for excellent research support and (without implicating them) to Kemal Dervis, Jean-Pierre Lehmann, Danny Leipziger, Sergio Marchi, Jessica Mathews, Moises Naim, Richard Newfarmer and William Shaw for helpful discussions and suggestions. A longer version of this note is published as a Carnegie Policy Brief.

on its promise. Sluggish WTO negotiations have been overtaken and sidelined by unilateral (i.e. autonomous) liberalization as well as bilateral and regional processes.

Though the Doha agenda is reduced to a shadow of what was launched in December 2001, its conclusion is critical to capturing the gains still on the table and to preserving the system's credibility. The G-8 meeting held in L'Aquila, Italy, in July 2009 called for a conclusion of the negotiations by the end of 2010, and given the long history of missed deadlines and the time needed for ratification, it is unlikely that implementation can begin before the end of 2011, the tenth anniversary of the start of the negotiations.

While Doha's conclusion – assuming there is a conclusion – will lend the institution a new lease on life, it will not end the need for reform. On the contrary, as members confront the need to move rapidly on issues that have only been dented by ten years of Doha negotiations, they will be looking hard for a better way, and this will make the need for WTO reform even more visible and pressing than it is today.

The successes of the WTO in important areas are widely recognized, starting with holding the fort against backsliding through the Dispute Settlement System. The accession of China and of twenty-four other countries, the conclusion of plurilateral agreements in telecommunications and financial services, and the establishment of an aid for trade agenda, are important achievements. However, to retain its relevance, the WTO must show progress on its core mission, the negotiation of lower barriers to trade and securing the liberalization that has occurred.

Outlining reforms

While there is no agreed blueprint for WTO reform,[1] the following steps are evidently needed.

---

[1] Numerous very good studies, including the Sutherland Report and the Warwick Commission, have provided a comprehensive view and a plethora of academic and policy studies have examined specific areas of the WTO's functioning, but they have only rarely gained traction among the membership.

The first step to dealing with a problem is to recognize its existence. Some have argued that actual negotiations on reforming the WTO cannot be initiated before concluding Doha, as they would compromise the conclusion of negotiations on the latter. But, stopping short of negotiations, it is surely possible to begin a serious process of analysis, reflection and consultation on WTO reform before concluding Doha. Serious discussions on the functioning of the organization would enhance its credibility, and might actually encourage negotiators to conclude Doha so as to move on to the next phase. WTO reform is likely to be at the top of the agenda of any realistic post-Doha scenario anyway.

Second, the WTO has to break its splendid isolation amid a sea of fast-changing trade relations. It must move from a single-minded focus on reciprocal multilateral concessions based on consensus – negotiations that are bearing insufficient fruit – and find ways to participate actively in arenas where actual liberalization is taking place. This implies addressing the following issues:

1. How can the institution assist its members in enacting autonomous trade reforms, in which experience shows they are inclined to engage? Contrary to the prevailing mercantilist logic of negotiators, trade theory and empirical evidence points overwhelmingly to the benefit. How can the WTO exploit its Trade Policy Review Mechanism to provide a platform for ongoing dialogue on trade reform, perhaps in collaboration with the World Bank and IMF?
2. How can the WTO reduce its reliance on the consensus rule and instead promote agreements among a critical mass of members that a) establish new rules or achieve new market access in important sectors; b) comply with some well-identified criteria to minimize the adverse effects on non-members; c) can be extended to non-members on reasonable terms, including favourable treatment for the poorest countries; and d) are subject to dispute settlement? Such 'plurilateral' agreements will be challenged – especially by the smallest and poorest countries – on the grounds that they discriminate or that they can pre-empt the broader agenda in favour of participants. Yet, the alternatives of vacuous global deals or immobility are surely worse. Moreover, small and poor countries may find that there are agreements of primary interest to

them. The answer is not to eschew plurilateral agreements, but to choose to proceed on a small set of such agreements that reflect the interests of smaller and poorer countries as well as larger and richer ones.

3. How can the WTO harness the energy behind regional agreements? While research has shown that many regional agreements are badly designed and implemented, and some exist only on paper, it has also shown that others – starting with the EU, NAFTA, CAFTA and even some South–South agreements, such as the Pan Arab Free Trade Area, the Gulf Cooperation Council and SAFTA – have been genuinely successful in removing barriers, increasing the certainty of access and creating trade. Regional agreements can more easily deal with behind-the-border impediments to trade, and provide ground for experimentation and broader application. How can the WTO cease viewing regional trade agreements (RTAs) largely as a threat and treat them instead – as do large segments of the business community around the world – as an opportunity to advance trade? Research has identified the essential characteristics of welfare-enhancing regional agreements that minimize discrimination: a low external tariff, simplified rules of origin and coverage of all forms of trade. How can the WTO promote the formation of welfare-enhancing regional agreements? How can it facilitate the harmonization of their external tariffs, and promote accession to them of poor and small countries that might otherwise be excluded?

Third, the WTO must decide on how the progress achieved along the unilateral, plurilateral and regional channels can be eventually 'multilateralized' and translated into a set of enforceable rules, without embarking on a decade of global negotiations on everything.

A realistic approach to multilateralization must first recognize that it is only an ideal. Multilateral agreements, not least the current Doha drafts, are rife with exceptions, special treatment and non-reciprocity. It is best to think of multilateralization as a continuum, rather than as an absolute. There are at least three non-exclusive ways to multilateralize:

• One approach is to encourage the 'flexible geometries' of agreements to become wider when possible, by including a larger group of members to plurilaterals.

- Another response is to seek specific opportunities to consolidate liberalization that has already occurred or requires modest steps across the board. For example, WTO members might agree to eliminate all tariffs under 3 per cent, to ban export subsidies in agriculture, to adopt a unified code for rules of origin to provide duty-free-quota-free access to least-developed countries (LDCs), and so on. More than one of these proposals could be promoted simultaneously to address a diversity of interests, without having a full-fledged negotiation on everything.
- Yet another approach is to promote agreements where one country or a group of countries bind actual tariff levels or service schedules in specific sectors, both as a self-restraint mechanism and as an inducement to others to do the same. One could imagine, for example, a G-6 group, the USA, EU, Japan, China, India and Brazil – accounting for over 80 per cent of world trade – agreeing on such a step and adopting a common approach to induce other countries to do the same.

Fourth, implementing a more flexible, multidimensional and opportunistic programme of global trade reform requires a more empowered WTO Secretariat, but also a more engaged membership, including more active and ongoing (rather than sporadic) participation of ministers. At the same time the institution would need to become more ideas-driven. The Secretariat's research and policy functions would aim to become *the* centres of excellence on matters related to trade reform, such that they become obligatory ports of call for negotiations generally.

The time to start is now

Urgent new issues confront the international community on which the WTO could be making major contributions, including climate change, trade in clean technology, financial regulation, and so on. However, it is simply unrealistic to ask the organization to tackle major new challenges when its ability to deliver on such a large part of its core agenda is unproven.

However, it goes without saying that in an institution as complex and deeply entrenched as the WTO, far-reaching reforms along the lines set out above would take time to define and implement.

The Geneva WTO ministerial held at the end of November 2009, whose declared purpose was to discuss all issues other than Doha, would have been a good place to start a formal discussion and launch a member-endorsed process of reflection and analysis. Given the importance of the institution and the hoped-for imminent Doha conclusion, ministers would probably find it easy to sell the start of a process of WTO reform to constituencies back home.

B4 'Murky protectionism' and the WTO

SIMON EVENETT[*]

Without international commerce living standards would be fettered by national resources, prejudices and spending. Perhaps more importantly, international commerce also provides new vistas to explore, creating opportunities unavailable in traditional, hidebound societies. It is no wonder that such freedom is feared by insecure rulers and elites, those unwilling or unable to compete, and those yearning for yesteryear. Until the recent sharp global economic downturn, the latter had been on the defensive for nearly twenty-five years as countries of all types integrated further into the world economy, so creating greater freedoms for their citizens and firms. Will the current crisis provide the pretext for limiting that freedom and what are the implications for the WTO?

The enemies of opportunity know that outright protectionism of the 1930s type is politically unviable. Smoot and Hawley are names that have gone in infamy; nobody wants to be their heir. So new tactics are employed and what better than to subvert the implementation of legitimate state functions to protectionist ends. In the first instance criticism can be deflected by pointing to the legitimate purpose of the measure in question, with the hope that the analyst, journalist, or voter in question is too bored or too lazy to ask whether any noble policy objective could be accomplished at less cost to international commerce. Murky protectionism has increasingly replaced outright protectionism as the reactionary's international economic policy of choice.

* Simon Evenett is Professor of International Trade and Economic Development at the University of St Gallen, Switzerland, and co-Director of the CEPR Programme in International Trade and Regional Economics. Evenett taught previously at Oxford University and Rutgers University, and served twice as a World Bank official. He was a non-resident Senior Fellow of the Brookings Institution in Washington.

Fortunately, the world economy is not completely defenceless against murky protectionism. Far-sighted trade diplomats negotiated accords in the early 1990s that require, in the case of health and safety standards for products, a scientific rationale for any permanent trade-restricting measure. Moreover, steps were taken at the WTO to promote transparency in government regulation and implementation, including the publication of evidential findings and notifications to relevant WTO bodies. These steps, plus a greater emphasis on evidence-based policy making in regulatory reforms, provide some defence against murky protectionism. Unfortunately the recent global economic downturn has shown these steps are not enough.

At the centre of many industrialized and developing countries' strategies during the 2008–2009 global economic downturn has been the goal of shifting as much of the painful adjustment on to others. Let the evident excess capacity in many sectors be eliminated by others, they say. The widespread resort to selective bailouts of firms by industrialized economies, the channelling of stimulus package funds to certain sectors by many governments and the growing reliance on WTO loopholes (such as anti-dumping investigations) reveal the limits of the WTO's current accords. A very expensive game of chicken is under way where the poorer nations are at a significant disadvantage. The solution, of course, is to extend over time the scope of binding multilateral rules, and completing the Doha Round will be a useful step in this regard.

Given the time it takes to negotiate what amounts to incremental improvements in multilateral trade accords, defenders of open markets must recognize that the set of WTO accords and practices will always be incomplete. There will always be government measures and WTO loopholes for those tempted by murky protectionism to exploit. This realization calls for a new three-prong approach to opposing protectionism in the decades to come. Fortunately, many of the building blocks are in place for this approach to be taken forward. None of what follows should be taken to mean that the era of negotiating binding accords at the WTO is over. Rather, the latter will never be enough.

First, the general principle should be agreed that transparent and evidence-based regulatory processes not only lead to better national decision making but also help build confidence of trading partners that any discretion is not being used for discriminatory ends.

Governments should get into the habit of publishing in a timely fashion what options were considered, why one or more options were preferred to others, and their assessment of the pertinent evidence. In the large number of regulatory areas where the right public policy measure depends on factors – such as consumer preferences, technology and innovation, and suppliers' costs – that change over time, reviews of prior decisions should be built into regulatory decision-making processes. These reviews, too, must be conducted in a technocratic, evidence-driven manner. WTO members could adopt these principles for regulatory and state decision making for all state functions, irrespective of whether there is a distinct WTO accord for a particular government function.

Second, greater transparency at the national level should be coupled with enhanced monitoring by third parties and international organizations. This monitoring will generate high-quality information that should feed into a more elaborate deliberative function at the WTO. Regulatory decisions should be scrutinized more often and best practices established where possible and reviewed from time to time. These deliberations should happen at the WTO rather than at global sectoral bodies – such as the International Competition Network – precisely because at the WTO each member has equal standing and it is harder to shunt difficult subjects to one side. But performing this deliberative function credibly will require a substantial change in the mindset and skills of trade diplomats and officials, many of whom see the WTO membership merely in terms of negotiating trade accords and resolving disputes that arise from time to time. Resisting murky protectionism is going to require trade diplomats with substantial regulatory expertise.

Third, whatever institutional innovations take place at the national and multilateral levels, the first line of defence against murky protectionism will be national body politics that are convinced of the benefits of open borders, not just economic benefits but also in terms of the freedom that it creates for all of a nation's citizenry. There is no institutional fix here. Vigilance, public campaigns and credible facts about the damage done by protectionism – whether outright or murky – must continue to be generated and discussed. The real threat protectionism poses to living standards and social as well as economic opportunities must be highlighted. There will be no end to the several hundred-year-old battle for openness.

In conclusion, resisting murky protectionism is about something much more important than defending corporate opportunities to sell abroad. Rather, it concerns defending the wider range of economic and social freedoms that citizens as well as firms experienced in the last decades of the twentieth century and take increasingly for granted. Falling costs of international travel and greater access to information about abroad have transformed many countries' political debates as the privileges that entrenched interests enjoy (and everyone else pays for) appear more and more anomalous. Although murky protectionism has been stimulated by the current global economic downturn, it remains the latest manifestation of the reactionary impulse to control national societies. For the sake of humanity, murky protectionism must be resisted and this short article lays out an approach to meet this challenge.

B5 | Preferential trade agreements: imagining a world with less discrimination

ELISA GAMBERONI AND RICHARD NEWFARMER[*]

Reducing the discrimination inherent in preferential trade agreements (PTAs) to make them compatible with the multilateral system is likely to be one of the main challenges facing the world trading system in the next ten years. PTAs are a now common feature of the world trading system. The number of reciprocal preferential agreements – free trade agreements and customs unions that involve reciprocal tariff reductions[1] – has jumped to 251. These now cover some 34 per cent of international trade (Figure B5.1). Over the next decade, it is safe to bet that PTAs will go from becoming a common feature to becoming a dominant trait of the world trading system.

To be sure, these coverage ratios exaggerate the impact on actual trade flows. They include trade that takes place with zero most-favoured nation (MFN) tariffs and so is unaffected by preferences. Moreover, another portion of PTA trade does not take advantage of preferential access because costs of provisioning compliance is greater than the tariff. Cadot and de Melo,[2] for example, estimate that the utilization rate for the EU's Generalized System of Preferences (GSP) was only 52% of eligible goods; for Cotonou, utilization was 50%, and for NAFTA, it was 80%. Taking into account both the zero tariffs and proxies for

[*] Elisa Gamberoni is an Economist at the World Bank and Richard Newfarmer is the World Bank Special Representative to the WTO and UN, Geneva. They would like to thank Jean-Pierre Chauffour and Jaime de Melo for thoughtful comments. This note is the sole responsibility of the authors, and does not necessarily reflect the views of the World Bank or its Executive Directors.
[1] This discussion excludes non-reciprocal preferences, such as the EU's Everything But Arms programme and the US AGOA programme.
[2] C. Carrere and J. de Melo (2004) 'Are Different Rules of Origin Equally Costly?' CEPR Discussion Paper 4437.

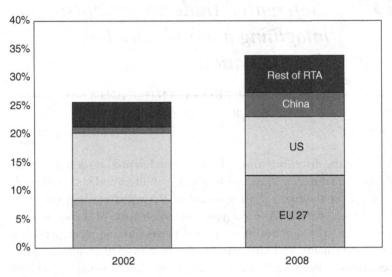

Figure B5.1: Share of import covered by RTAs
Source: Authors' calculation based on notified and non-notified RTAs.
Note: The graph shows the share of imports covered by Chinese, EU 27, US and all the other RTAs. The calculation excludes intra-EU 27 trade. The calculation for the EU 27 involves only agreements signed by all countries of the customs union. It therefore excludes trade under the Global System of Trade Preference or the Protocol of Trade Negotiation.

utilization would reduce coverage with actual trade effects to roughly about half of all PTA-covered trade.[3]

That said, few economists would argue with the proposition that weaving this overlay of discriminatory arrangements into a world trading system purportedly based on principles of non-discrimination will be a major challenge in the next decade. The 'multilateralization of regional trade agreements', to use the term of Baldwin and Low[4] who have undertaken the most comprehensive analysis of these issues, could be undertaken in four important areas:

- movement towards a simple and harmonized set of rules of origin and cumulation[5];

[3] World Bank (2005) *Global Economic Prospects, 2005: Trade Regionalism and Development*. Washington: World Bank, p. 41.
[4] R. Baldwin and P. Low (2009) 'Introduction' in R. Baldwin and P. Low (eds.) *Multilateralizing Regionalism*. Cambridge University Press.
[5] For a comprehensive review across agreements see A. Estevadeordal and K. Suominen (2003) *Rules of Origin: A World Map*, Mimeo.

- moving toward a common rules agenda;
- standardizing technical requirements (at least at the regional level);
- efforts to bring down external tariff peaks to promote more 'open' regional designs.

Politics makes convergence in each of the dimensions difficult. Specific provisions in each agreement are crafted to protect particular domestic constituencies defensively and/or win political support of special interests offensively. So how can these agreements be pushed toward convergence with multilateral principles?

We argue that leadership from the three leading traders – the USA, the EU and China – could realize the promise of converging regionalism. The reason is that these three economies are sponsors of agreements covering the great bulk of PTA-covered trade. If American, European and Chinese leaders were to apply some simple principles in their arrangements, they could have a marked impact in reducing the discriminatory 'noodles' in the spaghetti bowl and help drive PTA trade into convergence toward trade-creating MFN principles. As Baldwin suggests, the least line of resistance would be to focus as a first step on rules of origin and cumulation.[6] Unfortunately, a cursory overview of the critical features in recent agreements suggests all three powers are heading in the opposite direction.

The EU block: a good starting point but a dubious evolution

The EU has been a leading actor in the spread of PTAs. It sponsors agreements with a total of sixty-seven countries, grouped into some thirty agreements covering US$1.5 trillion of trade. Rules of origin in some of the early agreements permitted 'diagonal cumulation' – that is, any country with a PTA with the EU and sharing the same rules of origin could count imports from those countries as domestic value added and meet the EU rule of origin – and these minimized the 'hub and spokes' trading relations that undercut the value of PTAs for the

---

[6] R. Baldwin (2006) 'Multilateralising Regionalism: Spaghetti Bowls as Building Blocs on the Path to Global Free Trade', *The World Economy* 29: 1451–518.

'spokes' countries. The 1997 Pan-European System of cumulation was a case in point.[7]

The negotiation of Economic Partnership Agreements (EPAs) with about eighty African, Caribbean and Pacific countries took a different course. In late 2008, the EU concluded agreements with the Caribbean countries, a group of the East African Community (EAC) and Southern African Development Community (SADC) countries and a set of single countries, including Cameroon, Ghana and the Ivory Coast. Indeed, the EU agreed to modify rules of origin in clothing and textiles to eliminate some of the most restrictive provisions of the EPAs. However, the remainder of the agreements is complicated with different rules of origin, tariffs schemes and phase-in periods. These collectively tend to reinforce hub and spokes trading patterns rather than foment regional integration.

The US agreements

The USA has signed seventeen free trade agreements with a total coverage of some US$1.2 trillion in world trade. Three agreements are languishing in the US Congress, namely FTAs with Panama, Columbia and South Korea. These agreements have evolved toward a more standardized and comprehensive format than EU agreements. In addition, all include some new rules that go far beyond WTO disciplines on services, intellectual property, trade-related investments measures and, with the exception of Australia, investor-state dispute settlement provisions.[8] However, much like the EU agreements, variance in rules of origin across agreements and the absence of diagonal cumulation rules limit the market-widening effects of US FTAs. Carrere and de Melo[9] estimate that the distortion generated by rules of origin in NAFTA is equivalent to an average duty of 4.3 per cent. Also, unlike the non-reciprocal Africa Growth and Opportunity Act (AGOA) provisions, clothing arrangements require

---

[7] O. Cadot and J. de Melo (2008) 'Why OECD Countries Should Reform Rules of Origin', *The World Bank Research Observer* 23: 1; and P. Bombarda and E. Gamberoni (2008) 'Firm Heterogeneity, Rules of Origin and Rules of Cumulation', HEI Working Papers 09/20082008.
[8] See World Bank (2005).
[9] See C. Carrere and J. de Melo (2004).

the use of American-made yarn and textiles if these are not produced locally.[10]

Looking to the future, the fate of additional US PTAs remains
unclear. In 2008, the administration let its negotiating authority
for trade lapse in the face of certain Congressional opposition to
renewal. Moreover, the three negotiated agreements, Panama,
Columbia and South Korea, are stalled in Congress. The financial
crisis and recession, together with urgent long-term reforms such
as health and climate change, have commanded the attention of
the administration and Congress. Thus the opportunity for new
agreements, much less reconfiguring extant agreements in ways
that would make them more multilaterally compatible, remains a
dream deferred.

The China agreements

China began developing its own pattern of PTAs with its agreement with the ASEAN countries in November 2001. Since then it
has begun a dozen more negotiations. Today, China has bilateral or
plurilateral arrangements covering more than twenty economies and
about one-fifth of its total trade. Aside from trade with the special
administrative regions, it is the agreement with ASEAN that matters – and it covers 9 per cent of China's total trade. The Chinese
agreements contain fewer disciplines than either the EU or US agreements, and differ in terms of coverage, form and lack of specificity.
Generally they do not cover investment and intellectual property,
although some rules are under negotiation. Finally, because ASEAN
and Asia trade rules evolved around production chains, the rules of
origin did not defensively assume the restrictive character that US
and EU agreements have. The ASEAN–China FTA requires a 40
per cent local/regional content and allows for full cumulation while
for certain items the change in tariff heading criteria apply. While
estimations for the cost of compliance are still missing for China
RTAs, Manchin *et al.* estimate that exporters find it profitable to
use ASEAN preferences when preferential margins are higher than

---

[10] They also find that recent FTAs have undermined LDCs' access under other
preferential schemes (2009).

10–25 per cent.[11] Nonetheless, rules of origin in China PTAs have yet to be studied closely.

Conclusions: towards convergence

PTAs are likely to cover an ever-widening percentage of trade in the next decade. Enlightened leadership in the three largest trading economies could point the way toward MFN-compatible outcomes, opening the way for greater non-discriminatory competition and development impact. The most effective and actionable ways to expand trade and reduce discrimination would be to adjust rules of origin toward a common and less restrictive platform, perhaps using an across-the-board 10 per cent value added or change of tariff heading requirement.[12] This would simplify customs administration, facilitate greater participation in production chains and expand trade. Second, allowing diagonal cumulation among all members in their agreements would create trade and competition over a much larger sphere, and reduce the now dominant tendency toward hub and spokes trade in all three sets of agreements.[13] Third, in all agreements, removing certification requirements for rules of origin in all tariff lines with less than a 5 per cent MFN tariff would markedly expand utilization rates in PTAs.[14] Fourth, proving origin might be waived altogether for LDCs when the MFN tariff is less than 5 per cent. Finally, writing in MFN provisions in services agreements would ensure that access would be competitive for smaller services providers and that domestic markets would be maximally competitive.

If the three trading powers, realizing their common interest in the non-discriminatory multilateral system, were to adopt these provisions collectively – informally or formally – as part of a concerted effort, it would move the world trading system toward non-discrimination and increased competition. Moreover, working together in the WTO to

---

[11] M. Manchin and A. O. Pelkmans-Balaoing (2007) 'Rules of Origin and the Web of East Asian Preferences', World Bank Policy Research Working Papers 4273.
[12] P. Brenton (2005) 'Enhancing Trade Preferences for LDCs: Reducing the Restrictiveness of Rules of Origin', in R. Newfarmer (ed.) *Trade, Doha, and Development: A Window into the Issues*. Washington, DC: World Bank.
[13] See Bombarda and Gamberoni (2008).
[14] See Cadot and de Melo (2008).

strengthen recent new efforts to enhance WTO monitoring of PTAs would give impetus to a new effort to reform multilateral rules to the benefit of all countries. All of this may be the trade policy equivalent of John Lennon calling on us to imagine world peace. Perhaps. It would, however, give multilateralism a chance.

B6 | The G-20 after the Great Recession: rebalancing trade

BRUCE STOKES[*]

The 2009 global economic downturn poses an unprecedented challenge and a unique opportunity for China, the United States and the G-20. Just as the lessons of the Great Depression shaped post-World War II trade policy, contributing to a half century of unparalleled growth in world trade and economic activity, the experience of the Great Recession will shape globalization for years to come.

The financial meltdown that spawned the Great Recession was rooted in the record global current account imbalances that emerged over the last decade. These imbalances were, in part, a product of trade policies that had served the world well for years. Economists argued that unilateral import liberalization benefited consumers and thus should be pursued even if it was non-reciprocal and a nation's exports did not increase. But this economic reasoning eventually sowed the seeds that led to the recent crisis because it ignored the unintended economic consequences when non-reciprocity in trade created unsustainable current account imbalances.

Re-establishing more sustainable trade balances will require a new global economic growth paradigm, one in which debt-dependent countries, such as the United States, produce more of what they consume and export-dependent countries, such as China, Germany and Japan, consume more of what they produce.

The post-war trade regime was largely designed by the United States and a few of its European allies, reflecting their experience, insights and interests. The new trading system must draw on the forces driving the current global economy, in which nearly two dozen nations with differing perspectives and stakes play a major role.

* Bruce Stokes is the international economics columnist for the *National Journal* and a Transatlantic Fellow at the German Marshall Fund, United States.

In this process of rebalancing there will be a need for greater reciprocity and a balance of benefits in trade relationships. This contradicts an important underlying assumption of the current trade regime: that non-reciprocal trade was both beneficial and sustainable. The boom in the world economy over the last two generations conclusively demonstrated that non-reciprocal trade can fuel unprecedented growth. The Great Recession is evidence that non-reciprocity, when practiced in the extreme, is not sustainable.

About a decade ago substantial current account imbalances began to emerge in the world economy. In 2001 the US current account *deficit* was 3.8% of GDP. By 2007 it had nearly doubled from US$385 billion to US$739 billion, reaching 5.2% of the economy. Meanwhile, in 2007 China ran a current account *surplus* equal to 11.4% of its GDP, Germany a *surplus* of 7.6% and Japan a *surplus* of 4.8%.

These imbalances were a product of different patterns of national savings and investment that were produced by inflexible exchange rates, differences in monetary policy and financial regulation. They also reflected trade policies that assumed that non-reciprocal trade so benefited consumers, which it did, that the current account consequences could be ignored. This led Washington to discount its mounting trade deficit and Beijing, Tokyo and Berlin to assume they could build economies based on other people's consumers, not their own.

Most economists believe the United States can safely maintain a current account deficit of about 2–3 per cent of GDP. The US current account deficit is now declining, thanks to the recession, a dramatic rise in private saving and a fall-off in the trade imbalance. But the danger will come with eventual economic recovery. 'If we return to external deficits that led to this crisis,' warned European Central Bank President Jean-Claude Trichet, 'we'll have the recipe for a new crisis'.

Recasting trade policy to avoid that eventuality involves reviving the principles of reciprocity and balance of benefits, long embedded in the General Agreement on Tariffs and Trade, but long ignored.

Of course, blind pursuit of narrowly balanced trade would neither be workable nor economically sound. And reciprocity, with its implicit focus on promoting a country's exports rather than valuing imports, could lead to destructive mercantilism. Nevertheless, post-Great Recession trade policy will necessarily be more mindful of the need to avoid future build-ups in unsustainable current account imbalances.

A reduction of the US trade deficit will require an equal reduction in trade surpluses elsewhere. This might easily play out in a destructive manner. Washington could pursue beggar-thy-neighbour policies: weakening the dollar, imposing a variety of import barriers and slowing trade liberalization, effectively rebalancing trade by limiting it. China, in order to maintain its export market share and export-related employment, could continue to subsidize investment in export-oriented production, leading to increased trade tensions as governments around the world try to protect their domestic economies from 'unfair' Chinese competition.

But the rebalancing of the world economy does not have to play out that way. The G-20, nations with the most to lose if Beijing and Washington mishandle this challenge, could lead the redesign of the trading system, much as the United States and Great Britain did six decades ago.

As with many issues involving globalization, the most important thing the G-20 nations could do to rebalance trade is to get their own houses in order. Export-led growth spurred economic development in East Asia and enabled the Germans to bear the burden of reconstructing East Germany. But it also depended on the ability and the willingness of the American consumer to buy more and more by going deeper and deeper into debt. That proved unsustainable. Now it is time for the United States and for the other members of the G-20 to jointly develop rules of the road for the trading system that produce a more balanced outcome.

As Michael Pettis, a professor at Peking University's Guanghua School of Management, has written, 'the best hope is a well-coordinated set of policies acknowledging that the US savings rate must rise, and with it the Chinese [savings rate] must decline, but also recognizing that if this happens too quickly, or is accompanied by a collapse in trade, it will be bad for the US and terrible for China' and the world'.[1]

To that end the G-20 needs to move beyond denunciations of protectionism and squabbling over fiscal stimulus spending and begin

---

[1] http://mpettis.com/2009/08/what-should-have-been-discussed-during-the-sed-meetings-part-2/.

tough talk about changes in domestic policy that can reduce export and import dependency. Washington must be pressured to adopt a value-added tax (as have 153 other nations in the world) to discourage consumption and to eliminate the mortgage tax deduction that subsidizes the internationally non-competitive real-estate sector. Beijing must be leaned on to liberalize interest rates, allow workers higher wages and boost domestically oriented small enterprises and the service sector. Other members of the G-20 will need to make similarly difficult domestic reforms.

The orientation of trade liberalization will also necessarily need to change. Priority must be given to efforts to spur trade that does not depend on the US market. This may take the form of regional agreements in Africa, Asia and Latin America or plurilateral deals among complementary developing economies. Services trade must be accorded greater emphasis to spur, through international competition, greater efficiency gains in domestic services industries, which would in turn promote non-export-related economic growth.

None of this will be easy. Americans will want to return to their profligate consumer ways. The Chinese will worry about the regime-destabilizing unemployment consequences of a reduced dependence on export-led growth. And other members of the G-20 will be wary of changing the rules of the game before they get to the winner's circle. The temptation will be to do nothing and hope that a return to the *status quo ante* the Great Recession will somehow be more sustainable next time around.

But that would ignore the hard-won lessons of the last few years. Much as the late 1940s offered the victors in World War II an opportunity to redesign the global trading system based on the experience during the Great Depression, today the G-20 has an opportunity to draw on the lessons of the Great Recession to reshape the global economy to make it more sustainable and, ultimately, to ensure that it better reflects the interests of a broader cross-section of humanity.

B7 | The missing piece: global imbalances and the exchange rate regime

PAOLA SUBACCHI[*]

The exchange rate is the missing piece from the international debate on the reform of the financial architecture which has fallen under the remit of the G-20. Despite coming on stage briefly in October 2008, when President Sarkozy called for the reform of the Bretton Woods system and summoned the G-20 heads of state summit in Washington the following month, the issue of the existing exchange rate arrangements and their reform has still to be addressed through a deep and comprehensive discussion. Like a ghost waiting in the shadows, exchange rate arrangements and misalignments keep cropping up. Of particular concern, in the current monetary system, is the fact that the United States continues to provide global liquidity through its current account deficit – i.e. specifically the large flow of savings from developing countries into the United States. As a result the exchange rate remains at the heart of China-bashing in Washington. There is also discomfort about the volatility of the euro in the euro area. And the current account deficit and the critical fiscal position of the United States have raised worries among major emerging economies that hold substantial shares of US government debt. There is indeed a risk, albeit low, of the US inflating itself out of debt. As the risk of holding dollars has become more evident as a result of the financial crisis, questions have been raised on the soundness of the dollar-based international monetary system.

* Paola Subacchi is Director of International Economic Research at Chatham House (the Royal Institute of International Affairs), London. Her research covers a range of international economic issues, focusing in particular on the international monetary system, international capital flows and global imbalances. Her current work explores the emergence of new economic powers and the challenge that this poses to global economic governance.

Just before the G-20 London Summit in April 2009, China's central bank governor Zhou Xiaochuan suggested that the status of the dollar as the key reserve currency should be halted, as the costs of the current system may have exceeded its benefits: 'The price is becoming increasingly higher, not only for the users, but also for the issuers of the reserve currencies.' Instead, a new global system controlled by the IMF should replace the US dollar as the international reserve currency. Within such a scheme, the main global reserve currency would be represented by a basket of significant currencies and commodities – an extended version of the Fund's Special Drawing Rights (SDRs).

Governor Zhou's proposal for an overhaul of the global currency reserve system was positively received and deemed worthy of further analysis and discussion. Russia's President Medvedev seemed particularly keen and regarded it as an important building block of a new global financial architecture. Since then, however, China has moved on and taken the first steps towards the internationalization of the renminbi through a pilot scheme for the use of the renminbi in cross-border trade settlements in Shanghai, Shenzhen, Guangzhou, Zhuhai and Dongguan with Hong Kong and Macau (in June 2010 the scheme was expanded to include 20 provinces).

Even if the proposal for creating a new international currency may have become less feasible or relevant, Governor Zhou's comment on the urgency and need for an overall reform of the international monetary system remains highly relevant in the current situation in which a significant structural realignment in the world's external imbalances is unfolding – without, however, removing the structural cause of these imbalances.

China is keen to be engaged in the debate addressing the arrangements that underpin the international monetary system, and other countries and regions holding the main reserve currencies should be as well. An appropriate framework for further multilateral discussions should be set up within the G-20 remit given the latter's mandate with issues related to the international financial and monetary architecture and prevention of future crises. The most technical issues should, however, be addressed by a small caucus that would include, as a minimum, the USA, the Eurozone, Japan and China, and possibly the two largest foreign exchange reserves holders after China and Japan.

It is critical to recognize that economic and financial hardship could push countries into protecting their domestic markets as well as supporting their exports by any means available. In this respect, competitive devaluations could be as effective as trade barriers. Thus, if fighting protectionism is seen as a natural remit for a multi-lateral forum such as the G-20, then international policy cooperation should also be directed towards dealing with the negative spillovers resulting from exchange rate misalignments.

With a number of countries dealing with falling exports, the risk of competitive devaluations is all too real. Switzerland was the first developed economy to opt for intervention in foreign exchange markets. Beginning in March 2009, the Swiss national bank have tried, without much success, to curb the rise of the franc against the euro and, at the same time, tried to discourage the use of the franc as a haven currency. But unilateral devaluation is a zero-sum game and, given the limited number of reserve currencies that qualify for safe haven status, the scope for unilateral exchange rate policy is very narrow. The burden cannot be shifted without limit, in the hope that somebody else will take the strain; rather it should be fairly shared.

This becomes a pressing issue at the time of crisis. For instance, expansionary monetary policies in the USA could result in downward pressures on the dollar. As a result, countries in the euro area might be forced to share the burden of the US stimulus indirectly through the exchange rate. The developed country leaders should be vigilant to avoid the emergence of competitive devaluations. They should commit not only to eschewing protectionism but also to pursuing economic policies that do not generate beggar-thy-neighbour effects through currency devaluations.

Even if the sovereign debt crisis in Europe has raised many questions about the role and even the survival of the euro within the international monetary system, it still makes sense to look at the future of such a system as a multi currency one. This would reflect the fact that the international economic order is increasingly multipolar. Is this the way forward that should be central to the debate about the future of the international monetary system? A multi currency system, based on a number of reserve currencies in a complementary rather than rival role, is highly desirable. If properly developed it would ensure that pressure is defused and appropriately shifted from one currency to the other in time of crisis without triggering huge instability in the currency market. Such a system, however, will take a long time to develop. Monetary authorities and political leaders could prepare the ground for this, but cannot change the system by mandate. The current system is underpinned by a formidable combination of confidence, efficiency and inertia. This is a critical point, which seems to be missing from Governor Zhou's analysis.

B8 | Trading knowledge fairly: intellectual property rules for global prosperity and environmental sustainability

CAROLYN DEERE-BIRKBECK[*]

Innovation and creativity are vital to the world economy but the global intellectual property (IP) rules that govern trade in knowledge-related goods and services are a source of bitter dispute.

Creative industries – from entertainment and publishing to textiles and design – occupy an increasingly important place in many national economic strategies. Information technology companies are now among the world's most profitable. And the race to find better, cheaper cures for old and new diseases, develop greener energy sources and support more efficient production processes, has made policies that protect R&D investments and profits a top concern for business strategies. With one recent estimate valuing global IP assets at some US$300 billion, rules on intellectual property have grown rapidly in importance for many businesses over the past decade as they seek to gain legal security over the ownership of such rights and their enforcement.

But the global debate over IP rules, and especially over access to affordable medicines, has shown that IP laws can no longer be the domain of a small, specialized community of business lobbyists, IP officials, lawyers and international civil servants. Indeed, tensions over the appropriate rules for managing the creation, use and sharing of knowledge-intensive goods and services now engage a range

* Dr Carolyn Deere-Birkbeck is Director of the Global Trade Governance Project at the University of Oxford's Global Economic Governance Programme. She is the founder and Chair of the Board of *Intellectual Property Watch*. She is also the author of *The Implementation Game: The TRIPS Agreement and the Global Politics of Intellectual Property Reform in Developing Countries* (Oxford University Press, 2008) and the editor of *Making Global Trade Governance Work for Development: Perspectives and Priorities from Developing Countries* (Cambridge University Press, forthcoming 2011).

of stakeholders in a vast and expanding array of global public policy debates, spanning issues as diverse as the environment and climate change, innovation, access to knowledge, education, public health, agriculture, the Internet, creative industries, biodiversity and food security, traditional knowledge, and genetic resources, as well as competition, industrial development, and science and technology. In the wake of the financial crisis and facing the imperative of a low-carbon transition, the competitive struggle over the scope and distribution of IP rights is set to intensify.

In the global arena, the locus of rule-making on IP issues has been bilateral and multilateral agreements on IP, many of them set within the context of trade agreements. Multinational R&D companies argue for stronger international IP rules to protect their investments, profits and competitive edge, and to help them expand their reach into emerging markets. Heeding their call, developed country governments have been impressively persistent in negotiating new international agreements that raise IP standards beyond the minimum already set in the World Trade Organization's Agreement on Trade-Related Aspects of Intellectual Property Rights (TRIPS) – and sometimes beyond standards available within their own borders. They have also pushed for new initiatives to boost IP enforcement across the world, using both 'sticks' such as threats of trade sanctions and 'carrots' such as the provision of training and capacity building. In tandem, individual companies and their global associations have raised the alarm that IP infringement hurts their bottom lines and launched intense public campaigns to 'stop' piracy. Spurred by business frustrations with the pace of multilateral negotiating processes, such as those at the WTO and the United Nations' World Intellectual Property Organization (WIPO), a group of around twenty countries have broken away to negotiate among themselves a new, controversial Anti-Counterfeiting Trade Agreement (ACTA).

Up against public criticism for putting private profits before public interests and defending outdated business models in the face of rapidly changing information technologies, most of the world's largest entertainment, software and R&D companies stand defiant. To demonstrate good corporate citizenship and deflect attention from calls to rebalance global IP rules to boost access to medicines, the largest pharmaceutical companies have instead offered donations of products and joined various partnerships to address global health priorities.

In the coming years, companies will not be able to escape debates on intellectual property. The access to medicines debate, as one example, has spurred public understanding that IP rules require delicate and crucial trade-offs between public goods and private profits – and that debate is set to broaden. As such, the staunchest defenders of stronger and better enforced IP rights face at least four sets of challenges.

First, there is a growing acknowledgement that the IP protection pendulum has swung too far. While more property rights can stimulate innovation, they can also impose constraints, locking up too much knowledge and raising the costs of access to basic scientific building blocks (such as data and gene sequences). For many of the world's fastest growing companies – in telecommunications, consumer electronics, open-source software and biotechnology – the push for the strongest-possible IP protection defends outdated business models and holds back more promising growth areas. For some companies, circumventing current IP rules is their best bet for mounting a competitive challenge to the 'old guard'. But the most forward-looking companies are exploring innovative business models and research strategies, including those for sharing content online, patent pools, open licensing arrangements and prize funds to stimulate innovation. At the government level too, there is a new appreciation that greater support for healthy competition authorities to balance IP rules is needed to ensure the most dynamic companies can advance, while keeping the costs to public budgets as low as possible, such as for educational materials.

Second, as countries now work to ensure that the best technologies for addressing climate change are available where needed most, questions about appropriate IP rules and strategies for ensuring technology transfer are once again in the global headlines. Already, the anthrax scare of 2001, the avian flu scare and the recent swine flu crisis demonstrate that even the staunchest developed country proponents of strong IP regimes are willing to reconsider when urgency demands it. The question now is how national and global IP regimes can and should respond to the need for affordable access to cutting-edge technologies for climate mitigation and adaptation to developing countries.

Third, the 'old' IP system cannot escape the necessity to address the needs of the world's poorer countries. The global spread of infectious diseases, the massive pressures for global migration and the web of

terrorist shocks have reinforced the notion that collective global security will depend on our ability to secure a better future for the world's
poorest countries. The health of the global economy will rely on the
ability of developing countries to foster growth and development.
This in turn will demand balanced global IP rules and smart national
IP policies that boost innovation, build local technological capacity
and cultural industries, increase access to education, improve the diffusion of technologies, promote agricultural productivity, improve
public health and foster competitive advantages.

Yet, for developing countries, the unpalatable statistic is that over
90 per cent of the world's IP is currently held by companies, research
institutes and individuals in developed countries. Through WIPO's
suite of international IP treaties and the WTO's TRIPS agreement,
poorer countries are locked into a system of high prices, hefty licensing fees and royalty payments to the industrialized world to secure
access to the technologies they need to develop. The burden of implementing global IP rules is already more than many fragile economies
with limited resources can bear. Astonishingly, however, many of the
world's poorest countries have been bulldozed into IP protection levels equal to (or even greater than) those in industrialized countries.
And the push for ever-higher standards of IP protection continues
with little assessment of their likely impact on development or the
ability of countries to implement them. So intense have been developing country concerns that in 2004 they supported the launch of a
'WIPO Development Agenda' to foster a global IP system that puts
development more fairly at the heart of global IP rules. Meanwhile,
many countries and communities continue to suffer misappropri-
ation or theft of their knowledge and creative assets, such as in music,
design, or regarding medicinal uses of plants. Only in the past several
years have there been concerted efforts to help developing countries
themselves use the IP system to accrue local benefits, for example
by more effective use of trademarks on exports. Even still, few companies from poorer countries or indeed their governments have the
resources to defend their IP rights in the global marketplace.

Fourth, we need to acknowledge that the current approach to IP
enforcement is a losing battle. It is particularly unlikely to yield positive results in many developing countries. True, the proportion of
piracy and counterfeiting in developing countries is increasing, but
the greatest overall costs to IP right-holders come from developed

world markets. While affected companies rightly highlight that piracy is sometimes linked to problems of smuggling, organized crime and consumer risks through lower-quality products, their war on piracy is flawed. Good enforcement of reasonable laws would yield better returns than the push to enforce excessively strong laws in countries with far more crucial national economic and social priorities. All countries have an interest in the effective enforcement of their national laws and many local companies in developing countries also benefit from regimes where the rights of IP holders are clear and secure. However, we need first to ensure that the laws in question are appropriate to national circumstances. It is also time to better consider non-punitive approaches to securing greater respect for IP rights, such as lower prices for products and discounted collective licensing deals, and to help foster institutional arrangements within developing countries that place the implementation of international IP laws in the context of dynamic national strategies for development and innovation.

Businesses around the world – whether multinational, local, small, or medium-sized – need a global IP system that provides legal security and certainty. They also need a system that is responsive to change. Our global economy is one where new ways of doing business are constantly emerging and global public policy priorities shift over time. The IP system must be adapted to keep up with these realities. Gone are the days where it is helpful to have a binary debate with one side pretending that stronger IP protection is always good, and others insisting that the system must be overthrown altogether. Now is the time for a nuanced debate, where the public interest is paramount, small- and medium-sized businesses have greater say and the most cutting-edge, forward-looking companies assume greater authority than those struggling giants that have hitherto captured the rule-making process.

B9 | Trade and subsidies: undermining the trading system with public funds

MARK HALLE[*]

Despite the official optimism at the WTO, it is hard to hide the serious malaise that has taken grip of the multilateral trading system. Efforts to winch the Doha Round out of the ditch are proving much more strenuous than anticipated, and the feeling is spreading that there might be something more profoundly wrong with the system than we initially feared; or if not with the system, then certainly with our approach to expanding and consolidating it.

Ironically, this malaise strikes at a time when visible progress on concluding a trade deal could play an important role in helping put the world economy back on its feet. In fact, the loss of confidence in the trading system comes at the worst possible time. Trade offers a promising way for countries to grow their way out of the recession, and it offers to pay dividends faster than many of the other measures included in economic stimulus packages. Instead, there are ominous signs of resurgent protectionism. So far, most protectionist measures have been combated successfully, but no-one is sure how long the tide can be held off.

Surely, given both the dangers of protectionist escalation, and the role that robust trade could play in combating the recession, concluding the Doha Round and thereby rebuilding confidence in the trading system must be a high priority. But here is the paradox: there is broad agreement that expanding trade would be of great benefit at this time of economic downturn. It is generally agreed that it makes sense to complete the Doha Round and that the concessions required are not beyond the reach of enlightened leadership. Most agree that a final

* Mark Halle is Executive Director of the International Institute for Sustainable Development – Europe. Based in Geneva, his work explores how the global macroeconomic framework can be adjusted so that it facilitates the transition to sustainable development.

failure to secure a reasonable Doha package would not only weaken the WTO but also that it would land a body blow on multilateralism in general. And, finally, trade economists worldwide share a sense of danger on observing the proliferating signs of protectionism. So why can't we move forward?

Solving this situation is not simply a matter of all sides showing marginal flexibility. It is not a matter of stumbling across the ingenious formula that everyone has missed in their haste. It is not a matter of cutting a few bilateral deals in the corridors and forcing a consensus on the more recalcitrant WTO members. Instead, it requires recognizing that, in many ways, the current organization of both national and global economies seriously undermines the goals that trade liberalization is intended to serve and recognition that we must retool the trading system to confront these issues.

Nothing illustrates this challenge better than current patterns of subsidy use. The fact that gigantic sums are deployed in ways that distort trade and undermine the development of mutually beneficial trading relationships is nothing short of a scandal, both in the dimensions of public money deployed and in the impact on trade and sustainable development. While the subsidies involved range from those that are marginally useful or neutral to those that are outrageously destructive, there is little doubt that a significant majority of these subsidies undermine progress towards sustainable development. Agricultural subsidies approach US$1 billion a day. Subsidies to water provide incentives to waste a commodity that is not only growing more scarce but that is fundamental to agricultural and industrial production and, indeed, to life itself. Subsidies to fisheries have contributed to the depletion of one fish stock after another, pushing them over the brink so that they never recover. Subsidies to fossil energy reward behaviour that flies in the face of global efforts to combat catastrophic climate change, warping markets in ways that perpetuate wasteful and environmentally destructive energy practices.

Current subsidy budgets vastly outstrip the funding needed to address the world's major development challenges. Subsidies to agriculture, energy, water and transport annually total some fifteen times the sums needed fully to implement the Millennium Development Goals by 2015. They are an order of magnitude higher than the amounts needed to attain the goal – set back in 1966 – of devoting 0.7 per cent of GDP in OECD countries to development assistance. They represent over eight times the amount once calculated as being needed fully to implement Agenda 21 – the world's most ambitious plan to bring about sustainable development. Finally, if the public funds currently invested in energy subsidies were to be invested instead in the fight against climate change, they would largely suffice to meet the target that Lord Stern calculates is needed to stabilize greenhouse gases below the levels at which they risk causing irreversible damage.

These examples are deliberately chosen to shock. The simple fact is that public money is not only being mis-spent, it is being mis-spent in titanic proportions. It is being mis-spent in ways that undermine the credibility of the trading system and that saps the confidence developing countries have in trade as a potential solution to their development problems. As such it is preventing recovery of the world economy, and virtually guaranteeing that action on climate change will be too little, too late.

Wait, isn't the WTO able to combat subsidies, provided they are trade distorting? Of course it is – and at least the agricultural subsidies are on the negotiating table. The trouble is that WTO members do a poor job of notifying the subsidies they use and, when they do so, the reporting is patchy, out-of-date and generates non-comparable data. In fact, there is no incentive for members to notify subsidies, since there is no price to be paid for failing to doing so, whereas notifying their subsidies could leave them open to challenge.

So we have a situation where we are trying to urge countries to extend the multilateral trading system in the interest of relaunching the world economy. To do so requires raising the confidence of members – and especially the developing countries – that their concerns will be met. And yet we systematically refuse to address seriously one of the most massive, most damaging and most central of the reasons for the low level of confidence. Subsidies are a defiant slap in the face to developing countries that can't afford them, that can't compete because of them, and that see them as a monument to a system that is unbalanced, unfair and hopelessly stacked against them. They underline as hypocritical the endless political statements at the G-8 and elsewhere that action against climate change is the most urgent problem of humanity, or that alleviating poverty in Africa must take precedence over any other development challenge. And they cement the mistrust with which the developing countries regard institutions such as the World Bank or WTO that are dominated by the rich and powerful.

If we are serious about trade, we must get serious about how we use precious public funds. We must resolve that they should no longer be used in ways that undermine equitable, sustainable development and instead insist that they should only be used in ways that advance and protect the global public good. Where is the leader that will take us down that path?

B10 | *Trading labour: a dilemma for migration regimes*

PRADEEP S. MEHTA[*]

While international migration is an old phenomenon, its link with trade is a recent one. Earlier trade economists were of the view that trade in products could be a perfect substitute for trade in capital and labour. However, with increasing industrialization and the importance of services sector-led growth, it has become apparent that trade in factors of production can complement trade in goods, in which case freeing both would yield greater gains. Evidence also suggests that the greatest gains have come to countries that opened both. These developments are proving to provide win–win solutions to both exporting countries and importing countries, but political dimensions often queer the pitch.

Global trade and investment have spin-off effects on labour mobility. Reinforcing these developments, communication technology and modern transportation systems offer faster mobility. Consequently, our world is undergoing substantial spatial transformations, at a pace faster than anybody could predict. Trade expedites movement of labour both nationally and internationally. Internal migration is towards cities and towns, drawing surplus labour from rural to urban, motivated by opportunities to climb up the economic ladder. Such agglomerations throw up an immense amount of opportunities for businesses as they become 'thick markets', act as incubators for innovation and provide access to a wide range of consumables which otherwise could not be imagined of.

Along with internal relocation to urban centres, incidence of cross-border and intercontinental migration has increased manifoldly. Unlike uncontrolled intra-national migration, stringent migration policy regimes are in place controlling international migration.

[*] Pradeep S. Mehta is the Secretary General of CUTS International, a leading economic policy research and advocacy group. Joseph George of CUTS contributed to this article.

119

Economically advanced nations offer better living standards and, given their first-mover advantage, they can afford to be selective in screening and absorbing skilled labour.

Human capital embodied in labour is the most valued factor of production today. Countries the world over are keen to plan and control both internal and external migration of labour. But it raises innumerable managerial issues: urbanization and congestion, remittances and brain drain, job displacements and wage rates, cultural and civic challenges and so on. Importantly, it also raises the crucial question of how migration affects the trade capability of a country.

Duration of migration as a cause for concern

The association of migration in modern times with specialization and trade is not unidirectional; it could be both cause and effect of international trade. Theoretically, trade in goods between nations sustains when labour is immobile across borders and at the same time mobile within borders. In other words, there exists a fear that migrants may take the comparative advantage away with them to a foreign country. On the other hand, the free flow of nationally locked-in labour to export sectors with comparative advantages is essential to engage in and tap the benefits of international trade. International migration in this context can be seen as a cause of trade and intra-national migration as its effect.

The conventional issue of brain drain is generally discussed in this context. Countries may want to restrict permanent movement of labour abroad, since it may hamper production capacity, especially as international migrants are generally skilled workers capable of contributing to value addition in the fastest-growing sectors. At the same time, repatriation of income by cross-border migrants constitutes an important source of economic expansion in developing countries such as Bangladesh and Mexico. Very often, this trade-off is quite visible in the national contexts also. Within national boundaries, as in many areas in rural India, migration to the urban area does bring remittances to the impoverished hinterlands but migrants may drain out a substantial part of the productive activities left in such regions.

This brings us to the question of net gains from migration vis-à-vis trade. It is difficult to quantify the costs and benefits of migration in the long run for origin as well as destination countries. The question directly relates to skill levels of migrants, duration of migration and the amount of remittances. In specialized economies, skill locking and 'structural unemployment' is very common. It is counterintuitive for a nuclear physicist from the Maldives to stay in her homeland and practice her trade. A migration regime that permits labour trade so that skills may be best put to use avoids 'brain wastes' and is most certainly a win–win for trading partners.

The duration of migration and the amount of remittances are important points for migration regimes to consider from a practical point of view. It is essential to distinguish between long-term labour migration, which might lead to a change in the overall trade patterns of both origin and destination countries, and short-term migration, which in itself is trade in labour for the country of origin. The content of remittances defines the amount of trade in labour in both cases. Remittances are generally high in the latter case. As long-term migration translates into citizenry and becomes an integral part of all facets of national governance in the host country, and sometimes short-term migration becomes a pretext for long-term stay in attractive destinations, policy makers very often end up being disillusioned and over-rigid in screening even short-term migrants.

Treating migration in trade agreements

Trade renders certain sectors of production obsolete in an economy, but it also makes certain locales inhabitable. Freedom of physical mobility is an integral part of achieving efficiency through cross-border trade and investment. Should markets choose products, they must select places as well. In order to harvest the gains from consumption and production scale efficiencies, the migration of labour to centres where they deserve to be must be encouraged. By doing so, governments actually practice meritocracy at the international level for the benefit of businesses in their own jurisdiction.

Currently, cross-border labour migration of a short-term nature is negotiated in trade agreements through instruments of services trade liberalization. The origin of inclusion of such migration in trade talks is based on the premise that the delivery of service products in many cases entails physical proximity of the producer and consumer, and therefore the temporary movement of service providers is warranted. The principle for treating such movement is embedded in the definition of types of services (Mode 4) in the General Agreement on Trade in Services (GATS) under the WTO. Similar definitions are replicated in services negotiations in various regional trade agreements.

The multilateral arrangement under the WTO system thus takes care of only short-term migration. Besides, the system only deals with labour movement associated with service industries such as education, health, banking, etc. The scope and demand for migration goes far beyond this arrangement. While Mode 4 market access may prove to be crucial for opening up rigid migration regimes, alternative channels such as exclusive bilateral labour agreements could be more effective in framing quick and orderly movement, as in the case of region-centric accords like the Canadian Seasonal Agricultural Workers Programme. Bilateral agreements like this are inescapable requirements of our time given the massive scale of inefficient distribution of skills worldwide and the fast-changing demographic profiles across countries.

Globalization has indeed stimulated the movement of goods, financial capital, information and technology, enhancing efficiency in the way businesses are conducted. But liberalization of human capital movement is yet to catch up with these developments. Job-related insecurity and political standoffs build up numerous barriers for cross-border migration. Looking at the future, while trade policy instruments are used to attune market topography at the one end, migration policies must be used to equitably assist people to move and tap markets at the other.

Poverty and global inequities

Editorial introduction

Poverty and global inequities

Global poverty and the underpinnings of liberalization are tackled in this chapter. One of the questions of the early twenty-first century is whether lagging regions will follow the performances of the fast-growing, emerging economies. The immediacy of destitution implies that special attention must be paid to the weakest groups in society. Openness is generally considered to be a facilitating condition for income convergence on wealthier nations, but not a sufficient one. The strengthening of domestic institutional infrastructure, fairness in international rules and the extension of capabilities are all recognized as fundamental.

The first three authors introduce aspects of the trade–poverty nexus that remain controversial, highlight some of the issues to be addressed if trade policy is to be an effective instrument of social justice, and assess the globally observed increases in domestic income inequalities. The subsequent two articles offer contrasting perspectives on the rebalancing of trade rules, development potential in poor countries and the role of international aid.

We then turn our attention to three topics within a regional perspective: domestic institutional infrastructure in Africa, a focus on the Middle East and North Africa to provide a case study of the relationship between women and trade, and standards in the commerce of pharmaceuticals in vulnerable regions. This is followed by a commentary on the importance of entrepreneurship education. A challenge to the conventional view on the relationship between trade, development and security in the course of the past decades of reform closes the chapter. In consonance with other articles in this publication, it underlines the potency of the historical correlation between poverty, inequalities and conflict.

C1 Trade and poverty: an old debate rekindled

CARLOS A. PRIMO BRAGA*

The analysis of the relationship between international trade and poverty is as old as the economics profession. Adam Smith himself argued that growth would contribute to reducing poverty, and to the extent that trade can be characterized as the 'engine of growth' – a twentieth-century metaphor – the positive association between trade and poverty reduction has been an issue of 'faith' for most market-oriented economists. In contrast, those who perceived the growing integration of the world economy as a mechanism for the extension of capitalism had a much dimmer view of the role of trade in promoting poverty reduction. This dimension of the debate lost most of its stridency with the collapse of communism. Still other aspects of the trade–poverty nexus remain controversial.

The controversy is mainly associated with conflicting views on the implications of trade policy prescriptions for poverty. In short, to what extent does trade liberalization (as a mechanism to expand trade) reduce or increase poverty? Different answers to this question can be envisaged with the help of the 2x2 matrix below where views about the 'time horizon' of the analysis and presumed 'market structure' are identified. The signs in the cells indicate the expected impact on poverty of a trade-liberalizing reform.

For those that believe that markets operate efficiently and economic agents have limited market power, static efficiency should guide resource allocation. In this view of the world, trade liberalization will improve productivity, fostering economic growth and contributing

* Carlos A. Primo Braga is currently Director, Economic Policy and Debt Department, the World Bank. His department provides support to country programmes in the areas of debt, macro-policy and shared growth. He is also the Chairman of the Economic Policy Sector Board of the World Bank, which provides institutional guidance with respect to economic policy advice and professional development.

Trade liberalization and poverty

Assumptions/timeframe	Competitive markets (with a comparative advantage emphasis)	Imperfect markets (with a learning-by-doing emphasis)
Short term	+/–	–
Medium to long term	++	– –

Note: (+) indicates an expected reduction in poverty; (++) an even more significant impact in terms of poverty reduction; (+/−) an ambiguous impact on poverty; (−) an increase in poverty.

over the medium to long term to poverty reduction. It is recognized that in the short term trade liberalization may have negative implications for the poor, depending on the structure of the labour market (wage impacts and composition of labour dislocation) and the price effects on the basket of goods/services consumed and/or produced by the poor. The overall presumption, however, is that unless some unusual circumstances prevail (e.g. the possibility of 'immiserizing growth' associated with perverse terms-of-trade movements) trade liberalization will over time expand markets and contribute to poverty reduction.

A different perspective, however, can be derived from a view of the world that emphasizes learning-by-doing and the importance of market imperfections. In this case, inward-looking strategies (and government intervention) are rationalized as a mechanism to support the development of the domestic market. This school of thought can be traced back to Alexander Hamilton/Friedrich List and the arguments for infant industry protection, as well as arguments in favour of import-substitution industrialization and more recent theories in defence of industrial policy. In this view of the world, trade liberalization is often portrayed as having a bias against the poor by impacting factors of production controlled by poor households in the short term (e.g. unskilled labour), by increasing economic volatility and by constraining long-term structural transformation (to the extent that trade liberalization could impede movement away from 'myopic' prevailing comparative advantages).

Different 'stories' can be told by relying on each of these frameworks and by focusing on different timeframes. They can be more or less compelling, depending on data sets utilized and the skills of the storyteller. From the perspective of the public at large, however, the last two decades have been characterized by significant swings in the perceptions about the links between international trade and poverty. In the late 1980s, the 'end-of-history' triumphalism that followed the collapse of the communist bloc strengthened the appeal of market-oriented perspectives. This intellectual dominance – often associated with the so-called Washington Consensus – however, did not last long. The bumpy road travelled by transition economies in the 1990s and the East Asian crisis in 1997 provided a reality check to the more extreme predictions about the benefits of international market integration.[1]

By 1999, the debate had gained a new edge as trade became the focal point for a broader discussion about the benefits of globalization as illustrated by the 'battle of Seattle' that engulfed the WTO Ministerial. The next two years were characterized by growing confrontations between those that saw globalization as a positive force for change (in the tradition of the market-oriented perspective) and those that saw it as a destabilizing force with an anti-poor bias (a perspective that went well beyond heterodox economists, including a diverse coalition of civil society organizations (CSOs), environmentalists and organized labour).

The tragedy of 9/11, however, provided a new impetus to the search for mechanisms to harness the positive forces of globalization. In November 2001, at the Doha WTO Ministerial, an agreement to launch a new multilateral round of trade negotiations was reached. It could be argued that such an agreement, considered a pipe dream just a few months earlier, reflected less a renewed consensus on the positive role of trade in promoting economic efficiency and development, and more an attempt to engage the tools of trade diplomacy in the

---

[1] The criticisms of globalization were mainly driven by concerns about the implications of financial liberalization, but in the popular debate trade and financial liberalization were often seen as part and parcel of 'market fundamentalist' ideas. See, for example, R. Kanbur (2001) 'Economic Policy, Distribution and Poverty: The Nature of Disagreements', *World Development* 29(6): 1083–94.

promotion of peace and economic goodwill. The initial enthusiasm of reaching an agreement on launching the Doha Development Agenda (DDA), however, was soon replaced by the realization that there was no consensus on what a development round would really mean. The early momentum was soon lost and as most deadlines for the negotiations were missed, cynicism about the ability of the WTO process to deliver a substantive result increased.

It is worth noting that at least one dimension of the debate about the potential benefits of the DDA revealed a limited convergence in the thinking between the opposite sides of the policy spectrum. Most analysts and CSOs would agree that industrialized countries should improve conditions of market access to products of interest to developing countries – particularly agricultural products. The debate about the role of trade liberalization at the level of developing economies, however, remained as divisive as before. Special and differential treatment proposals advanced by developing countries would often emphasize the concept of 'policy space', arguing, for example, that developing countries should be granted greater freedom to protect their infant industries than what was allowed under WTO disciplines.

The deadlock in the negotiations – with the DDA bound to earn the dubious record of the longest multilateral trade round ever – could be interpreted as additional evidence that policy preferences have swung decisively from viewing trade liberalization as a good thing to something to be feared. I would argue, however, that the problems of the round have more to do with the difficulties of employing the 'mercantilistic logic' of trade negotiations to an increasingly complex agenda involving a growing number of stakeholders.[2] In fact, the post-2001 era continued to witness progress in unilateral trade liberalization. Measures such as the overall trade restrictiveness index (which captures ad valorem tariffs, specific duties and non-tariff measures) declined for most countries between 2002 and 2007. And low-income countries achieved the greatest progress in overall trade liberalization during this period![3]

[2] For details on the DDA negotiations, see C. A. Primo Braga and E. Grainger-Jones (2006) 'The Multilateral Trading System: Mid-Flight Turbulence or Systems Failure?' in R. Newfarmer (ed.), *Trade, Doha and Development: A Window into the Issues.* Washington, DC: The World Bank.
[3] See World Bank (2009) *Global Monitoring Report: A Development Emergency*, p. 152.

The financial crisis, however, has rekindled the debate on the links between trade (and trade policy) and poverty. For developing countries, the growth slowdown, coming on the heels of the food price increase of 2005 to mid-2008, is expected to have a negative impact on the prospects for poverty reduction. To the extent that international trade has been one of the main channels of transmission of the crisis from the centre to the periphery of the world economy, outward orientation has often been identified as an indicator of vulnerability. Moreover, new arguments for the adoption of industrial policies in developing countries are presented as necessary steps to promote modernization in an environment that will be less accommodating to large current account imbalances.[4] The record decline in world trade volumes (between October 2008 and March 2009) and growing unemployment around the world have, in turn, reawakened fears that the beggar-thy-neighbour policies and the protectionist temptation may become too strong to resist, particularly in industrialized countries.

The latest economic developments suggest that the 'pendulum' of economic perceptions is likely to move against those that see economic integration as an instrument for poverty reduction. The current backlash against globalization, however, is mainly associated (as was the case during the East Asian crisis) with concerns about financial liberalization. If history serves us well, this will be another temporary swing. Actually, outward-oriented economies are likely to be the first ones to emerge from the global economic downturn.

The links between trade and poverty will always have to be analysed in a country-specific context, by evaluating not only how trade affects the relative prices of products and factors of productions relevant to poor households (in the short term), but also its impact on growth (and income distribution) over the long term. Empirical analyses confirm that side-by-side with economies where trade liberalization has had a positive impact in terms of poverty reduction (e.g. Mexico) one can find others in which the effects have been less favourable (e.g. India).[5]

---

[4] See, for example, D. Rodrik (2009) 'Growth After the Crisis', paper prepared for the Growth Commission, mimeo.

[5] See, for example, A. Nicita (2004) 'Who Benefited from Trade Liberalization in Mexico? Measuring the Effects on Household Welfare' Policy Research

In sum, for organizations such as the International Chamber of Commerce, the promotion of international trade as a lever to advance the goals of peace and prosperity remains as important today as it was a century ago. In spite of the current stresses, globalization (and trade expansion) will continue. International trade after all is akin to technological change. And as pointed out by Winters *et al.*, '[with] care, trade liberalization can be an important component of a "pro-poor" development strategy'.[6] The challenge is to calibrate such a 'prescription' in a way that takes into account the circumstances of the 'patient', to recognize that the outcomes will vary from case to case, and to complement it with policy interventions that facilitate the adjustment of the poor.

Working Paper Series, 3265, The World Bank; and P. Topalova (2007) 'Trade Liberalization, Poverty, and Inequality: Evidence from Indian Districts', in A. E. Harrison, *Globalization and Poverty*. University of Chicago Press.
6   See L. Alan Winters, N. McCulloch and A. McKay (2004) 'Trade Liberalization and Poverty: The Evidence So Far', *Journal of Economic Literature* 42 (March): 108.

C2 | *Trade policy as an instrument of social justice*

VEENA JHA*

Trade is an important instrument, not a goal in itself. More trade will not necessarily result in expanded national income or poverty reduction – this is a function of the whole set of the economic, social and political conditions that influence development. This article will highlight some of the issues to be addressed if trade policy is to be an important instrument of social justice.

Trade and poverty reduction

For developing countries, one of the most important aspects of social justice is poverty reduction. Trade can play a role in poverty reduction. On average trade constitutes 30 per cent of global GDP. Poverty reduction requires sustained economic growth, which in the context of trade generally denotes export expansion. Import bottlenecks hamper the full utilization and efficient development of domestic productive capacities. Hence, exports and imports facilitate sustained economic growth, development of productive capacities, expansion of employment opportunities and sustained livelihoods.

Three types of trade-poverty relationships can be identified:

1. Virtuous trade effects, where backward and forward linkages to traded products are established leading to an overall increase in consumption.
2. Immiserizing trade effects, where few linkages are established with domestic industry, and domestic consumption actually decreases.
3. Ambiguous trade effects showing no clear trend.

---

* Dr Veena Jha is a visiting professorial Fellow at the University of Warwick and a Research Fellow at IDRC, Canada. She is the Director of Maguru Consultants Limited, UK, and is currently engaged in working on issues related to trade and climate change, trade-related technical assistance with bilateral donors such as the EU, and on inclusive growth issues. She worked for the United Nations and its specialized organizations for over twenty years.

Export growth can play a number of different roles in support-ing economic growth. These include: (a) static efficiency gains, which arise through specialization according to current comparative advantage; (b) increased capacity utilization, which arises if exter-nal demand enables the employment of previously idle labour and land resources; (c) increased physical and human capital investment owing to improved returns to investment; (d) productivity growth, which can arise through the transfer of technology or increased effi-ciency owing to the pressure of exposure to international trade com-petition; (e) export-accelerated industrialization, involving a labour re-allocation from agriculture into manufacturing; and (f) relaxation of the balance of payments constraint on sustained economic growth. However, none of the above gains are automatic. In fact quite the reverse effects could also take place.

The relationship between trade and poverty is asymmetrical. Although developing countries with declining exports are almost cer-tain to have a rising incidence of poverty, increasing exports do not necessarily lead to poverty reduction.

Trade adjustment costs

In moving towards a more open trade regime, adjustment costs also need to be taken into account. While more trade will help increase aggregate real income over time, some groups in society will lose in the short run, and others may confront a permanent reduction in expected income. While trade adjustment costs in industry and services have been the central focus of a number of discussions in the developed countries, food security concerns related to trade have occupied centre stage in developing countries. Measures to safeguard the interests of poor households, particularly with respect to food security, and especially in the wake of the global food crisis of 2008, deserve further analysis.

Trade and food security concerns

Food security refers to the capacity of a country to ensure that its whole population will have enough food on a stable basis, whether domestically produced or imported. Cheap imports may displace domestic production. As production decreases, employment in rural areas will fall, thus increasing poverty. The aggregate effects depend on the rate of urbanization, which along with other factors will determine whether a country is a net importer of food. Barring a few countries, nearly 80 per cent of the world produces its own food.

The positive effects of liberalization depend upon the supply response in agriculture. This supply response in turn depends upon a host of factors, most of which are determined by national conditions and policies, such as infrastructure investments, well-functioning credit and other input (seeds, fertilizers) markets and the existence or absence of anti-agriculture and anti-export biases. Typically, developed countries have an elastic supply response and most developing countries an inelastic one in agriculture.

On the issue of food security, a rigorous definition evolved by notable economists points to the fact that food security risks largely affect economies such as India and China.[1] The average level of food security risk (1 being the highest level of security risk, and 12 the lowest) is 2.5 for the poorest countries, 4.5 for China and India, 6.4 for the middle-income developing countries, and 10.6 for the OECD countries. This does argue for careful and calibrated liberalization in agriculture for large developing countries.

Most farmers produce for local markets, a dimension hard to fully integrate in trade calculations. Improving food security could be dealt with by an open trade policy coupled with the possibilities of *ex ante* adjustment of bound tariffs and of building *ex post* emergency food stocks. Development of complementary policies requires analysis of the prevailing situation, and identification of the sources of rigidity in markets and of the balance between rural net sellers (including the importance of subsistence farming), rural net buyers and the urban poor.

Trade liberalization and loss of tariff revenue

In several, if not most countries social protection measures are administered and paid for by the government. Thus loss of tariff revenue may be a serious consideration and may reduce a number

---

[1] E. Diaz-Bonilla, M. Thomas and S. Robinson (2002) *Trade Liberalization, WTO and Food, Security*. TMD Discussion Paper No. 82. IFPRI. January. Washington, DC.

of social protection measures also reducing social justice. However, a tariff decrease does not necessarily lead to reduced revenue. The actual outcome will depend on the response of import demand to changes in price due to the tariff cut. Indeed, sometimes revenue can increase as very high tariffs do not generate revenue, but may either encourage smuggling or wipe out imports entirely. Empirical evidence from major trade liberalization programmes suggests that revenue implications are not always significant, in part due to accelerated import growth. Trade facilitation improvements in collecting existing (particularly more uniform) duties can also boost revenue in the face of tariff cuts.

Finally, the structure of the initial tariff structure of the country concerned will also affect the impact on government revenue. Where bound rates are significantly above applied rates, cuts in bound rates could well have no effect on revenue. There is also scope to increase trade without reducing tariff revenue by focusing initial cuts on high tariff rates on price-elastic goods (increasing trade and welfare), while levelling tariff rates on price-inelastic goods. This would also have the benefit of creating a more uniform tariff profile. Equally, the choice of method for tariff reduction can impact on the extent of revenue loss.

Addressing social justice concerns through trade policy

The most important trade policy for administering social justice in the international trade arena has been trade preference schemes for poor countries. Contrary to widespread perception, preferential (duty-free) access to the European or US markets, be it through the Generalized System of Preferences (GSP), Everything But Arms (EBA) initiative or African Growth and Opportunity Act (AGOA), has not been really helpful to the least developed countries (LDCs). But GSP schemes did help East Asian countries and helped them to trade their way out of poverty. The limited ability of preference schemes to deliver social justice at the international level has been traced to behind-the-border measures – price support and other domestic production subsidies – which keep OECD farmers producing and selling in their own OECD markets. The presence of heavily subsidized OECD producers in the market makes it very hard for exporters from the poorest countries to compete in those markets, despite their preferential tariffs.

The poorest countries (excluding China and India) are much more affected by farm protection than other countries. For countries such as Benin, Burkina Faso, Burundi, Chad, Malawi, Mali, Rwanda, Sudan, Tanzania, Uganda and Zimbabwe, 60–80 per cent of their total exports comprise goods subsidized by OECD countries.

There are several other reasons why utilization rates of preference schemes tend to be low: complex regulations; exclusion of key exports from the recipients; uncertainty and conditionality of the preferences; non-production of relevant goods; or administrative failure. Further, many LDC exports remain unable to meet relevant standards; few preference schemes currently include any capacity-building programmes to assist in this regard. Lastly, countries must have a minimum base of production and supply capacity in order to be able to take advantage of preferences – the low level of industrialization and diversification in many African, Caribbean and Pacific (ACP) countries has contributed to the low utilization.

In the aftermath of the 2008–2009 economic crisis and the widespread structural adjustment that will have to take place in advanced economies, it is essential that moves towards trade protection in developed countries be strongly resisted. As pointed out above there is a need for rebalancing the gains from trade towards developing countries. Trade protection in developed countries cannot be treated on a par with food security concerns or trade adjustment policies in developing countries. Social justice requires that trade policy be cognizant of the differences and some countries will necessarily have to yield more than others. Unfortunately the political climate for such give and take is diminishing.

C3 | Trade, employment and global responsibilities

MARION JANSEN[*]

Over the past decades trade has played an increasingly important role in the world economy and has contributed significantly to economic growth both at the global level and within individual countries. Many have taken advantage from trade through increases in wages and household incomes, and this has in particular been the case for those involved in export-related activities. Being connected to the world economy may not give any guarantee for economic growth, but there have not been many examples – if any at all – of countries that managed to significantly enhance their growth performance while staying disconnected from global production and financial networks.

Through its contribution to prosperity, trade has certainly contributed to political stability and peace in this world in the past decades. In order to continue to do so, though, a number of challenges need to be overcome. Failure to overcome those challenges may turn trade into a destabilizing factor. It is especially important that we reflect upon these obstacles in times of economic instability. I want to focus on two challenges here: the need to provide protection to those who become more vulnerable in an open world and the need to guarantee that the gains from trade are distributed in a way considered acceptable by societies.

After having continuously outpaced growth over a period of three decades, export growth was negative in 2009 and dropped by

* Marion Jansen is a Senior Specialist on trade and employment in the Employment Sector of the International Labour Office. She previously worked for many years in the Economic Research and Statistics Division of the WTO and has been active in public sector consulting notably for the UK government and the European Commission. Her publications cover the areas of trade and labour, trade in services, temporary migration and domestic regulation in the context of trade.

Disclaimer: The opinions expressed in this article should be attributed to the author and are not meant to represent the position of the International Labour Office.

12.2 per cent in volume terms.[1] Through drops in trade and FDI, the 2008–2009 crisis – that started as a financial crisis in the industrialized world – was being transmitted to other countries without home-grown problems in the financial sector. As a consequence, the housing bubble in the USA has, for instance, led to slumps in the demand for cars and caused significant lay-offs in Liberian rubber plantations that produce the stuff car tyres are made of. The slump in economic growth may be more significant in the USA than in Liberia, but the individual hardship caused by the crisis is likely to be more significant in the latter country where the loss of one job may bring an entire family below the poverty line.

Even in the 1990s, Dani Rodrik drew our attention to the fact that 'open economies have bigger governments'.[2] When looking at the impact of the 2008–2009 crisis on developing and emerging economies we understand why: openness tends to increase exposure to external shocks and social protection systems play a crucial role in providing shelter against the negative effects of such shocks.

So trade contributes to growth but the growth effects are not evenly distributed over time, which is a problem for those who cannot prepare themselves for the bad periods. Growth effects are also not evenly distributed across individuals and trade may therefore contribute to increases or decreases in within-country distribution. Although the story has already been told hundreds of times, let me repeat that there seems to be agreement that trade has contributed to increased income inequality in the industrialized world in the 1980s and early 1990s but that the contribution of technological change has been much larger. Let me also repeat that trade seems to have contributed to decreases in inequality in 'early liberalizing' Asian economies such as Indonesia, Malaysia and Thailand.

What do we know about changes in income distribution in more recent years? Concerns about increasing income inequality persist in the industrialized world and have become more acute in countries such as the United States. Developing countries are also increasingly experiencing upward movements in inequality and this includes most

---

[1] WTO (2010) 'Trade to Expand by 9.5% in 2010 after a Dismal 2009, WTO Reports', press release, 26 March.
[2] D. Rodrik (1998). 'Why Do More Open Economies Have Bigger Governments?' *Journal of Political Economy* 106(5), October.

Asian economies.[3] Some even express concerns about income 'polarization' associated with the 'disappearing middle class'.

   Indeed, even in countries that are large exporters of labour-intensive
goods, such as China, trade seems to be only one among other potent
drivers of changes in labour demand. China is often called the 'world
factory', because of the massive increases in manufacturing exports
the country experienced in recent years, with average annual increases
of 20 per cent in the period between 2000 and 2007.[4] Yet, in China
the share of manufacturing employment has remained rather stable
in the past ten years.[5] The two phenomena together probably reflect
significant productivity improvements. So while exports contribute to
growth and while jobs are probably created in exporting industries,
the effect is not large enough to tip the changes in relative demand for
production factors in favour of (low skilled) workers. More generally,
with the observed advances in production technologies, it is hard to
see how growth in emerging and developing countries – in particular those with strong population growth such as India – will manage
to generate enough labour demand to increase the relative returns to
(low skilled) labour.

   From the industrialized countries' point of view trade liberalization
in large countries such as Brazil, China and India has represented a
massive surge in the 'global supply of labour' with ensuing pressure on
wages in the industrialized world. Medium-income and least developing countries together account for 73 per cent of the world's labour
force and this number reaches 80 per cent when focusing on the world's
young workers.[6] Although this picture may change in the future, notably
as a result of the one-child policy in China, pressure on industrialized

[3] P. K. Goldberg, and N. Pavcnik (2007) 'Distributional Effects of
   Globalization in Developing Countries', *Journal of Economic Literature*
   115: 39–82; International Monetary Fund (IMF, 2006) 'Rising Inequality
   and Polarization in Asia', *Asia and Pacific Regional Economic Outlook*,
   September, pp. 63–78.
[4] WTO (2008) *International Trade Statistics 2008*, Geneva: World Trade
   Organization.
[5] L. Chen and B. Hou (2009) 'China: Economic Transition, Employment
   Flexibility and Security' in Sangheon Lee and Francois Eyraud (eds.)
   *Globalization, Flexibilization and Working Conditions in Asia and the
   Pacific*. Geneva: ILO.
[6] A. K. Ghose, N. Majid and C. Ernst (2008) *The Global Employment
   Challenge*, Geneva: ILO.

country wages is unlikely to cede in the coming decade and in several European economies recent cohorts of entrants in the labour market are expected to receive lower incomes than their parents in real terms.

If it is true that workers in open economies, in particular the smaller ones among them, are increasingly vulnerable to external shocks and if it is true that trade cannot counterbalance the effects of technological change on income dispersion or even contributes to globally observed increases in domestic income inequality, what can be done about it? Stopping or reversing trade openness and technological change do not seem to be viable options.

The difficulty is that answers to the two mentioned global phenomena (volatility and inequality) driven by two other global phenomena (technical progress and trade) have so far been sought for at the domestic level. We may still be wondering whether US wages are set in Beijing or German wages in Warsaw,[7] but we take for granted that national governments are responsible for social protection and redistribution policies. Yet the tools at their disposal are strongly influenced by two other global phenomena not mentioned so far: global capital mobility and the presence of increasingly powerful global private players. Notwithstanding the 2008 financial crisis, capital has been *the* winner of the most recent globalization phase,[8] but it is difficult to redistribute from a mobile winner to an immobile loser, as the winner can always threaten to leave the country to avoid taxation.

In this context, the question therefore arises whether global answers are required to the two global challenges outlined in this article. Could the answer lie in increased international collaboration of governments in matters of public finance, maybe in the context of global or regional institutions? Could global private actors play a role? When comparing the role of private foundations such as the Gates Foundation in development aid with the role of the UN, it would probably not be far-fetched to say that private global actors can have a similar role to public actors when it comes to 'cross-country redistribution'. Would

---

[7] R. Freeman (1995) 'Are Your Wages Set in Beijing?' *Journal of Economic Perspectives* 9(3): 15–32 (Summer) and H. Brücker (2001) 'Werden unsere Löhne künftig in Warschau festgesetzt? Eine empirische Analyse der Arbeitsmarkte®ekte der Osterweiterung', *LIST-Forum* 27(1): 71–92.

[8] K. Rogoff (2005) 'Hollywood's Favourite Villains', Project Syndicate.

it then be far-fetched to ask the question of what the responsibility and role of those private players can be in meeting the two challenges emphasized in this article?

A popular recent French song says, 'quand le financier s'enrhume ce sont les ouvriers qui toussent' – when the banker catches a cold, workers start coughing. If this is the case let's make sure the latter can take sick leave and see a doctor without putting the living standard of their families at risk.

C4 | *Misconceptions about the WTO, trade, development and aid*

FAIZEL ISMAIL[*]

This article will address three misconceptions about the WTO, trade, aid and development. First, development is equal to Special and Differential Treatment (S&D)[1] and aid. Second, aid does not belong to the WTO. Third, developing countries want to make the WTO a development institution. And in the conclusion I will set out a vision for where we should be on these issues in ten years' time.

Is development equal to S&D and aid in the WTO?

My proposition is that S&D and aid do not constitute the core development content of the WTO.[2]

S&D issues are related to three main concerns of developing countries. First, market access (mainly concerned preferences); second, flexibility in the rules; and third, aid for technical assistance and capacity building. These concerns are reflected in over 150 provisions in the GATT since 1947. Market access was mainly about preferences which served to ameliorate and compensate somewhat for the increasingly high barriers erected in the USA, Japan and the EU against agricultural imports and textiles. Preferences were based on the colonialist system preferring some developing countries and not others, and were thus fundamentally discriminatory.

As the GATT developed, the rules reflected the competitive capacities of developed countries. In manufacturing, where developed

---

[*] Faizel Ismail is the Head of the South African Delegation to the WTO in Geneva. He has written a book entitled *Mainstreaming Development in the WTO: Developing Countries in the Doha Round*.

[1] Special and Differential Treatment referred to those provisions in the GATT, which preceded the WTO, that made special exceptions in the Rules for developing countries, enabled trade preferences and promised donor assistance to build developing country capacity to trade.

[2] F. Ismail (2005) 'Mainstreaming Development in the World Trade Organization', *Journal of World Trade* 39(1) February.

countries were very competitive, the Uruguay Round (UR) Trade-Related Investment Measures (TRIMs) agreement abolished subsidies. Whilst in agriculture the boxes created in the UR agriculture agreement (Amber, Blue and Green), to provide some disciplines on trade-distorting subsidies, contained large loopholes to allow the EU and USA to actually increase their expenditure. On intellectual property rights, the Trade-Related Aspects of Intellectual Property Rights (TRIPS) agreement provided increased protection for largely developed-country research and development. Thus the call for S&D flexibilities by developing countries in the TRIMs agreement and TRIPS were largely to ameliorate this inequity.

Capacity building was largely a best endeavour effort in the GATT and was directed mainly at the capacity of countries to participate and implement GATT rules rather than address supply-side issues.

As the Chair of the Committee on Trade and Development Special Session (CTDSS) for two years, it took me some time to ponder why it was that developing countries were so keen on resolving the eighty-eight S&D proposals that were put on the agenda at the Doha Ministerial Conference. These proposals called for the existing S&D provisions to be made more precise, mandatory and operational.

However, these issues, in my view, do not constitute the development dimension of the GATT/WTO. They remain important in the system and are still valid. Their basic purpose is to recognize that vast differences remain in the economic and trade capacities of developed and developing countries.

So what then does constitute development in the WTO?

I drew on the work of Amartya Sen and developed four essential dimensions of development in the WTO. Sen defines development as 'the removal of unfreedom'.[3] Development in his view is the process of expanding human freedoms. Thus, for Sen, development is understood as the process of removing unfreedoms.

We have identified four types of unfreedoms or deprivations, in Sen's work, that are relevant to our discussion of development and the multilateral trading system. First, Sen argues that deprivations can result when people are denied economic opportunities. Second,

---

[3] A. Sen (1999) *Development as Freedom*, New York: Anchor Books, p. 3.

he maintains that poverty should be understood not so much as low incomes but as a deprivation of basic capabilities. Third, while Sen argues for government regulation to enable markets to work more effectively, he states that a system of ethics, based on social justice, is required to build vision and trust for the successful use of the market mechanism. Fourth, he argues that the deprivation of the opportunity to participate in crucial decisions regarding public affairs is to deny people the right to develop.

Therefore, in the ongoing Doha Round, how should we translate this perspective? First, it does mean that to provide developing countries with opportunities to export in global markets, we have to tilt the balance towards a level playing field and, in line with the promise of the Doha Mandate for a development round, somewhat in favour of developing countries this time. In agriculture, we have to remove the distortions caused by subsidies in developed countries that prevent and undermine developing countries from pursuing their comparative advantage. Second, we all have the responsibility to ensure that the poorest countries are provided with the capacity to produce and export, thus allowing them too to benefit from the opportunities in the global economy. Third, the rules of the trading system also need to be balanced while strengthening a rules-based system for all to benefit. The system should provide sufficient flexibilities to prevent developing countries from bearing the cost of these rules without the benefits. Fourth, the participation of developing countries in the process is crucial to ensure that they are engaged in negotiating the new rules in a fair and democratic manner.

Does aid belong to the WTO?

There are many provisions on technical assistance and capacity building in the GATT.

Paragraph 2 of the Doha Declaration states that: '... well targeted, sustainably financed technical assistance and capacity-building programmes have important roles to play'.

The Hong Kong Ministerial Declaration[4] recognized the importance of 'Aid for Trade' and called on the Director-General of the

---

[4] WT/MIN (05)/DEC Para 57 of the 'Ministerial Declaration'. Doha Work Programme, 22 December 2005.

WTO to: a) create a Task Force that 'shall provide recommendations on how to operationalise Aid for Trade'; and b) consult with members as well as the IMF and World Bank and other relevant international organizations 'with a view to reporting to the General Council on appropriate mechanisms to secure additional financial resources for Aid for Trade'. This Task Force[5] submitted its recommendations to the General Council at the end of July 2006.[6]

So, aid is very much a part of the WTO and, I have argued, an essential component of the development dimension of the WTO.[7]

Do developing countries want to make the WTO a development institution?

No! Developing countries do not want to make the WTO a delivery mechanism for aid but do want to utilize it a) as a point of leverage to increase Aid for Trade; b) to build coherence between the WTO and the aid agencies; and c) to build transparency and mutual accountability.

Conclusion

In ten years the WTO should have advanced sufficiently in concert with the developments in the UN System and the reforms made in the Bretton Woods institutions to have adopted development as an over-riding goal and objective of the WTO. Thus in this context development would be mainstreamed into the WTO. The WTO agreements would thus become fair, balanced, strengthen the capacity of developing countries, and become inclusive and transparent in its decision making. Aid for Trade would thus be seen as a necessary and essential element of the WTO. It would be an instrument to leverage overall

---

[5] The task force is composed of thirteen members – Barbados, Brazil, Canada, China, Colombia, the EU, Japan, India, Thailand, the USA and the coordinators of the ACP (African, Caribbean and Pacific) Group of States, the African Group and the LDC (least-developed countries) Group.

[6] WTO doc. WT/AFT/1, Recommendations of the Task Force on Aid For Trade, 27 July 2006.

[7] F. Ismail (2007) 'Aid for Trade. An Essential Component of the Multilateral Trading System and WTO Doha Development Agenda', *World Economics* 8(1) January-March 2007.

Official Development Assistance for developing countries. The WTO Aid for Trade work programme would be used to encourage ownership, transparency and accountability, of both developed and developing countries, as the Paris Principles have agreed. Aid would not be used as a substitute for trade solutions but as a necessary complement to them.

C5 Two hundred years after Jefferson

IQBAL QUADIR*

In any discussion about international trade, we should remind ourselves of one of Thomas Jefferson's maxims: 'Commerce with all nations, alliance with none. That should be our motto.'

One of the principal authors of the Declaration of Independence and one of the most influential Founding Fathers of the United States, Jefferson left office as third President two hundred years ago in 1809. Deeply influenced by Adam Smith, Jefferson was a champion of commerce who wanted to promote trade to open markets for US agricultural products, thereby improving farmers' welfare and furthering general prosperity. Although Jefferson was philosophically opposed to such action by the central government, he compromised and purchased the Louisiana Territory from France so that he could promote trade via the port of New Orleans.

During the last two hundred years, trade – especially trade involving goods whose production puts people to work rather than trade based on the extraction and sale of mineral wealth – has been an engine for prosperity, proving Jefferson's wisdom. On a theoretical level, many economists since Smith have articulated the merits of trade. In the early nineteenth century, David Ricardo established that, when two parties engage in trade, both benefit – even if one party is stronger in all areas – as long as each concentrates on its respective strengths.

On a practical level, trade has yielded many benefits for the USA and its trading partners. For the USA, trade has resulted in cheaper consumer goods, larger export markets, investment opportunities, gradual democratization of governments that the USA has engaged in trade, and an overall expansion of the US economy and US influence.

* Professor Iqbal Quadir is the founder and Director of the Legatum Center for Development and Entrepreneurship at MIT and the founder of Grameenphone in Bangladesh.

Although some argue that the North American Free Trade Agreement has not helped enough, the size of the US economy doubled during the first ten years of the agreement. East Asian economies have made tremendous economic progress in recent decades, largely through trade, and pulled hundreds of millions of people out of poverty.

Born and raised in Bangladesh, I have witnessed trade's positive effects on poor countries. Over the last two decades, Bangladesh has exported apparel to the USA and Europe, generating US$11 billion of Bangladesh's annual export revenue of approximately US$14 billion. Entrepreneurs in Bangladesh – about 5,000 of them in apparel alone – capitalize on low-cost labour, creating millions of jobs. The vibrant, dispersed apparel sector in Bangladesh has, in turn, boosted activities such as banking, trucking, shipping and insurance. American consumers have also benefited from lower apparel prices.

Despite trade's many benefits, the USA has strayed from Jefferson's maxim, often pursuing short-term interests to the detriment of broader, long-term ones. In fact, the USA has discouraged trade in at least three ways.

First, the USA generally adheres to the principle of reciprocity, extending tariff reductions on imports from certain countries in exchange for tariff reductions on US exports to those countries. However, poor countries with smaller markets are usually unable to bargain for reductions in US tariffs on imports to the USA. This is why the average US tariff on Bangladeshi imports is over fifteen times higher than that on imports from France, which obviously has greater bargaining power than Bangladesh.

This reciprocity game attempts to protect jobs in industries where Americans fear losing to cheaper labour. But, when technology changes, jobs are naturally gained or lost. Bureaucratic protection of jobs only cages people; conversely, freely operating economic forces spur innovation that propels people into new jobs. Despite this, certain industries have used their leverage to pressure the US government to levy tariffs on imports from countries where low-cost labour is a perceived threat.

However, as has been the case in China, powerful American companies have outleveraged American labour, effectively overcoming the reciprocity game. Strapped for foreign exchange in 1979, China established export processing zones where foreign companies could build factories and operate tariff-free. American companies took advantage of the low-cost Chinese labour and filled American shops with goods made in China. Even today, foreign firms produce about half of China's exports, with the USA levying an average tariff on Chinese imports that is only one-fifth of the average tariff on Bangladeshi imports.

A more consistent treatment of trading partners, in line with Jefferson's 'commerce with all nations', could have led to varied levels of economic progress worldwide. This would have slowed down China's emergence as a genuine rival for the USA, reducing inequity among nations and benefiting the entire world, including the USA.

Second, the USA and Europe spend US$1 billion daily on agricultural subsidies. Even two hundred years ago, Jefferson understood the importance of farmers competing in the international market. Yet today's subsidies harm the USA and poor countries in agriculture, trade and other areas. Three-quarters of US agricultural subsidies go to the largest 10 per cent of farms. Subsidized corn syrup in many US foods contributes to obesity, which apparently accounts for 10 per cent of US healthcare costs.

The USA could follow New Zealand, which in 1984 removed agricultural subsidies. Subsequently, its farmers innovated and prospered. If US farmers were not subsidized, they would innovate. Farmers in poor countries could also better compete with American farmers and contribute to development in their countries. This would increase US exports to those markets.

Third, the USA discourages trade by providing 'aid' to governments in poor countries. Aid is intended to boost, artificially, the purchasing power of these countries so that they buy equipment and consulting services from those giving the aid. Aid hurts trade in many ways. Poor governments receiving aid have little incentive to earn tax revenues, so they do not promote the trade that would yield such funds. Aid strengthens bureaucracy, impeding entrepreneurs pursuing trade. Finally, aid recipients have a weaker hand in negotiating fair trade with the aid providers.

Aid is actually provided for geopolitical purposes such as facilitating alliances of the very sort that Jefferson viewed with suspicion. When the USA, in its formative years, was weaker than France and Britain, Jefferson worried that alliances strengthened central power, making government less accountable. Today, this dynamic still plagues poor countries with strong central governments. When the USA allies politically with unaccountable governments through aid, the USA, in effect, makes it harder for citizens of those governments to improve accountability. Pakistan and Egypt are examples where state power, bolstered by aid and alliance, has contributed to corruption and stagnation.

Trade can cure the malaise caused by aid. The opportunity to trade empowers entrepreneurs, giving them the clout to demand and get greater cooperation, accountability, and pro-growth policies from government. Otherwise, in the absence of such demanding citizens, governance deteriorates. According to the World Bank's *Doing Business* report, Bangladesh ranks 110 out of 181 countries in its ease of doing business index. Transparency International ranks Bangladesh 147 out of 180 countries in its corruption perception index. Despite Bangladesh's apparent barriers to business and the country's reputation for bad governance, its apparel sector is thriving with 20 per cent annual growth. This proves that government bodies involved in trade are functioning better, thanks to the countervailing force of entrepreneurs, than the rest of the government. In short, trade not only generates growth, but also improves governance.

Trade leads to jobs, innovations, prosperity and an empowered citizenry. The ensuing democratic forces lay the foundation for durable alliances that are both made possible and reinforced by trade. Jefferson, an intellectual giant who understood the fundamentals of economics and politics, must have grappled with these issues in formulating his maxim. In 1962, when President Kennedy welcomed forty-nine Nobel laureates to the White House, he said, 'I think this is the most extraordinary collection of talent and of human knowledge that has ever been gathered together at the White House – with the possible exception of when Thomas Jefferson dined alone.'

The world has changed significantly during the past two hundred years. Because of the US economy's size, our errors, while perhaps less visible to us, have a magnified impact beyond our borders. And, in a world that is profoundly more connected, the consequences of our actions quickly come back to us. These complexities make guiding principles even more necessary today than they were two hundred years ago. Because Jefferson's maxim addresses long-term US interests, those who argue that we must deviate from it for practical, short-term reasons must think deeply and debate broadly before deviating from it.

C6 | Trade, coercive forces and national governance

FRANKLIN CUDJOE*

Trade has not ceased to be the single most important activity that brings people together voluntarily. Naturally, this voluntary exchange rests on a market principle based on a willing seller and a willing buyer at an agreed price.

At the height of their glory, many pre-colonial African states and empires found trade to be a better way to prosperity than conquests. Gold was shipped from Wangara in the Upper Niger across the Sahara desert to Taghaza, in Western Sahara, in exchange for salt, and to Egypt for ceramics, silks and other Asian and European goods. The old Ghana empire controlled much of the trans-Sahara trade in copper and ivory. At Great Zimbabwe, gold was traded for Chinese pottery and glass. From Nigeria, leather and iron goods were traded throughout West Africa.

Today, many trading posts have been brought together through conventions and rules, culminating in the establishment of a supra-national authority such as the World Trade Organization (WTO). Globalized trade has lessened suspicion, promoted multicultural-ism and peace. Nonetheless, we are at the edge of losing it to special interests groups and lobbyists seeking all manner of favours from the WTO and individual member nations. The inability of the WTO to revive the collapsed Doha trade talks points to the deep schism and mistrust among trading nations. Such staggering inertia in deepening trade ties has been made worse by the global financial difficulties.

Pascal Lamy, Director-General of the WTO, has said that a US$250 billion financial package to revive a global trading system crippled by

* Franklin Cudjoe is Founding Director of IMANI Center for Policy & Education, a Ghanaian think tank dedicated to fostering public awareness of important policy issues concerning business, government and civil society. Mr Cudjoe is also editor of www.africanliberty.org and an Earhart Fellow at Buckingham University.

the credit crisis has begun to bear fruit. The WTO has still announced a 12 per cent contraction in global trade volumes in 2009 as a result of the financial difficulties. However, the same absurdity that partly brought down the house is pretty much in place. Offensive and blanket subsidies in the developed world are no excuse for developing country blindness to domestic reform. Preferential trade arrangements are not sacrosanct. Some of them have packages that inhibit the sensible growth progression of smaller nations.

Giving aid in exchange for access to 60 per cent of a local market is a defeatist notion of development. The history of aid has not been palatable anywhere, not least in Africa. But that is exactly what the European Partnership Agreements (EPA) seek to achieve. In June 2009, a trade communiqué signed in Abuja, Nigeria, stated that the Economic Community for West African States (ECOWAS) and Union Economique et Monétaire Ouest-Africaine (UEMOA, West African Economic and Monetary Union) must take all the necessary steps to finalize the study on the regional EPA fund including the modalities and mechanisms for mobilizing financial contributions for the region to the fund. Again, the two commissions must obtain from the European Commission and the EU member states a clear commitment to the financing of the EPA.

Instead of demanding that the Common Agricultural Policy of the EU be scrapped in order to allow market access for poor African farmers, our politicians have cut a deal for themselves. One such absurdity these misdirected funds will be applied to is a project to ban the importation of second-hand refrigerators into Ghana. So far a US$2.7 million support from the Multilateral Fund of Canada, Global Energy Fund and the government of Ghana has been acquired for the commencement of the project. It seems that a common sense approach to better the lives of poor Ghanaians would be to advocate a liberalized trade regime that has the capacity to unleash individual wealth. After all, that is why we have governments: to facilitate trade deals for their citizens, not to dupe them by making self-serving deals.

Not having the courage to call off external trade barriers means the absence of incentives to fight higher barriers at home. After thirty-four years in existence, West African countries, through the regional trading bloc, ECOWAS, have only attained 3 per cent trade penetration into a regional market comprising 250 million people. In comparison, their European counterparts have achieved 40 per cent. What is offensive is ECOWAS' shifting mandate to enhance greater integration within the region. Having missed the 2007 deadline for eliminating barriers to free movement of goods and people, the regional trade bloc reports that this may be achievable in 2017.

Subsidy to cotton farmers in the West has damaging prospects for the so-called C4 West African countries of Benin, Burkina Faso, Mali and Chad, which consistently argue that US subsidies depress world prices and rob their farmers of export sales. Somehow the Africa Growth and Opportunity Act (AGOA) of the USA gives preferential market access in the USA to textile manufacturers in Africa. Despite AGOA not being a full liberalizing arrangement, it has helped grow the apparel and textile industries and created more than 300,000 jobs across the continent. Sadly, last year the forty-eight countries of Sub-Saharan Africa represented only 1.2% of the US$95 billion US apparel import market. Bangladesh alone captured 3.8%, more than triple the trade of AGOA's African beneficiary countries combined. Last year apparel exports from Africa to the USA dropped by 10%, a decline over three times greater than the contraction in the overall US textile and apparel market. This is why supporters of AGOA are urging the US government to resist pressure from some development advocates and members of congress who declined to support legislation that extends the duty free access to the US market enjoyed by AGOA to all least developed countries.

However, preferential market access at guaranteed prices cannot be a substitute for direly needed reforms at home. Try as AGOA would, it cannot help African textile manufacturers outdo the Asian apparel market, which, quite frankly and understandably, has eaten into many local markets in Africa. China and Bangladesh, for instance, have superior economies of scale backed by a large cheap labour sector and increasing FDI. Conversely, many African countries have higher production costs that range from inadequate and expensive credit facilities to prohibitive taxes.

There clearly cannot be competition here, save special interest lobbying. So the vested interest song goes, cheap textile imports have plunged the local industry into an even more serious crisis with a

drop in production from 130 million metric tonnes in the 1970s to
25 million metric tonnes thirty years later, and a further 60 per cent
drop in textile sector employment. The woes of the textile industry
began in the 1980s as a result of a shortage of raw materials and foreign exchange. High-quality fabrics sell at US$20 a piece; the cheap
imports may go for US$10 a piece.

Ghana's deputy Minister for Food and Agriculture (Livestock
division), Dr Alfred Tia-Sugri, has expressed concern about the large
importation of cheap livestock products, particularly meat, into the
country. He noted that 30% of the meat required is produced locally.
He explained that presently livestock contributes just 5% to the agricultural gross domestic product out of the expected 35%.

It is true that in the case of certain food staples such as rice and
meat, developed country subsidies help depress local markets. One
may argue that given the higher cost of production on the continent, subsidised products that come in cheaply help locals who have
to spend a portion of their meagre incomes on food in order to save
and reinvest in other sectors of the economy. It is possibly the same
reason why a 100 per cent increase in import taxes on rice imported
to Nigeria did little to stop the importers because the taxed rice from
America, Japan and Thailand was still cheaper than the locally produced rice. As I have argued, fighting off subsidies is a noble cause,
but it has to be balanced with the depression effect on local production costs.

One of such opportunities is the World Expo held in Shanghai in
2010. It is hoped that West African trade ministers and diplomats
will have used this event, in which an Africa Joint Pavilion was con-
structed, to market the subregion in order to reverse the trade imbalance with China at least.

Ultimately, regional trade integration is the best way to affect the
economic destiny of Africa. Some regional trading blocs point the
way. Since the formation of the Free Trade Area within the Common
Market for Eastern and Southern Africa (COMESA) in 2000, for
fifteen out of the nineteen members, trade volumes have increased
fivefold, from a paltry US$3 billion in 1997 to US$15 billion in 2008.
It is expected that a customs union will eventually harmonize trade
deals. Conversely, within ECOWAS, with sixteen member countries,
trade volumes have increased by 10 per cent in the last couple of years
to a paltry US$2.9 billion.

For Africa to benefit from globalization, it is important first to urge domestic reforms. African leaders must reduce economic intervention, free financial markets, remove bureaucratic obstacles to setting up businesses, establish property rights and enforce contract law. These are the forces that release entrepreneurial energy and make trade free from coercive powers.

C7 | Gender equality in trade

HAIFA FAHOUM AL KAYLANI[*]

Forget China, India and the internet: economic growth is driven by women.

The Economist, April 2006

At around 30 per cent, the ratio of world trade to GDP is higher today than ever before. While trade is bringing immense gains to increasing numbers of people across the world, a major challenge for policy makers aiming to reduce poverty and inequality is to enable a more equitable distribution of these gains. This requires understanding and accounting for factors that prevent some regions, countries and social groups from benefiting equally from expanding trade flows and their concomitant benefits.

Gender is a key factor linked to poverty, particularly with regard to patterns of employment in the labour market. Trade benefits are differentiated between women and men, and between various groups of women, impacting gender equality as well as poverty reduction. While trade expansion is improving employment opportunities open to women and increasing their income-earning possibilities, vulnerable women often lack access to favourable employment opportunities and disproportionately occupy irregular and insecure positions with low earnings and few labour and social protection regulations.

Despite this, research findings show a close correlation between greater female participation in society and improved economic

* Haifa Fahoum Al Kaylani is founder and Chairperson, Arab International Women's Forum. She is well known in international government and business circles as a high-impact change agent focusing on leadership in cultural and gender issues. She holds senior roles in several organizations in the UK and internationally as well as seats on the boards of educational and cultural institutions, NGOs and charities. She has also received numerous international awards in recognition of her role as an influential leader.

outcomes and indicate that women-led businesses increase economic diversity and productivity as well as bring wider human resource development. Women's role in trade expansion is thus central to economic and social development due to their integrity and ingenuity.

Women and trade: evidence of reciprocal benefits

Trade as positive for women

The expansion of trade has benefited women overall. It has *created many jobs* for them both absolutely and relative to men. Earning outside of the household environment has increased women's *influence on household decisions.*

Growth in trade expansion has seen an expansion in labour-intensive industries in developing countries. As these industries frequently favour women as employees, this has usually seen a significant *increase in female wage employment* in the formal sector. This also has multiplier effects on *employment creation* in the informal sector, an area in which women frequently find work. Women also *earn more* in export industries than they would have in traditional sectors, thus contributing to a *decrease in the gender wage gap.*

Studies suggest that trade also benefits women in social terms. It offers increased *economic autonomy,* greater *influence within their households* and more choice to *enter or leave marriages.*[1]

Women as positive agents for economic and social development

Women business leaders can play an important role in economic diversification and in ensuring that international trade realizes its potential to enhance social gains. Indeed, a 2006 study by the World Economic Forum showed a close correlation between greater female participation in society and improved economic outcomes.

By offering new ideas, production methods and technologies, women-led businesses can *boost productivity growth* and productivity

[1] M. Fontana, S. Joekes and R. Masika (1998) *Global Trade Expansion and Liberalisation: Gender Issues and Impacts.* Brighton: Institute of Development Studies.

across the economy. In some countries, they are more *open to foreign investment* and participation in export markets. Studies of developing countries have found a strong positive correlation between female participation in manufacturing and *export growth*.

More female business leaders *increase economic diversity*. For example, in tracing the 20 per cent productivity gap between the United Kingdom and the United States, the UK Department of Trade and Industry identified slower business formation as the cause. While the rate of business formation by men is roughly equal in the USA and the UK, the gap in the rate of business formation by women is of around the same magnitude as the productivity gap.[2]

The role of women in trade has *wider human resource development* implications. As women tend to have more family- and socially oriented expenditure patterns than men, their increasing income and employment from trade expansion can increase *child nutritional status* and other human development indicators. An increase in women's income-earning capability also strengthens incentives for investing in the *human capital of girls*.[3]

Thus the potential for women-owned firms to contribute to economic growth, women's empowerment and poverty reduction is great, but only if policy makers remove the barriers that continue to undermine their effectiveness.

The MENA region

Our work at the Arab International Women's Forum focuses particularly on the Middle East and North Africa (MENA) region, which provides a particularly interesting case study of the relationship between women and trade. While economic growth has been impressive in recent years, women's participation in the economic and political spheres remains the lowest of any region.

This fact poses significant barriers to economic growth for the Middle East, as women are very well-educated. Indeed, progress in education has been impressive and women outnumber men at universities in eleven countries out of eighteen. Despite these investments,

---

[2] World Bank (2008) *The Environment for Women's Entrepreneurship in the Middle East and North Africa Region.*
[3] See Fontana *et al.* (1998).

medium and higher education is consistently associated with higher unemployment for women. Governments and policy makers are working to advance women entrepreneurship, particularly given that women have strong economic rights in Islam and there is a tradition of women in business.

A 2008 World Bank report surveyed over 5,100 formal-sector firms in the Middle East regarding perceived barriers in the investment climate. Of the firms surveyed, women were principal owners of only 13 per cent. However, contrary to popular perceptions, more than 30 per cent of the female-owned firms surveyed are very large firms employing over 250 workers.[4]

The study found that female-owned firms in MENA are as large, successful, well-established and tech-savvy as male-owned firms, at times more so. They are active exporters, and also hire more women, with a higher share represented at professional and managerial levels.

The World Bank report found that business and trade laws and regulations in the MENA region are not as gendered as presumed, but that neutral barriers have gender-differentiated effects that are more difficult for women to overcome. The MENA region thus illustrates the need to address barriers inside and outside the labour markets preventing women's full participation, including negative social norms.

Limiting factors to full participation

While increasing openness to trade has seen overall positive effects for women, these vary with resource endowments, educational levels, labour market institutions and policies, and sociocultural norms.[5]

While trade itself may offer immense benefits to women, discrimination in other areas may hinder the ability of certain groups of women to benefit. For example, there is some evidence that married women are particularly prejudiced against in terms of job opportunities and wages, while negative employment effects from cheap import displacement most negatively affect women in small-scale subsistence agriculture, particularly if they lack control over land, labour and the income generated by export production.

[4] See World Bank (2008).   [5] See Fontana *et al.* (1998).

Laws and attitudes outside the business sector can also disadvantage women entrepreneurs and limit the role of women in participating in the trade industry. For example: women's opportunities are significantly influenced by the overall governance environment and the investment climate; social attitudes about women and work influence female labour force participation; gender roles and prejudices in inheritance, land ownership and constitutions can constrain women's independence and access to employment and entrepreneurship; high capital requirements are likely to exclude many women; the World Bank's 2008 *Doing Business* report notes that countries with more cumbersome environments have smaller shares of women entrepreneurs and vice versa.

Policy implications

If we are to see international trade contributing to solving pressing societal and environmental challenges over the coming decade, policy makers will need to harness more effectively the potential of increased trade and the unique skills of women towards this end. A broad range of policy considerations is needed to enable women to fully benefit from the economic and social opportunities that trade expansion offers.

Gender-neutral recommendations should take into consideration the following points: addressing discriminatory laws and regulations outside business law as well as social norms that limit female economic opportunity; providing social protection for the poor, particularly those vulnerable to unemployment due to frequent job turnover as a result of rapid trade liberalization; and reducing barriers to entry for all firms.

A broad set of *gender-specific recommendations* include: investing in women's education and skills accumulation; removing gender distortions in labour markets to ensure proper returns to education; promoting gender equality in employment and promotion practices; enhancing women's control over resources, particularly women's property rights in land; encouraging voluntary company codes of conduct to extend to gender discrimination concerns; including gender-equality labour standards in fair-trade networks; supporting effective women's organizations; increasing representation of women in decision-making bodies in trade organizations; and instituting social clauses in trade agreements, recognizing gender-differentiated experiences.

Conclusion

Trade expansion has the potential to be a powerful conduit for economic growth, women's empowerment and social development. However, where structural problems and unequal gender relations remain in market and non-market spheres, the opportunities that trade expansion offers both women and society as a whole to address issues of poverty through trade will not be fully realized. As a result, attention to gender equality in trade should be part of a holistic social strategy to overcome gender discrimination.

Trade offers a powerful arena for women's empowerment and the economic and social development of entire societies and its expansion should be celebrated and encouraged. The challenge is therefore to pursue patterns of trade most likely to offer all sectors of society equal opportunity and sustainable development.

C8 | *Trading health for comfort*

BRIGHT B. SIMONS*

If you listen regularly to much of the debate around major multilateral trade initiatives, such as the so-called 'Doha Development Round', or the multiple variants of 'Aid for Trade' schemes that every now and then come into fashion, you have probably on many occasions concluded that we have, as a global people, barely snapped out of the self-indulgent 1960s.

You can almost hear Samuel Huntington's typewriter clattering away, 'modernization theory' after 'modernization theory' dribbling down the ribbon like so much cheap ink. The high notes are of course Wallersteinian, with every chord striking home such strong points as: 'core', 'periphery', 'metropolitan', 'dependency', 'de-industrialization' etc., though of course it is also true that the language in current use has done away with certain words and brought in a considerable number of new ones.

That the structure of world trade has not changed – as far as inequity, underdevelopment and exploitation are concerned – is nearly the most uncontested truism in modern-day written and oral geoeconomic literature. The enduring relevance for many a latter-day global theorist of the Polanyis, Habermases and even the Gadamers in the description of the North–South imbalance of power, influence, sovereignty and authority speaks powerfully to the relentless persistence of that intellectual ideology.

Like all truisms, however, this grand consensus disintegrates very shabbily when it leaves the *mantelpiece* and enters the *toolkit* of enquiry. We find that we can hold it together with patches of strawman argumentation in the case of East–West exchange, but only at the risk of great ridiculousness when any attempt is made to use it as

* Bright B. Simons is a Director at the Ghanaian think tank IMANI Centre for Policy & Education, and the innovator of the world's first direct-to-consumer, technology-based, anti-counterfeiting system, mPedigree.

a probe for revealing any of the meaningful features of South–South trade.

Working with the above notion, it is the case of the South–South trade in pharmaceuticals and health products that, in several important respects, is the most striking.

Nearly every global theorist worth her salt has cut at least some of her empirical teeth prying into the regime of standards and how they stifle the movement of otherwise competitive southern hemisphere trade products into northern markets. In the context of northern governments' regulatory complicity, the passions of anti-poverty campaigners have frequently boiled over into steamy confrontations with institutions perceived to be fronts for northern capital interests. When it comes to trade in the other direction – i.e. North to South – standards are this time frequently cited as factors stifling the flow of vital resources into the social economy of southern communities. The issue of TRIPS (Trade-Related Aspects of Intellectual Property Rights) in the North–South trade in pharmaceuticals is probably the handiest illustrator of this phenomenology.

Which is why it is extremely surprising that the issue of standards in South–South trade, particularly in the crucial commerce of pharmaceuticals, receives so little attention.

True, private and transaction-level, as well as 'transient', standards are increasingly the determinative factors in the flow of global trade generally, and there is no doubt that inherent in this trend is a certain deconstruction of the very notion of standards as coherent modes of control, but that fact is in no way suggestive of an imminent redundancy of the standards paradigm of trade facilitation or anti-facilitation.

Hence, a recent spate of legislative measures in Uganda, Kenya and Tanzania that admit notions of intellectual property rights (IPRs) as relevant in the proscription of counterfeit pharmaceuticals and other regulated health products from entry into these East African markets is, in the view of this author, of fundamental importance in highlighting the lopsided discourse about the role of standards in moderating the flow of resources along the various hemispheric axes.

It is fascinating that some campaigners, confronted with obvious evidence of this incoherence, have chosen to retreat to their comfort zone in global theory by construing the pursuit and passage of these legislative measures in these countries as a case of successful hijacking by Northern pharmaceutical interests of policy processes in captive Southern states as part of the effort to preserve the exploitative North–South pharmaceutical trade. The supposed victims in this construal are poor patients in peripheral Southern states and marginalized pharmaceutical producers in semi-peripheral states, such as India or China. Very 1960s.

As was mentioned earlier, however, such an extension of 'dependency theory' to the anti-counterfeiting aspirations of African countries can barely withstand the light of scrutiny.

It is far from the case that campaigners against the import or smuggling of counterfeit and substandard medicines into African countries are the lackeys, puppets, or instruments of multinational drug makers in the North; nor are they useful idiots blindly and ignorantly facilitating the emergence of a system that is injurious to the interests of their own societies.

The evidence from Nigeria, for instance, depicts a highly sensitized national regulator, the NAFDAC (National Agency for Food & Drug Administration & Control), and its dedicated corps of technocrats, gradually and persistently growing a national consciousness of 'zero tolerance for counterfeiting'. Where intellectual property rights have been mentioned, the context has usually featured the concerns of local producers of medicines to at least the same extent as the concerns of multinational producers.

The same is the case in Ghana, where the Coalition Against Counterfeiting & Illicit Trade (CACIT) has driven a local multi-stakeholder effort to the stage where the national regulator now feels compelled to take centre stage in the process of evolving a national consciousness strong enough to match the situation in Nigeria. Indeed, a former director of the local regulator in Ghana, the FDB (Food & Drugs Board), once reported a counterfeiting incident involving a brand of a multinational producer, and was amazed to discover that the multinational company involved, in direct contrast to the attitude of the FDB, was extremely reluctant to press the case.

We now see also, to indulge the outmoded 'dependency theoretic' model of global protest discourse, the emergence of a clash of interests within the *semi-periphery*. Recently, in the wake of a major counterfeiting incident, involving Chinese-made fakes mislabelled as Indian generic drugs, India, naturally outraged, felt obliged to push for new transfrontier protections in the global trade in pharmaceuticals that very lucidly rise above petty squabbling about peripheral IPR issues.

There should be greater clarity about what is at stake here. A recent report by the London-based International Policy Network, citing empirical work carried out in conjunction with the IMANI Centre for Policy & Education in Ghana, and the Free Market Foundation in South Africa, asserts that at least 700,000 deaths annually can be directly attributed to the proliferation of counterfeit and substandard pharmaceuticals in many of the global South's vulnerable regions. These conservative estimates are more than borne out by related investigations into the quality of pharmaceuticals in seven Sub-Saharan African countries, which turned out that in many of these countries, up to 50 per cent of anti-malarial medication failed to pass rudimentary quality tests such as dissolution and uptake.

Simply put: it is the very lives of African patients that are at stake here.

Moreover, every objective assessment of the state of counterfeit drugs proliferation in the world today must identify the rise of truly 'global' cartels who owe no alliance to national flags and give scant regard to the fine points of hemisphere-defining ideologies.

We cannot as a global people attack this menace if we remain trapped in the comfort zone of venerable but largely irrelevant grand theories and systems of thinking even as the health of some of the world's most vulnerable communities is imperilled by profiteering murderers from all continents who couldn't give a damn about the latest fashion in 'global poles' theory.

C9 Unlocking entrepreneurial potential

KAREN WILSON*

Stronger and more sustainable economic growth is more critical than ever in today's environment. In the wake of the economic crisis many developed and developing countries have shifted their focus to domestic challenges, including unemployment. At the same time, global challenges such as environment, health and poverty have become more urgent. Entrepreneurship and innovation provide a way forward for addressing these challenges on the local and international levels.

Entrepreneurship is increasingly recognized as an important driver of economic growth, productivity, innovation and employment, and it is widely accepted as a key aspect of economic dynamism.[1] Entrepreneurs fuel innovation in developing new or improving existing products, services or processes. As first described by Schumpeter, new technologies and their applications stimulate the growth of new firms, and improve the efficiency and productivity of existing ones.

Tariff and non-tariff trade barriers can hinder entrepreneurship by limiting opportunities for internationalization, which is important to the competitiveness of enterprises of all sizes – large firms expanding across borders, SMEs integrating into global supply chains and entrepreneurial ventures seeking high growth. Innovative firms need access to international markets not only for revenue growth but also for the development of knowledge, skills and networks necessary for long-term growth and competitiveness.

The role of entrepreneurship education

The development of entrepreneurial skills is a core component for building socially inclusive and highly participatory economies.

* Karen Wilson is founder, GV Partners and Senior Fellow at the Kauffman Foundation.
[1] OECD (2009) *Measuring Entrepreneurship: A Digest of Indicators*, November.

Innovation and economic growth depend on being able to produce future leaders with the skills and attitudes to be entrepreneurial in their professional lives, whether by creating their own companies or by innovating in larger organizations. It is imperative to develop entrepreneurial skills, attitudes and behaviours in school systems (primary, secondary, higher and vocational education) reaching across all ages as part of a lifelong learning process.

Interest in entrepreneurship education has grown dramatically around the world in the past 5–10 years. Schools, universities and other training organizations have increasingly been integrating entrepreneurship into their programmes. In addition, national governments and international organizations such as the UN, the OECD, the European Commission and others have begun to put a greater focus on entrepreneurship education. These initiatives bode well for ensuring sustained momentum to encourage educational institutions to make commitments in this area.

There have been many recent studies which have all pointed in similar directions.[2] It is time to leverage these initiatives to have a greater impact in implementing entrepreneurship education programmes on the ground where they are needed. More sharing of models being tested around the world, both inside and outside of formal educational systems, is needed to fuel new and more effective approaches to entrepreneurship education.

Globalization of education

Higher education has become increasingly international as more and more students choose to study abroad, enrol in foreign educational programmes, or leverage opportunities to take courses at colleges or universities in other countries. The latter can involve cross-border distance education, including e-learning, generally supplemented by face-to-face teaching in local partner institutions, but mainly takes

[2] World Economic Forum (2009) *Educating the Next Wave of Entrepreneurs*, April. OECD (2008) *Entrepreneurship and Higher Education*. Ewing Marion Kauffman Foundation (2008) *Entrepreneurship in American Higher Education*.

the form of traditional face-to-face teaching offered via a partner institution abroad. Institution mobility, in the form of foreign campuses and learning or research centres set up by universities, is also increasing.

This international growth of education is the result of several different, but not mutually exclusive, driving forces: a desire to promote mutual understanding; the migration of skilled workers in a globalized economy; the desire of the institutions to generate additional revenues; or the need to build a more educated workforce in the home countries. Cross-border higher education represents one way of increasing access to higher education through the different forms of cross-border educational provision (student, programme and institution mobility).[3]

Developing entrepreneurship education

Entrepreneurship has various forms both across and within countries around the world. While these require differing types of educational programmes and content to reach young people both inside and outside of formal education systems, there are some emerging approaches and success factors which appear to be effective for entrepreneurship education across all areas. There are also some key challenges which remain.

Key success factors

One of the key success factors for entrepreneurship education is the effective development of the entrepreneurial ecosystem, in which multiple stakeholders play a role in facilitating entrepreneurship. This includes business (large and small firms as well as entrepreneurs), policy makers (at the international, national, regional and local levels) and educational institutions (primary, secondary and higher education).

Access and exposure to entrepreneurship within educational systems at all levels is important, as is outreach to target audiences

---

3 OECD (2004) *Internationalisation of Higher Education*.

outside of traditional educational systems. Entrepreneurial learning should be deeply embedded into the curriculum, rather than only offered as stand-alone courses, to ingrain a new entrepreneurial spirit and mindset among students.

Entrepreneurship is not only about business and/or for business students. It is critical in all disciplines and sectors. Entrepreneurship education needs to be expanded across disciplines – particularly to technology and science, where many innovative ideas and companies originate, as well as to design, healthcare, public policy and other areas. The world is not divided into functional silos so neither should the educational process be. All students should be required to take an entrepreneurship course to open their minds to entrepreneurial approaches whatever their employment choices might be later in their lives.

Entrepreneurship education requires a different approach to teaching and learning. In particular, it requires experiential and action learning with a focus on critical thinking and problem solving. The pedagogy should be interactive, encouraging students to experiment and experience entrepreneurship through working on case studies, games, projects, simulations, real-life actions, internships with start-ups and other hands-on activities that involve interaction with entrepreneurs.

Effective entrepreneurship education programmes focus on developing entrepreneurial attitudes, skills and behaviours. This includes building self-confidence, self-efficacy and leadership skills. Curriculum development is critical and must be based around local materials, case studies, role models and examples. These should include appropriate representation along the lines of gender, youth, indigenous people and people with a disability, as well as informal enterprises and those based in rural areas.

Entrepreneurship education should be very closely linked with practice. Educators should be encouraged to reach out to the business community and integrate them into the learning process. Outside speakers and case studies provide role models for students considering an entrepreneurial career path. This is an important part of creating entrepreneurial drive: if students see that people 'like themselves' were able to successfully create companies, it helps to demystify the process and make that option more feasible.

There is a need to grow the number of entrepreneurship educators as well as further develop them by providing the appropriate training, particularly in interactive teaching methods. Entrepreneurs and others with entrepreneurial experience should also be allowed, encouraged and trained to teach. They not only provide great value in the classroom, but also enhance entrepreneurial spirit within the institution overall and create stronger links with the local community and ecosystem.

Challenges

Despite the tremendous growth in entrepreneurship education around the world, many challenges remain. One of the predominant challenges is to address the culture and mindset in countries and regions around the world in which business and entrepreneurship are either not viewed favourably and/or are not understood. The low exposure to business and entrepreneurship, combined with the lack of role models, makes the barriers to entry in many countries seemingly high.

At the same time, there is no 'one size fits all' solution for entrepreneurship education. The challenges and opportunities for entrepreneurship vary dramatically in different parts of the world as well as for different segments of the educational journey. Local context must be taken into account in devising and tailoring a set of programmes and initiatives relevant for each area.

Entrepreneurship is still trying to secure its academic credibility, which can create difficulties in efforts to embed entrepreneurship into the school systems. In most countries, the bulk of the funding for schools and universities still comes from governments, although this is beginning to change as companies, foundations and alumni have begun to contribute. The field of entrepreneurship education is still relatively young and it is therefore important and necessary that public and private support is continued until entrepreneurship is embedded in a sustainable manner in schools and universities as well as through informal education systems.

More effective measurement and evaluation of the impact of entrepreneurship education programmes is needed. These should be based on a broadly defined set of outcomes, not only on narrow measures such as the number of start-ups created which focus on short-term results without measuring the longer-term impact.

While an increasing number of entrepreneurship education programmes exist today compared to a decade ago, scalability and penetration remain key challenges. Technology and media provide mechanisms for reaching greater economies of scale as well as providing greater access and sharing of practices. Not only can technology and media facilitate the development of innovative interactive programmes and materials, they also can help reach larger audiences, including those in developing countries or regions who might not otherwise have access to entrepreneurship education.

Conclusion

Entrepreneurship has never been more important than at this time, not only to solve our pressing global challenges but also to address the issues of unemployment and growth. Entrepreneurship is a great enabler which can help level the playing field between developed and developed regions. Embedding entrepreneurship in education and providing greater access are the first and arguably most important steps for building an innovative culture and creating a new wave of entrepreneurs, entrepreneurial individuals and organizations. Tariff and non-tariff trade barriers should not block the growth of entrepreneurial ventures or the development of the critical skills and mobility of people and institutions necessary for building entrepreneurial economies.

C10 | Trade and security: a vital link to sustainable development in a troubled world

TALAAT ABDEL-MALEK[*]

The link between trade and security remains, for many, a controversial or at least an ambiguous issue. One school of thought argues that trade promotes security through increased welfare; the other views free trade as a potential trigger of insecurity and conflict. Neither school has a monopoly over truth.

What have trade and security got in common? Not much, at first glance. Trade is for business and security is the concern of the state which is responsible for protecting its citizens. So much for the conventional, narrow-minded view. It does not require a Nobel laureate or a rocket scientist to unveil the inherent two-way relationship between trade and security. Let's examine this relationship using sheer common sense, and staying away from fancy theories and frameworks.

The essence of security lies not so much in how many police forces, guns and hi-tech intelligence gadgets are around to sniff out potential terrorists and mete out harsh punishments to deter them from carrying out their evil acts. This militaristic approach might provide a sense of security for some but – for many, including myself – it bestows a frightening image of a fragile peace, a tense environment and an artificial truce between the state and its presumed adversaries.

Sure enough, these measures have so far provided a robust deterrent and foiled many potentially deadly schemes (but not without notable exceptions, as demonstrated by recent bombings in India and Indonesia, military conflict in the oil-producing Nigeria Delta, piracy off the Somali coast, not to mention Iraq, among many others). But what has been the cost? And to what extent have these tools and underlying strategies been effective in dealing with the root causes of

* Talaat Abdel-Malek is Professor of Economics at the American University in Cairo and Economic Adviser to the Minister of International Cooperation, Egypt. He is also co-Chair, OECD/DAC Working Party on Aid Effectiveness.

insecurity? My answer is: the cost has been too high and unsustainable and the long-term impact extremely modest. We are not talking about national defence here, but about the special actions against terrorism and other forms of violence (external and internal).

We only need to consider what has become a huge security 'industry' in control of our airports, harbours, public buildings, research centres, etc. Ironically, our conventional national income accounting treats expenditure on security as a contributor to GNP. While this is understandable, think of the more genuine and lasting contributions these same resources would have made had they not been diverted away from real development endeavours: alleviating poverty, improving education, eradicating illiteracy, combating chronic diseases and cleaning up our environment.

My take on the current approaches to better security is simply this: it is untenable, it is wasteful of scarce resources and it is very fragile and superficial. One cannot dismiss the impact of the huge lobbying groups that have developed very profitable vested interests in maintaining the status quo. These have become a formidable challenge to reforming our ways to achieve long-lasting security. But this challenge is not insurmountable. Once a better alternative to the militarization of our societies has been articulated and well accepted by the average citizen, winning the battle for genuine security becomes a more achievable goal. President Obama's refreshing approach to addressing global hot issues is creating a more conducive and potentially productive setting that is winning widespread support. It can be instrumental in disposing of unilateral gun-slinging methods based on 'axis of evil' perceptions and replacing these with a more inclusive and mature dialogue to reach agreement on how to address the real issues. While it is too early to be assured of its positive outcome, this new approach is the best option we have.

Against this background, where does trade fit in? We must first recognize that neither trade nor any other activity by itself is capable of creating sustainable peace and security. Trade, however, can and should become a critical ingredient in a broader composite of policies and actions aimed at achieving security. We need to look at the whole range of development issues, not economic growth alone, and identify the means necessary to improve welfare of the masses, not only that of the few. The record of global development since 1950 shows that high growth rates are insufficient to attain and sustain economic and social development. This is where globalization's image has suffered great setbacks in the minds of the masses in many countries. Open markets, massive privatization, rolling back of government functions and drastic de-regulation have been blamed for increased poverty, widening income gaps, persistence of illiteracy and damaging the environment. The recent food and financial crises and the 2008–2009 global recession have added to the public perception of a 'free-for-all' global playground for the giants that has gone out of control. The short-term profit motive and the greed and irresponsible acts of a few key corporate executives have caused incalculable damage to private and public assets and shaken confidence in vital institutions, besides leaving developing countries reeling from the consequences of the ensuing global malaise.

While there is more than a grain of truth in these perceptions, they run the risk of 'throwing the baby out with the bath water'. Millions of new jobs have been created with more liberalized trade; greater efficiencies in using scarce resources have been gained, and international competitiveness has compelled governments and businesses everywhere to put their houses in order as a means of surviving in the new globalized era. The other side of the coin, of course, has been the loss of jobs in ailing industries, drops in tax revenues, increased government deficits and dismantling of social welfare programmes. These, and other negative effects, have been blamed on the more open trading system and sweeping privatization measures carried out in developing countries.

However, many lessons have been learned during the past two or three decades of reform. Three stand out as pivotal. First, a private sector-driven economy does not imply a lesser but a modified role of government. In many cases, especially early in adopting a more liberalized reform strategy, governments have more or less 'abdicated' their responsibility to govern, believing this was an integral part of letting the private sector run the show. It was only a few years later that the undesirable consequences of this abdication became painfully clear, causing increased public disgruntlement and social unrest. Some countries have learned this lesson and are currently mending their approaches. While the private sector's goals of profit making and realizing decent returns on investment are being respected (and in many cases, also protected), government has to strengthen its role of ensuring a development-friendly climate in which various actors play their respective roles in society. The state has to ensure efficient and independent judiciary, and see to it that law and order is instituted as a fundamental condition for social stability and protecting human rights. Many challenges remain, but we seem to be making progress towards striking a more proper balance in the roles between the state and private sector, as well as other stakeholders in society.

Second, we have also come to realize that – no matter what developing countries do to reform policies – the fuller rewards of more open markets cannot be had without a more level global playing field, requiring, among other things, reforming existing outdated global governance architecture, led by the World Bank, IMF and the WTO. The rise of China, India and Brazil as regional and potentially global powers, and the emergence of more developing countries as significant international players, suggest it is high time to translate statements of good intentions into real actions, by giving these countries more say in global and regional affairs. This has not happened yet. As long as rich countries, which remain in control of the global agenda, drag their heels on reform and maintain the trade policies and practices that have brought the Doha Development Round to a halt, there can be no genuine global security. The uneven rewards of the current trading regime(s) and huge injustices generated, as any one can clearly see in Africa, and the increasing maldistribution of incomes pose real threats to peace and minimize the impact of reforms undertaken in developing countries, often at huge economic and social costs. In this context, we should remember Amartya Sen's saying that 'equal rules for unequal partners constitute unequal rules'. Finally, as long as the arms trade and the drugs trade remain unchecked (not to mention trade in blood diamonds and illegal timber), they will continue to fuel regional and civil conflicts.

The third lesson is the urgent need for more engaged and enlightened corporate leadership in development and trade policies – nationally and internationally. Good corporate citizenship must be translated into more than slogans and token events. Many good examples are emerging in different countries but much more is needed, including a longer-term perspective to replace short-term profit making and a 'development vision' that views business as an integral part of the social fabric of society, without compromising on the goal of earning an acceptable rate of return on investment and risk taking.

Championing the cause of more liberalized trade and a level playing field is a must in the current state described at one of the Evian Group's recent events as *global disorder*. The continued leadership of the International Chamber of Commerce, as merchant of peace through world trade, is of paramount importance in promoting this cause.

The long view on interlocking crises

Editorial introduction

The long view on interlocking crises

A theme running throughout the book is the need to restore balance between the benefits and risks of globalization. Many of the articles in the previous chapters make reference to the issues presented in this section, which aims to take the long view. Serious doubts exist about the environmental sustainability of our global growth models while many poor countries are hit by critical food security concerns. This chapter considers some of the contributions international trade can bring to tackling a set of intractable interlocking crises: climate, water, food and energy. All will have an incidence on welfare and future prospects for peace and prosperity.

The chapter opens with the observation that we have so far failed to establish international arrangements that ensure an enabling distribution of the benefits of global relations. The following two articles offer differing opinions on global trade rules and negotiations in the context of climate change and a planet constrained by resources. Four contributions on energy, agriculture and water then complement this debate. The first offers a scenario for a new clean energy deal in which trade and energy could be mutually reinforcing drivers of the global business environment, the second looks at the major distortions in the international trade of agricultural products, while the third and fourth concentrate their analyses on securing an efficient allocation of the water needed to grow food for an increasing world population.

The chapter concludes with two macro considerations. The first presents an economic examination of the role of trade in the dispersion of innovation and the fluid exchange of technologies. The second underlines the absence of a geopolitical process to tackle urgent global problems such as climate change.

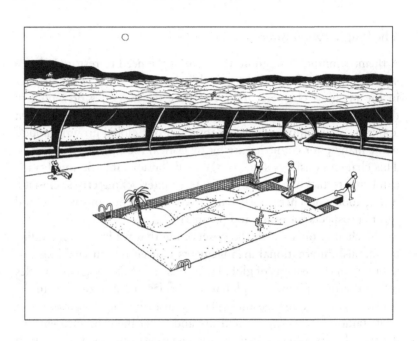

D1 | Trade and sustainable development: the ends must shape the means

RICARDO MELÉNDEZ-ORTIZ*

'Free trade is like heaven,' goes an old tease among trade negotiators. 'We all want to get there – but not just yet.' The reverse is the case when it comes to sustainable development; we wish we were there already. We all aspire to economic growth that is resilient, equitable and doesn't come at the expense of the health of our environment. But despite having a fairly good idea of how consumption, investment and production patterns need to change to make our growth trajectories more sustainable, societies have been lamentably slow to shift direction. Unsustainability can be aggravated or reversed through policies, domestic and international. In this context, it now seems clear, persistent unsustainability is partly the result of embedded inertia in lifestyles, allocation of resources and technological change; partly a consequence of inadequate institutions to deliver social primary goods, and of the inability of governments to agree to and establish international arrangements that ensure an enabling distribution of benefits of global relations. In the absence of a global state, a world operated collectively by and for actors of greater or lesser economic stride, requires performing global regulatory and incentive frameworks and institutions to manage economic and physical interdependence.

Our failure to achieve sustainable development is writ large across the world. While economic growth in China and India has propelled hundreds of millions of people out of poverty, 2009, for the first time in history, saw our planet host to over one billion hungry people while large swathes of the developing world remain mired in economic stagnation or outright decline, environmental degradation and crippling

---

* Ricardo Meléndez-Ortiz is the co-founder and has acted as Chief Executive of the International Centre for Trade and Sustainable Development (ICTSD), Switzerland, since 1996. Previously, he co-founded and held the position of General Director of Fundación Futuro Latinoamericano (Quito).

185

conflict. And the industrialized and emerging economies have for the most part pursued resource-intensive, high-carbon growth, a pathway that cannot be sustained indefinitely. Contemporary economic governance scaffolds have over-emphasized efficiency and growth, and paid scant attention to our prime social and environmental texture. Crippling widening gaps in income and capabilities, exacerbated by deficient institutional infrastructures, characterize the pre-crisis world of the first decade of the twenty-first century, as much as rapid growth and dynamic trade.

This has direct implications for peace and security everywhere. The nature of conflict has changed since the middle of the eighteenth century, when Montesquieu first wrote that trade promotes interdependence and consequently peace. War is no longer waged primarily by armies marching across international frontiers. Today, most conflict occurs among rival factions within a poor country's borders. And threats include shadowy non-state actors who order or inspire people to strap on bombs to detonate in faraway cities. Development and conflict are deeply linked, and the correlation between wealth – or rather destitution – and conflict has been historically confirmed: poor countries are more often the arenas of civil wars. Based on empirical data, Paul Collier, the Oxford economist, has estimated that a percentage-point increase in the growth rate of a low-income country knocks approximately one percentage point off its risk of conflict in a five-year period. The reverse is true, too: downturns are correlated with a higher risk of war.

Without development, security is precarious. And in places without security, there can be no development. Furthermore, environmental factors, from resource mismanagement to water scarcity, climate change and natural disasters, are now well recognized as potential drivers of conflict. In our present world, which is interconnected in ways Montesquieu could not have imagined, greenhouse gas emissions in the United States and China can affect weather patterns in Africa, increasing the likelihood of too little or too much rain, which in turn hammers growth, raising the potential for conflict. Unsustainable development in one part of the world can compromise prospects for development and security elsewhere. More complex but particular to today's world as described by Krugman's approach to the 'new trade' economic environment, policies to address those carbon emissions through cost internalization in one region and not in another, say in Europe but not in North Africa, would by definition affect competitive conditions and eventually prompt the relocation of productive capacity.

So where does trade enter into this? As we have said, availability of means – natural, human and financial capital – continue to be a factor of development; in today's world, the poorest countries need economic growth in order to make sustainable development possible. Trade could help them rise out of poverty. To be clear, wealth and growth do not automatically lead to sustainable development: a range of deliberate policies and conducive international support and regulatory frameworks are necessary to ensure that social primary goods are generated in an equitable manner. Also, natural resource use must be conducted in ways that don't compromise their renewal and ensure the integrity of natural energy and biological functions.

We have some experience now on what works and what doesn't, particularly at the domestic economy level. Incorporating the very poor into the economy and enabling them to contribute and benefit has been the focus of much policy reform and innovation in the decades either side of the millennium. Exploring use of market instruments to acknowledge ecosystem services and better manage the complex linkages between economic activity and sustainability of resources has also been the object of much policy attention. But relationships are not straightforward, particularly on the emerging challenges. For instance, responses of employment to traditional trade policies are dynamic and determined by the nature of formality or informality of labour, and differ in the urban, manufacturing or services economies. And, while certain pollutants decrease as a society becomes richer, this so-called environmental Kuznets curve is less apparent for carbon dioxide. Sweden is a rare country in that it has increased national income while reducing emissions in recent years, but has only been able to do so through deliberate policy measures, not automaticity.

Export-oriented industrialization has been a crucial element in the rapid growth and unprecedented poverty reduction witnessed in much of Asia. Aggressive reform to integrate national economies to global markets has also been a characteristic of a growing Latin American region. Most of Africa is now going through a proactive quest to turn around its chronic imbalance as net exporter of resources into

a future of vigorous domestic and subregional markets and net gains
from integration into global markets. All successful economies are
actively engaged in global trade and, with the exception of Russia,
they are part of the rules-based, multilateral framework of principles
and norms on trade, the World Trade Organization.

The 2008–2009 global financial crisis has confirmed the notion
that liberalization is not a one-size-fits-all prescription, and that it
doesn't work if unaccompanied by a very aggressive, autochthonous
building-up of institutional infrastructure. Rodrik points out that economic globalization's star examples – China and India – are far from
its best pupils, with the former's heavy state intervention and dubious
property rights, and the latter's relatively high levels of trade protection. Openness to imports is not in and of itself enough to produce
good outcomes, or else Haiti would have grown faster than Vietnam.
Other obstacles hindering poor countries' ability to benefit from trade
should be easier to overcome (except they haven't been): distortions
in production and trade arising from massive farm subsidies in the
industrialized world, and relatively high tariff and non-tariff barriers
facing the agricultural and labour-intensive products, such as clothing, that poor countries can make competitively. These distortions are
bad for development, bad for the credibility of the trading system and,
often, bad for the environment.

The Uruguay Round negotiations failed to live up to their promise
to curb the overproduction that Northern governments were shunting
out to world markets on the back of lavish export subsidies. Subsidy-
fuelled overproduction in rich countries continued apace through
the 1990s, lowering prices and undermining incentives for developing country governments or the private sector to invest in agricultural production and rural infrastructure. Years of low productivity
and low farm prices pushed farmers in poor countries to look for
other sources of income, becoming net food buyers. The spike in food
prices in 2007 and 2008 laid the consequences of this shift painfully
bare: many of these farmers, instead of benefiting from high food
prices, were squeezed in the middle. The icing on the cake is that some
of these farm subsidies are environmentally harmful, encouraging the
overuse of land and chemical fertilizers.

The Doha Development Round, launched in 2001, was supposed to
tackle these distortions, and deliver a host of other measures to help
developing countries participate profitably in international commerce.

But the round has languished amidst a sense that no major economy except Brazil really wants an agreement. The deal that seems achievable would modestly restrain trade-distorting farm subsidies (and developing countries' manufacturing tariffs) at around current levels. Progress on two totemic issues for the poorest countries – cutting the cotton subsidies that undermine livelihoods in West Africa and providing duty- and quota-free access to all exports from least developed countries – has been derisory.

More through omission than commission, the business community, particularly in the United States, Europe and Japan, deserves some of the blame for this lack of enthusiasm. If the Doha Round ultimately fails, it would represent a significant (though not fatal) blow to the multilateral trading system. It would be one that could not come at a worse time: job losses resulting from the worst economic downturn in decades are fuelling economic nationalism and protectionist sentiment everywhere, and unilaterally imposed tariffs linked to climate policy could further strain trade relations. The scope for legal increases in trade protection remains great, particularly in the emerging economies. This would not be good for business. Yet, Northern business groups have let the conversation on trade be dominated by special interests, none more than the farm lobby. A vice-like grip by agricultural interests on trade policy might be understandable in India, where farmers make up over 60 per cent of the population. But in the USA and the EU, the figure is no more than 2–4 per cent.

To the protectionists' chorus, those business voices that have waded into the debate could be called perfectionists. Like the farm lobby, they don't like what's on offer. The difference? They think there is too little liberalization on offer, not too much. Protectionist/perfectionist coalitions have a long history in trade negotiations. The late William Diebold attributed the 1948 stillbirth of the International Trade Organization, the GATT's predecessor, to the formation of such an alliance in the US Congress. Today, business would be better served by pragmatism. Companies know that the beating heart of the world's economic future lies in the fast-growing emerging economies of Asia and Latin America (and hopefully Africa, eventually). At a time of major geopolitical upheaval, with the emergence of new great powers, strong institutions lashing everyone together are particularly important. Doha or no Doha, business stands to benefit from a multilateral trading system that is respected. And the legitimacy of the system would be greatly enhanced if it were seen to help, and not hinder, countries' pursuit of sustainable development. Sustainable development is the end; trade, simply a means. We should act accordingly.

D2 | Trade and climate change: the linkage

DOAA ABDEL-MOTAAL[*]

Can trade policy support climate policy? The answer depends on how we define the linkage. In my view, there are three sets of linkages that the world must consider. First is the 'carbon footprint' of the international trading system, and whether trade policy can somehow be directed at reducing this footprint. Second are the issues of 'carbon leakage' and of 'competitiveness effects', which some would like to use trade policy to curtail. These are issues that are of particular interest to countries that consider themselves to be 'first-movers' on climate mitigation, and who do not wish to see their competitiveness impacted by being the ones to take the 'first step' so to speak. First-movers also argue that their efforts would be undermined if polluting industries were to simply migrate from carbon-constrained economies to the non-carbon constrained. After all does the planet care about the identity of the emitter of CO_2?

I hasten to add that the competitiveness effects of climate mitigation and the issue of carbon leakage are not issues that will immediately be resolved with the conclusion of a new post-Kyoto climate accord. The principle of 'common but differentiated responsibility' which currently applies in the negotiation will by definition mean that uneven carbon constraints will continue to prevail in different parts of the globe, even after an agreement is reached. Third is the relationship between the rulebook of the World Trade Organization (WTO), the Doha Round of trade negotiations and climate change. Can that rulebook, and can these negotiations, support climate adaptation and mitigation? They surely can, as I will explain below.

* Doaa Abdel-Motaal is Counsellor on agricultural and environmental issues, including climate change, in the Cabinet of WTO Director-General, Pascal Lamy. This article is written in her personal capacity, and does not represent the views of the WTO.

Let us start with the trading system's carbon footprint. Does it make any sense for a tomato to be transported all the way across the globe, from South to North, Africa to Europe, with the release of CO_2 in the course of its transportation? Today many consumers would say no, and this is but one of many examples. While there is no doubt that internalizing negative environmental externalities is a laudable goal which must be pursued, we must nevertheless be careful in how we go about doing so.

First, the carbon footprint of the international system cannot be measured in terms of transportation emissions alone. It is the entire life cycle of a product that must be considered. It may in fact make 'carbon sense' for a tomato to travel across the globe, if that tomato will be grown in natural sunlight instead of an energy-intensive green-house somewhere in the North. An examination of the entire life cycle of that tomato may show that it has a lower carbon footprint than a tomato grown in the North, and which has not travelled at all.

Second, even if we were to focus on transportation alone, then we must remember that 90 per cent of international trade takes place through maritime transport; one of the lowest carbon-emitting forms of transportation. Third, a simple look at a map shows that inter-national trade between countries with shared borders can actually reduce the distances travelled by products as opposed to increase them. Think of how much road or air transport international trade between the northern United States and southern Canada saves. Would it be better for the northern United States to systematically trade with the South instead?

Finally – and this is an issue that is particularly close to my heart – we must not forget about positive environmental externalities. After all, international trade can be water- and natural resource-saving. In early 2009 Saudi Arabia decided to call off its attempt to achieve self-sufficiency in wheat because of the heavy toll it took on its scarce water resources. For Saudi Arabia, imports were water-saving. In short, we cannot afford to be myopic on the question of 'food or carbon miles', as this issue has now been called. And surely the term 'water miles' deserves to be coined too. I say this with every hope that bunker fuels will come under the coverage of a post-Kyoto regime, so that negative transportation externalities will indeed be internalized.

So what of carbon leakage then, and of the competitiveness effects of climate mitigation? Should trade policy somehow deal with them?

First, it is important right from the start to distinguish between competitiveness concerns and carbon leakage. These issues are not the same: one is an economic goal and the other is environmental. Second, it is important to recall that the rules of the WTO are not there to guarantee that a particular company, sector or country stay in business, so to speak. The role of the WTO is to establish a level playing field in international trade, giving countries equal opportunities to compete; but without guaranteeing the competitiveness of anybody in particular. Competitiveness is what an industry must itself prove on an open market. I say this because we must beware of creating industrial policy, instead of environmental policy, in the fight against climate change.

Preventing carbon leakage is an environmental goal, and as we all know the WTO rules provide ample space for environmental protection. The preamble to the WTO rulebook enshrines the concept of sustainable development, and in dispute after dispute the WTO has shown itself capable of upholding legitimate health and environmental goals. However, were trade measures to be used to prevent carbon leakage, the WTO would ask a number of questions in their regard if these measures were to be challenged. It would explore, for instance, the compatibility of border tax adjustments, the free allocation of pollution permits, or other trade-related climate mitigation measures, with the relevant set of WTO rules.

Having said that, the WTO compatibility of trade measures taken to prevent carbon leakage may not be the most important issue at stake, in my view. The international community would need to ask itself a whole host of other questions regarding these measures, if it were to be really serious about the task at hand. Prime amongst them would be whether such measures can truly prevent leakage. Do importing countries import carbon-intensive products in significant enough quantities so as to have leverage over exporters? Are importing countries always more carbon-competitive than their trading partners? The answer may sometimes be no.

And what about the type of carbon leakage that cannot necessarily be addressed through trade? What I mean by this is the fact that carbon-constrained economies will, by definition, consume less oil with time, reducing the international price of oil, and inducing the non-carbon-constrained economies to raise their consumption. How will the international community address this problem?

In my view, there can be no answer other than the conclusion of an international climate accord, with as broad a membership as possible. I hasten to add that controversial issues such as border tax adjustment would be likely to receive an entirely different reception if they came in the wake of a consensual international accord, than if they came before. I have in mind the implementing of border tax adjustment measures that some countries put in place after the Montreal Protocol on ozone-depleting substances, and which have largely gone by unnoticed in the WTO.

Finally, a word on the WTO rulebook and the Doha Round. I believe that the non-discrimination principle of the WTO will itself help the international community in its fight against climate change. It will help weed out industrial policy from environmental policy, forcing a focus on the real environmental goal. I always thought that the non-discrimination principle should have been an environmental principle at the Rio Earth Summit, since the environment, as I said earlier, does not care about the nationality of the polluter. That said, the Doha Round will itself have a contribution to make in climate mitigation and adaptation, in particular, through trade liberalization in environmental goods and services. It will help make clean technology more accessible to all. I have also been struck by the International Energy Agency's studies which show that many of the obstacles to implementation of the Clean Development Mechanism are trade barriers, such as bureaucratic customs procedures which delay the access to green technology. These measures too can be addressed through the 'trade facilitation' chapter of the Doha Round. Clearly trade policy can support climate policy, but we must be clever in defining our goals.

D3 | *Destructive trade winds: trade, consumption and resource constraints*

CHANDRAN NAIR*

Any article which attempts to suggest that trade is destructive is going to be controversial. It will attract the attention of the pro-globalization and trade lobby whose attacks on the underlying arguments will be swift and stacked with conventional arguments. The reality though is that both directly and indirectly free trade encourages the unrestrained consumption of goods and services, thereby playing a potentially negative role in the world by increasing the pressure on resources in a constrained planet.

Conventional wisdom holds that trade over the centuries has been the great integrator of societies and has been the catalyst for human advancement and global prosperity creation. This is even if one discounts the fact that in the pursuit of trade colonial powers sowed the seeds for many current day inequalities in numerous parts of what is now the developing world.

The common response to any suggestion that this issue needs to be considered seriously is to dismiss it as naive and unrealistic. The often-used retort is: 'If there is less free and open trade, then what?' But is that the question we should be asking ourselves in the twenty-first century, knowing what we now know with the benefit of modern science about resource constraints?

No one is denying that trade in its numerous forms and shapes is needed, that it is very much part of what drives the human desire to be resourceful, that it creates much needed economic activity and thus is

---

* Chandran Nair is a true internationalist, having lived and worked in Asia, Europe and Africa. His Global Institute For Tomorrow (GIFT) is an Asian first: an independent social venture think tank dedicated to advancing understanding of key issues and challenges of globalization in Asia – the role of business in society, governance and ethics, and leadership development. Before founding GIFT in 2004 he built Asia's leading environmental consultancy, ERM.

even essential for human development. However, in the early twenty-first century, with a population of 6 billion that may peak at 9 billion by 2050, the question is whether we will need to cast aside many previously held beliefs and redefine trade by bringing in new rules of trade and commerce that recognize resource limits. The acknowledgement of the limits to consumption due to resource constraints needs to now take centre stage at the global trade framework for the twenty-first century. Conscious and even rules-based consumption will need to replace that which is simply conspicuous.

Therefore the questions we will need to ask are as follows. What sorts of trade activities should we encourage, on what aspects might we even impose restrictions, how do we make it fair as opposed to just free, and how do we ensure it is less destructive given that growth in trade is dependent on encouraging consumption and thus depletion of precious but finite resources?

Examples abound but let us just consider sectors such as fisheries, industrial meat production, forestry and vegetable oil production, while leaving aside energy. Most of these sectors are on an unsustainable path as their trade and consumption push the resource base to the brink. But if we are truly concerned it is entirely possible to put in place economically viable schemes which make most ocean-caught fish certified to sustainable standards and meat priced to take account of the carbon footprint of current inefficient conversion processes. The same can be achieved with forest-related products certified to sustainable standards and limiting the production of vegetable oil to essential needs so that more forests (carbon sinks, etc.) are not destroyed. If we are to suggest this is not possible then all discussions on resource protection and planetary wellbeing should stop now.

In addition it must also be blatantly obvious to all except the most fundamentalist of free marketers that peace in the twenty-first century will be shaped by resource ownership issues and the challenge of our times: climate justice.

These questions are often discussed among academics and intellectuals but rarely within trade negotiating circles. Even the best books on the history of trade and globalization rarely examine the issue of consumption and resource constraints even when they superficially address environmental issues. It seems just too uncomfortable to address this perfectly logical question with its harsh realities. The deniers typically revert to the tired old arguments that the solutions are to be found in the workings of efficient markets, the role of technology and even finance, and somehow find ways to ignore all the evidence accumulated since the 1980s and even the lessons of the 2008–2009 crisis.

But let us be very clear that trade in itself is a good thing. However, we must now be honest if we are to act and re-examine the conventional wisdom that has held sway for so long. Promoted by economists this has created the myth that trade naturally contributes to sustainable development by promoting efficient allocation of resources, economic growth and increased income levels. On the economic growth front the jury is still out as to whether trade promotes growth, though in developing countries it has undeniably had a positive impact.

Even if conventional wisdom to date has been largely true, the current evidence on resource depletion demands an honest re-examination driven by the harsh reality of our current economic model. This is the gross underpricing of social and environmental costs in a resource-constrained planet in which the population has more than quadrupled in just one hundred years. Climate change due to ever growing emissions of greenhouse gases driven by unrestrained consumption is just one example of this failure and it is unlikely that market instruments (cap and trade mechanisms) and/or technology are going to help solve this problem.

As the volume of world trade has increased by nearly 32 times since 1950 and its share of global GDP grown from 5.5% to 21% in 2001, the issue of limits, constraints and sustainable development must be thrust at the heart of all discussions about promoting trade, both fair and free. A fundamental rethink is needed at the heart of global trade negotiations. This is not a sidebar discussion about going green or environmentalism where it is normally relegated. The answers are not going to be easy and the journey will create huge tensions but the issues are far too important to be left to trade negotiators only.

While there has been in recent years a wider recognition that trade does have an impact on the environment and climate change this discussion typically centred on the impacts from the production side, conveniently sidestepping the question of resource exploitation because of the need to see growth in consumption by driving demand. The production-side initiatives have paid attention to supply chain issues of using more resources and energy for production and transport resulting in more pollution, carbon emissions and environmental destruction. Even there progress has been slow.

Trade, by encouraging consumption beyond meeting needs (not just basic needs), is creating too many losers as it creates elite winners. The losers at the bottom of the pyramid are usually also on the wrong side of the resource ownership and control equation. They are typically the developing countries and in these the most marginalized populations.

A challenge is that the current trade regime, led by the WTO, is often characterized by developing countries as being run by the developed nations to serve their appetite for cheap consumer goods while protecting their own industries, environmental quality and resources. At the same time the WTO does not have any special provision for the environment with onus put on its member states. It is common knowledge that at the Doha Round, even discussions about reducing tariffs for environmental goods and services did not amount to any action. Enabling policies that allow for easier transfer of clean/climate-mitigating technology, while important, do not address the real resource constraints issue. This approach has been the usual response from international agencies ranging from the WTO to the UN and World Bank even as the latter two acknowledge that trade increases the speed and scale of resource consumption and therefore consequences such as climate change.

The World Bank report on 'International Trade and Climate Change' states that 'the trade-environmental debate has so far considered little in terms of global-scale environmental problems – declining biodiversity, depletion of fisheries, overexploitation of shared resources. These public goods which require international cooperation can lead to trade tensions.'

For an organization such as the WTO, which is meant to help frame the international laws to govern trade, this significant omission and inability to direct action to the most pressing challenges of our time very clearly highlights the old world thinking which has dominated trade discussions and which is now in need of urgent and major surgery.

Tired arguments have been used by both sides to explain the background to this lack of attention but they only go to show how the members are caught in a vicious cycle of legal arguments about trade and the inequalities of the numerous current and proposed rules.

This is akin to villagers arguing about how many wells there are in the village and who has rights to what, while ignoring the fact that the wells are already drying up and not at all appreciating that the watershed surrounding the village which feeds the wells is being destroyed by illegal loggers.

Resource constraints will take the wind out of the sails of global trade unless we act now before the trade that we will all badly need to prosper in a resource-constrained planet is truly endangered.

D4 | Trade and energy: a new clean energy deal

ALEXANDER VAN DE PUTTE[*]

Trade is as old as humanity. Initially based on barter, markets emerged to facilitate the exchange of goods and services. Trade became international, then global, and the globalization process continues today.

Sometimes, however, markets don't work effectively, or they just fail – the 2008–2009 financial crisis being a perfect example of the interaction of market and policy failures – and a regulator needs to step in to provide a solution. Ideally, this enables the market to rebound, without distorting it in the process, and provides the framework to address problems. Failing to do so could lead to fundamental discontinuities or tipping points. Markets also don't deal well with 'externalities' such as climate change and sustainability, issues increasingly driven by trade globalization and the rise of the BRICs (Brazil, Russia, India and China) and other high-growth emerging markets.

Trade and energy: an enduring dilemma

Globalization proponents argue that trade has created wealth and enabled millions of people to escape poverty. From 1990 to 2005 alone, the number of people living on less than US$1.25/day fell from 1.8 billion to 1.4 billion, an unparalleled achievement – although the World Bank expects the 2008–2009 crisis to trap tens of millions more in poverty. Overall, human development improved as economies grew and living standards rose.

* Dr Alexander Van de Putte is Senior Director and Head of Scenario Processes & Applications at PFC Energy International, an Associate with the US National Intelligence Council and a Brains Trust member of the Evian Group at IMD. Alexander is also a visiting professor of scenario planning and energy economics at several leading business schools and technical universities in Europe.

The author would like to thank David Gates, Senior Advisor at PFC Energy; Jonathan Story, Emeritus Professor of International Political Economy at INSEAD; and Ann K. Holder, researcher/editor with ERMI, for their comments.

Alexander Van de Putte

Opponents argue that world trade and the endless corporate search for natural resources, markets and profits, has impaired the Earth's ability to support its inhabitants (current and future). Globalization accelerates the depletion of natural resources while the wealthy get wealthier and the poor are increasingly marginalized. Detractors can also point to the events of 2008–2009: the greatest financial crisis that humanity has (to date) experienced, the gravity of which cannot be underestimated.

As global trade grows we encounter higher levels of energy consumption which, given our reliance on fossil fuels, generate higher levels of GHG (greenhouse gas) emissions. More trade, more pollution. Princeton-led research estimates that just 700 million people generated half of the world's emissions in 2008, most coming from wealthier citizens – regardless of where they live.[1] This problem will intensify over the next twenty years as growth accelerates in other countries (e.g. VISTA[2] economies).

The historical relationship between energy consumption and economic growth follows an S-curve:

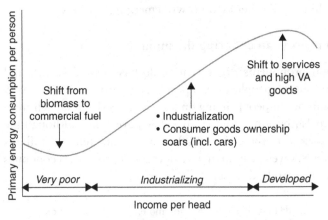

Figure D4.1: Historical relationship between energy, consumption and growth
Source: Shell's 'Energy Ladder' concept (early 1980s).

[1] S. Chakravarty, A. Chikkatur, H. de Coninck, S. Pacala, R. Socolow and M. Tavoni (2009) *Sharing Global CO$_2$ Emissions Among One Billion High Emitters*, Proceedings of the National Academy of Science (published online, 6 July 2009).
[2] Vietnam, Indonesia, South Africa, Turkey and Argentina, a group of emerging countries considered by many analysts to have huge development potential.

The energy ladder illustrates how energy consumption levels and energy demand growth rates reflect the process of moving from pre-industrial to modern, developed economies. In a modern economy, little incremental energy is required to grow the economy, yet energy use may continue to rise with increasing living standards. Thus, as income levels rise in poorer nations, so shall global energy demand.

The US Energy Information Administration's *International Energy Outlook 2009* projects a 44% climb in global energy demand by 2030, with an almost 75% rise in non-OECD demand (versus 15% in the OECD). Unsurprisingly, most (two-thirds) of the non-OECD energy use will come from the BRICs (85% rise), where China's energy consumption is forecast to more than double (+111%).

How can we sustainably meet these energy needs? Should emerging markets follow the same energy-intensive path as the industrialized nations, or instead leapfrog technologies and bend the energy ladder curve downwards? Fossil fuel supplies (given current technologies) are rapidly dwindling, and renewable, clean energy sources cannot yet fill the void: where will this energy come from?

Creativity takes courage

World trade has regained momentum as economies have started to recover, leading us to a crossroads. While it will remain unclear for a while exactly how deep and long-lasting this recession will prove to be, emerging markets such as China and India have proven quite resilient to the crisis. If properly designed, stimulus packages in emerging markets have much higher economic multipliers than in industrialized nations as they can invest in infrastructure projects and continue to manage the rural-to-urban shift.

However, the global economy and trade system that we've experienced since the mid to late 1990s is unsustainable:

1 With historically low, sometimes even negative, saving rates, America consumes a large portion of world trade, while China produces/exports finished goods.
2 Thus, the US runs a deficit, China has an unquenchable thirst for natural resources, and the rest of the world finances the system.

When the global economy is no longer in crisis mode, the new balance of power might reflect Giovanni Grevi's 'interpolar' world

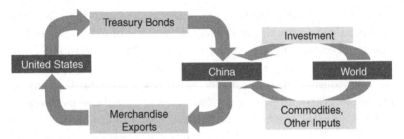

Figure D4.2: Schematic view of the global economy and trade system
Source: PFC Energy, Markets & Country Strategies Group.

(i.e. multipolar and interdependent)[3] where this triple threat – economic, energy and ecological crises – exposes our Achilles' heel: no major power can effectively tackle these challenges alone, thus both established and emerging powers have a strategic interest in cooperation. We sink or swim together.

Trade and energy in 2019: a new clean energy deal

Realizing a sustainable global trade environment will take time and the necessary steps should be implemented during the next decade. This section paints a single scenario – a plausible alternative future – about how trade and energy could be mutually reinforcing drivers of the global business environment, ultimately contributing to peace and prosperity. This future won't organically materialize since it requires a diverse group of stakeholders to coordinate their efforts across several dimensions.

To effectively reconcile trade and energy, a *new clean energy deal* is required. Here, a core group of nations take the reins of leadership on climate change and implement a series of eco-sustainable economic strategies, supported by sophisticated, non-fossil resource (cleaner) technologies.

The trigger for this is the current global recession: a unique opportunity for leaders to make the strategic investments needed to generate long-term solutions for sustainable growth. Using policies that stimulate growth by investing in new industries/infrastructure to create jobs, this coalition sets the tone by creating clean energy partnerships

[3] G. Grevi (2009) *The Interpolar World: A New Scenario*. EU-ISS Occasional Paper No. 79, June.

to transition to a low-carbon economy. Action is driven by an interpolar group – major powers plus several emerging economies – not just by America, since even under the Obama administration, Congress is seemingly more focused on immediate domestic issues rather than sustainability.

OECD countries will focus on reducing energy intensity through energy conservation and more stringent emissions standards (especially Europe and Japan) as well as longer-term levers such as funding new research. More initiatives and funding to develop clean energy technologies, with enormous potential for (highly skilled) job creation and the ability to address the trade–energy dilemma, plus more large-scale, international scientific collaborations such as CERN (i.e. capital-intensive, long lead times) will occur.

Professors at Princeton's Carbon Mitigation Initiative have developed a global emissions allocation framework ('stabilization wedges') to stabilize and reduce GHG emissions for the next fifty years. Some combination of carbon-management schemes is required and focusing on the 'one billion high emitters' when considering emissions standards is a possible point of departure.

For emerging markets to really internalize a clean energy strategy, several things need to happen:

• *Energy Technology Revolution*: co-evolution of technology. China, and increasingly India, rely heavily on coal for (cheap and easy) power generation. Emerging markets need to access clean(er) power generation technologies. In June 2008, International Energy Agency chief Nobuo Tanaka called for an energy technology revolution: 'The world faces the daunting combination of surging energy demand, rising greenhouse gas emissions and tightening resources. A global energy technology revolution is both necessary and achievable, but it will be a tough challenge.'
• *Global Energy Leadership (GEL) and the E-20*: a coherent, inclusive global energy leadership policy designed by those with the relevant expertise/talent, possibly convened under the aegis of the United Nations Framework Convention on Climate Change (UNFCCC).

The core leadership should include Brazil, India, China (the BICs), the United States, Japan, France, Italy, Germany, the United Kingdom, Canada and Saudi Arabia. Other high-growth emerging economies will join over time. Perhaps instead of a G-20 it's time for an *E-20, the Energy 20.* The IEA expects virtually all (97 per cent) of the projected rise in energy-related CO_2 emissions from 2010 until 2030 to come from the non-OECD with China, India and the Middle East alone generating three-quarters: their active participation is critical for any chance of lasting success. Initially, it will be difficult to get Russia on board. Also, other nations need to take the initiative if the USA will not, though it behooves America to lead in partnership in this global climate crisis. It is probably too hopeful to expect a concrete reversal in US energy policy in the near future despite Mr Obama's best intentions.

Given our complex reality, i.e. the very diverse interests and priorities of peoples and states in the world today, this poses a significant challenge. But a consensus on the 'this world is our only boat' notion at the 2009 London Summit was a major step forward and symbolically very powerful. By 2019 we can be well on our way to a future characterized by vigorous global trade, sustainable economic growth, clean energy and energy security – with a good strategy. An appropriate twenty-first century mantra is surely that *global challenges require global solutions.* And let us remember that Planet Earth's proverbial biological clock is ticking.

D5 | *Agriculture and international trade*

MANZOOR AHMAD[*]

One billion people in the world were chronically hungry and mal-nourished in late 2009, more than at any time in history. This flies in the face of the target of the Millennium Development Goal (MDG) to reduce by half the proportion of people who suffer from hunger by 2015.

Fortunately the world leaders recognize the problem and are giving the issue the priority that it deserves. At all the recent major international conferences, the leaders have been making pledges to take practical steps to meet the challenge. At the July 2009 G-8 summit in L'Aquila, Italy, for instance, they agreed to formulate a *comprehensive strategy* for *sustainable agricultural development* and decided to mobilize US$20 billion over a three-year period. This is a significant step, even though the amount committed falls far short of the Food and Agriculture Organization (FAO)'s estimates of US$30 billion required *per year* for investments in rural infrastructure and other needs such as providing access to modern inputs for food production, guaranteeing food safety and quality and food safety nets.

Any strategy to reach these goals must start where the prevalence of hunger and poverty is the highest; in rural areas in general and agriculture in particular. The ultimate goals of these strategies must be to raise agricultural productivity and output so that agriculture incomes will become comparable to those attained in other sectors. And, where people are able to produce enough output, they often lack the means to store, transport and process their primary products with the result that almost one-third to one-half of the agricultural produce perishes

---

[*] Dr Manzoor Ahmad served as Director of the FAO Liaison Office with the United Nations at Geneva. Previously, he served as Pakistan's Ambassador and Permanent Representative to the WTO from 2002 to 2008.

in the field. If the farmers could be made more productive, if there was more predictability in the prices of agricultural commodities and the wastages could be reduced, a large number of people dependent on farming could be lifted out of poverty and hunger.

There is abundant evidence that international trade and economic growth are interlinked. Agricultural trade can also provide a cushion against volatility in food production and prices. Under the prevailing practices of high tariffs and non-tariff barriers, however, agricultural trade has yielded much less benefit than it has potential for. Only a quarter of the world farm output is traded globally compared to 50 per cent of industrial goods, and as a share of the world trade, agriculture accounts for less than 10 per cent. The sensitivities of agriculture have resulted in flexible international rules, which can be manipulated to distort international trade. Whereas the rules for global trade in industrial goods have been in place for sixty years and have been gradually tightened with each successive GATT round, agriculture was practically treated as an exception to GATT rules. The Agreement on Agriculture concluded during the Uruguay Round (1986–1994) was not ambitious enough, with the result that no significant progress could be made towards its goal of a fair and a market-oriented system. The hopes are that this could change to a large extent with the successful conclusion of the Doha Round.

What are the major distortions in international trade of agricultural products that deny a level playing field to farmers from developing countries?

- First, it's the subsidies given by OECD countries to their farmers which could add up to an estimated one billion dollars a day. Such subsidies cannot be matched by the poorer countries, with the result that their farmers cannot compete globally. The Doha Round has to ensure that these subsidies are non-trade distorting and are substantially reduced.
- Second, high tariffs hinder developing countries from exporting their surplus produce. Tariffs on the import of agricultural commodities into OECD countries average about 14 per cent, compared to tariffs on industrial goods, which average only 3 per cent. The tariff levels on agricultural products have to be reduced to about the same level as for manufactured products.

- Third, tariff escalations (where tariffs increase on processed products with the degree of processing) ensure that developing countries are unable to export processed and more value-added goods. On average, tariffs on processed products are two to three times higher than on unprocessed commodities. All tariff escalations should be addressed in a manner so as to ensure that developing countries share more of the value added of their produce.
- Fourth, tariffs are not the whole story. Agricultural exports to OECD countries face several kinds of non-tariff barriers as well. Some studies indicate that non-tariff protection is double that of tariffs. Furthermore, the standards applied by some OECD members for imports into their countries are much more difficult to meet than the international ones. As standards have been gradually becoming more onerous to all trading partners, they have become particularly difficult to meet for countries with less advanced food systems.
- Fifth, there is the undisciplined bilateral food aid especially at times of low prices. Many donors buy food in their own countries and dump it in developing countries, which prevents farmers in those countries from earning enough from their agricultural products.
- Finally, there are no binding disciplines on restricting exports or giving huge subsidies to convert food crops to biofuels even at times of food crisis. The potentially large detrimental effect on international food security calls for reform in these areas.

While the Doha Round will be a step forward to correct some of these distortions, it may not fully achieve a reduction in the current applied level of domestic support or improve the objective of market access. This is because the cuts in trade-distorting subsidies being negotiated are not in the actual applied levels but the bound levels which are much higher than the current levels. In the case of tariffs too, the tentative agreement to cut them by an average of 54 per cent for developed countries would not apply across the board. They could be much lower for many important products of export interest to developing countries, which would nullify any additional market access. Furthermore, for most other issues such as non-tariff barriers, restricting exports from developed countries and diverting food crops with the help of subsidies for industrial usage such as biofuels even at the time of food crises, there seems to be no solution in sight.

Finally, more emphasis has to be placed on achieving long-term goals rather than merely reacting to emergencies. The UN's Food and Agriculture Organization has the objective of improving agricultural productivity. Its budget is a fraction of that of the World Food Programme, the main mission of which is emergency aid. If a lasting solution is to be found, the global community has to adopt a long-term outlook on agriculture, and more resources have to be provided for achieving this.

D6 | *Water scarcity: how trade can make a difference*

HERBERT OBERHÄNSLI[*]

In 2008, the city of Barcelona ran short of water; several shiploads of water were imported from Marseille to supplement the Barcelona city supplies during the summer months.[1] This news attracted a lot of attention, and the media as well as the world became aware of the gravity of the water issue like never before.

But this story also diverted from the real issue – the water needed to grow food for an increasing world population. Seventy per cent of all freshwater withdrawn for human use goes into agriculture, as producing one calorie for an average diet requires one litre of water. Water stress and shortage, falling tables of underground aquifers and rivers running dry for ever-longer periods over the year will therefore, in the first instance, endanger the production of basic foodstuffs.

In 2003, Frank Rijsberman, the then-head of the International Water Management Institute, formulated what this could mean: 'If present trends continue, the livelihoods of one-third of the world's population will be affected by water scarcity by 2025 ... We could be facing annual losses equivalent to one-third of global grain crops today.' A map published by the UN in 2006 shows where the problems lie currently: in the US Great Plains, the Middle East and North Africa, and parts of Spain, Pakistan, North-Western India and North-Eastern China. These are all important agricultural production areas. To illustrate orders of magnitude, it would require more than 35 million 'Barcelona'-size shiploads of water per year to be transferred to the water-stressed areas still growing food today in order to avoid the worst, once the water crisis does erupt.

---

[*] Herbert Oberhänsli is Assistant Vice President/Head Economics and International Relations, Nestlé SA and assistant for economic affairs to the Chairman of Nestlé Group.
[1] 19,000 tonnes of water per each of the ten boatloads from Marseille, also Tarragona, as well as a desalination plant in southern Spain.

In early 2008, Saudi Arabia decided that it would no longer grow
cereals but import them from countries with sufficient water.[2] The
underlying reason for this decision was the fact that Saudi farmers
used to pump up non-renewable fossil water. The government realized that, for them, water was more valuable than oil, and decided to
stop this type of water exploitation.

There is a wide range of rain-fed land still unused or massively
underused in the world today, particularly in Sub-Saharan Africa
(about 600 million hectares) and Latin America (about 300 million
hectares).[3] According to the Food and Agriculture Organization,
average per-hectare productivity in Latin America is 45 per cent
lower than that in North America, and yields in Sub-Saharan
Africa are even up to 80 per cent lower. Bringing the negotiations
on agriculture within the World Trade Organization (WTO) to a
conclusion would give a strong signal that efforts towards higher
agricultural productivity are worthwhile, particularly so in rain-fed
areas of Africa. The OECD estimates that full liberalization of trade
in farm products would lead to a 10 per cent reduction in freshwater
withdrawals for agriculture, due to open markets allocating scarce
water for global agricultural production more efficiently. But as is
true in other areas, in certain instances multilateral liberalization
of cross-border transactions only works efficiently if it goes hand-
in-hand with some necessary internal measures, including liberalization, modernization of regulations and, in certain instances, also
privatization.

The mere term 'privatization of water' is highly contentious, and
hence needs some further explanation. Water for fundamental human
needs – for drinking, cooking and basic hygiene – is a human right.
Governments have to make sure all people have adequate and affordable access to that minimum amount – which, if necessary, should
be provided free of cost. Any use beyond basic needs, for instance
in a private household for watering the lawn or filling a swimming
pool, should carry with it at least the full cost of the infrastructure.
And freshwater use for production (industrial or agricultural) is most
efficient and sustainable when water usage depends on opportunity
costs.

[2] 'Saudis to Phase Out Cereals', *Financial Times*, 11 April 2008.
[3] IFPRI and IIASA, 2001.

There is only one way of getting users to consider opportunity costs and that is to give users well-specified, transferable water rights. Such rights have long existed in the arid Western US, for decades in Chile, Australia and Mexico and, more recently, in parts of India and Pakistan. Once users have these rights, they automatically decide whether to forgo use of water in exchange for compensation from another user who may place a higher value on the water. Reallocating water then becomes a matter of voluntary and mutually-beneficial agreements between willing buyers and willing sellers and not a matter of confiscation via pricing at the scarcity value of the resource, or the endless search for new sources of supply.[4]

One outstanding example of how well tradable water usage rights work is the Aflaj water supply and irrigation system in Oman. The farmers of a village build the system and cover the cost of mainten-ance themselves. Water is captured in underground sources and then, through gravity, brought in tunnels up to 20 kilometres long to the village. For a few metres after the water comes into the open, it is freely accessible for drinking, both to villagers and to passing travel-lers. The canal then runs through the courtyard of the mosque, where the water is still free for ceremonial purposes and for the schoolchil-dren (the mosque also often serves as a school). Only after that does the water become private property, with days, hours and minutes of the water flow for irrigation belonging to individual farmers. Needless to say, their contribution to building and maintaining the system is proportional to the share of the water they own.

What is important in the Aflaj is that the water rights can be inher-ited, which is a strong incentive for sustainable use. What is equally important is that the water usage right can be traded, sold or tempor-arily rented out. A farmer with an idea for more efficient use of his water can sell some of his rights and use the proceeds to finance the investment to become more water-efficient. Similarly, a farmer who temporarily does not need some of his water can rent it out to a fellow farmer who still needs some more for his fields.

As opposed to this, in Valais in Switzerland where private water rights have been in existence for 800 years, a farmer will flood his

---

[4] John Briscoe, Harvard University, in *Wall Street Journal*, 23 June 2008. Typical examples including spot markets and permanent transaction markets are the Australian Murray-Darling basin in South Australia and the Chilean Limarí basin.

fields anyway, because he cannot rent his share of water out. Trading water among farmers has contributed significantly to the sustainability of Aflaj.

Undistorted, efficient local water markets would be the starting point for the global liberalization of the water-in-farm-products trade, the aim being to help avoid the severe food crisis as forecasted by Frank Rijsberman. But a truly multilateral solution of liberalization of international trade in agriculture combined with the right local water governance is still a far cry from actual government action. Major new policy trends point instead to new and highly restrictive forms of bilateralism. Countries and government-sponsored companies are buying and leasing land where water is still available. Among the countries involved are China, Japan, Korea, Libya, Egypt and countries of the Arabic peninsula as investors acquiring farmland in Laos, Cambodia, Burma, Mozambique, Uganda, Ethiopia, Brazil, Pakistan, Central Asia and Russia. The media has been reporting this, but has largely been lacking an overall perspective. Over the last two years, we have counted more than a hundred news messages pertaining to this issue. In some forty of them the size of the land was defined: it adds up to about twice the total cereal cropland of Germany. But again, it is not so much about land; it is about the right to withdraw the water linked to the land. Estimated on the basis of one crop per year, the acreage transferred represents 55–65 km^3 of embedded freshwater, i.e. 3 million 'Barcelona-type' shiploads per year.[5] And since this water has no price, the investors can take it over essentially for free.

Exporting food grown in countries with unused or inefficiently used land for rain-fed agriculture to countries that suffer increasingly from water shortage is a positive development. But it should be based on the global liberalization of agriculture within the WTO, rather than on bilateral linkages that will further restrict the free market.

Water embedded in farm products is currently being traded in large volumes across borders, but in highly distorted markets, with new

---

[5] Despite these high numbers, it is still a perception underpinned by the Barcelona water story that made the headlines. It even triggered the interest of Hollywood, with a James Bond movie and several 'documentaries' constructing a story of tap water barons withholding water resources from the population in order to increase personal profits.

distortions being added rather than existing ones being removed. Thinking in terms of water for agriculture is a challenge – but a major risk if we remain in a mode where politicians avoid thinking and talking about water because of the political risks involved. On the other hand, and to end on a positive note, it is a huge opportunity to stimulate the global liberalization of trade if we accept a new way of thinking.

D7 | Water resources: a national security issue for the Middle East

NIDAL SALIM AND NINA NINKOVIC[*]

Water resources in arid and semi-arid regions face the greatest pressure to meet growing needs. The Middle East is in fact 'the most concentrated region of (water) scarcity in the world and the most vulnerable to water shortages'.[1] The problem is further compounded when one considers demand and supply in the context of future socio-economic and natural changes that may occur such as population growth, urbanization and climate change.

The lack of water resources and the increase in consumption give this resource a strategic quality that has contributed to conflict in the region. The Middle East is characterized as water stressed, increasingly suffering from water shortages and environmental pollution. The last decades have witnessed many instances in which groundwater pollution or groundwater level declines have had serious negative impacts on the health of people, the economy and the environment.

Food security fears loom large in public policy discussions in the Middle East and North Africa (MENA). The ability of most countries to maintain national food security depends on import capacity. The Middle East is the most dependent region in the world on imports of food staples and buys a quarter of all cereals traded

* Dr Nidal Salim is Director and founder of the Global Institute for Water Environment and Health (GIWEH), Geneva, Switzerland. Before forming GIWEH, he was involved in collaborations with different research institutes, universities and international organizations, such as the Middle East Peace Process/Water Working Group/EXACT, the World Health Organization (WHO), the World Meteorological Organization (WMO) and the United Nations Environment Programme (UNEP). Prior to joining the University of Geneva for his Ph.D. in September 2002, he worked as a Director at the Palestinian Water Authority (PWA).

Nina Ninkovic is from the Geneva School of Diplomacy and International Relations, University Institute, Switzerland.

1 N. Salim (2007) 'Water Cycle from Theory to Practice, Derivation of a Basic Concept of Groundwater Recharge in Palestine' *Terre & Environnement* 70, section des science de la terre, University of Geneva.

globally. Households are food insecure, largely as a result of poverty. Agriculture utilizes 85–90 per cent of the region's water, as security is partly sought through domestic production at often unsustainable and inefficient water usage rates.

Water security is not only a challenge of physical scarcity, but also an issue deeply rooted in power, poverty and inequality. There is therefore a major difference between the concept of actual physical scarcity of water, and that of lack of access to water attendant to economic, political, social and environmental reasons. On top of this, there are hydro-political and trans-boundary considerations.

Community frameworks

The main concern of this article is to present 'water sustainability and security' as a concept which can highlight water challenges and be applied to the development of a framework for all stakeholders in a community in order to address their current and future water needs. These frameworks, formulated by the communities themselves, should form the foundation of a national water policy based on sustainability and security for all. Only then can regional and international agreements make progress and be implemented to enhance the water security of the region. The water cycle itself should link us in a common effort to protect and share our resources equitably, sustainably and peacefully.

Sustainability and security

A large proportion of the water resources in the Middle East are trans-boundary. Final arrangements on water allocation, which guarantee 'fair and equitable apportionment' between different countries in the region, are not yet in place. The Middle East region's natural water is not only threatened; it is also threatening!

The gap between water demand and water supply is growing due to population growth, higher living standards, climate change and the expansion of irrigated agriculture and industrial activities – which leads to potential decreases in fresh water availability.

When water resources in one community become scarce or threatened, the economic, social and environmental risks increase for all. Thus, a proactive integrated management approach is needed to balance the competing needs for this limited resource. 'Water sustain-ability' is a collaborative community-driven initiative, which requires the active participation of all members in the community. It seeks to establish new creative and coordinated water management strat-egies based on value addition and security for all stakeholders in the community.

The manner in which a community chooses to best use its resources to achieve its economic, social and environmental goals depends on a unified vision, leadership and objectives that are specific and meas-urable. A responsible and committed private sector should lead this change within the community.

Future perspectives (integrated water resource management)

The key aspect to be considered when looking at future perspectives is the role of governance and sound decision making. Water effi-ciency can be improved by adopting structural measures, for instance improved technologies, and non-structural measures, such as water pricing, better awareness and enhanced cooperation.

Another level of efficiency is related to the allocation and realloca-tion of water resources. Water allocation is the process used to decide how water should be shared between industrial, agricultural, munici-pal and domestic uses. Ideally, water will also be allocated to sustain-ing the environment. Efficiency at this level is generally achieved with government interventions in the form of different public regulations in the water sector.

The highest level of efficiency is related to the inter-basin trade of water. As water is quite a bulky item to transport, trading it in its real form is costly, which is the reason why the concept of virtual water comes into the picture. The economic argument behind the virtual water trade is that, according to international trade theory, nations should export products in which they possess a relative or compara-tive advantage in production, while they should import products in which they possess a comparative disadvantage (Wichelns, 2001).[2]

[2] D. Wichelns (2001) 'The Role of "Virtual Water" in Efforts to Achieve Food Security and Other National Goals, with an Example from Egypt', *Agricultural Water Management* 49: 131–51.

In a constantly changing socioeconomic, political and natural environment, water resource management in the MENA region has to satisfy a variety of needs, including through common water management strategies and their implementation. These strategies have to take into account current gaps in water availability and the need for equity. International involvement and the exchange of information are also of essence, especially in light of the fact that water resources have contributed to conflicts in the region. We consider, in this context, that an approach in which water acts as a catalyst towards peaceful cooperation is highly desirable. The best approach should be a message of peace and not a message of conflict over a scarce resource. We therefore recommend the following.

• Increase international involvement and support in the region, mainly in the fields of training, research, data exchange and scenario building aimed at the resolution of water conflicts.
• Desalination and wastewater treatment technology should be considered a strategic industry and could become a major exporter. Industry and business should lead this effort within their organizations and integrate water sustainability principles and goals within their business plans.
• Academia and other community leaders should play a leading role in increasing community awareness on water sustainability.
• The media also has a critical role to play in raising the awareness of the public at large. A fair and independent media could serve as a watchful eye over the abuse or misuse of limited freshwater supplies or unsustainable management practices.

Conclusion

The critical aspects to be considered for water resource management in the region are good governance, international involvement, cooperation and solid framework agreements. The key to increased national and household-level food security is pro-poor growth, driven by export-oriented, labour-intensive sectors.

Agricultural sector policies should be subordinate to the pro-poor growth goal and not to the goal of food self-sufficiency. Such a strategy requires conflict resolution, macroeconomic stability, physical and human capital accumulation, reliance on markets and the private sector, and the diffusion of ecologically friendly farming practices.

This could be achieved through: adopting production techniques and shifting to consumption patterns that require less water per unit of product; shifting production from areas with low water productivity to areas with high water productivity; adopting and expanding new green technology in wastewater treatment, desalination plants and rainwater harvesting; reducing water use through trade by importing from countries with higher water productivity; and building regional infrastructure, encouraging cross-border economic interaction and expanding from the national scale to a regional framework.

Meeting the water gap to satisfy the different needs and produce enough food by 2020 requires a water management approach which recognizes the value of water. All members of the community are accountable for its success. All countries in the region should embrace water sustainability to drive a new culture that is responsible, accountable and balances the short-term quality of life and development needs of the community with the needs of future generations. This is the essence of sustainable development. This new culture will also lead to closer collaboration among communities and countries in the region and thus diffuse the potential for conflict and adverse competition for this vital finite resource.

D8 | Trade, technology transfer and institutional catch-up

MARC LAPERROUZA*

Starting with David Ricardo, economists have examined how national differences in technological capabilities give rise to specialization and trade. Since then a large strand of the economic literature has been concerned with the intricacies of the relationship between trade and technology. Three types of interaction can be envisaged:[1]

- In **learning-by-doing**, trade increases the size of markets and the scale of specialization with positive spillovers on the domestic production of knowledge and accumulation of experience. Specialization may switch from sectors with low technological spillovers (e.g. primary goods) to sectors with important learning-by-doing effects (e.g. low-tech manufacturing goods).
- In **learning-by-importing**, foreign technology gets used or imitated. Trade transfers foreign technologies to the domestic economy or lets domestic firms improve their own technologies or products through reverse engineering and imitation.
- In **learning-by-exporting**, exporting firms learn by observing their competitors on international markets and aim to reach the same efficiency as their competitors by adopting their technologies.

Trade as a channel of technology diffusion

Together with foreign direct investment (FDI) and the diaspora, trade counts as one of the most important mechanisms for transferring technologies and diffusing innovation. In fact, trade and innovation are mutually reinforcing. Innovation gives birth to technological advantage which, together with differences in factor endowments,

* Marc Laperrouza is Senior Advisor, the Evian Group at IMD, and Senior Research Associate, Swiss Federal Institute of Technology.
[1] See G. M. Grossman and E. Helpman (1994) *Technology and Trade*. Cambridge, MA: National Bureau of Economic Research.

is the source of comparative advantage which in turn drives trade. Trade and investment affect innovation through technology transfer, competition effects, economies of scale and spillovers. Intellectual property protection matters too in stimulating technology diffusion. Improvements in intellectual property rights (IPR) can create an environment that attracts more foreign patents.[2] One important and open question is whether developing countries' implementation of TRIPS obligations (the World Trade Organization's Agreement on Trade-Related Aspects of Intellectual Property Rights) increases their exposure to foreign technologies. In certain cases, the existing IPR regime may lead to a paradoxical situation where access to foreign technologies is facilitated but their exploitation in developing countries is reduced.[3]

The nature and usefulness of trade differs significantly between countries. While developing economies and smaller economies are generally more reliant on foreign technology, more developed economies also benefit from trade as it increases the pool of technology available for domestic innovation processes.

Not all countries are able to benefit the same way from the international diffusion of technology.[4] The absorptive capacity of the importing economy matters greatly for technology to be effectively transferred.[5] Substantial efforts can be required to match foreign technology with domestic productive assets. Trade can nonetheless stimulate the process in several ways. First, it facilitates the transmission of knowledge embodied in traded capital and intermediate goods. Second, trade in services (as well as FDI) can be important

[2] Some studies even show that, overall, a change in IPR policy brings more productivity gains to middle and low income countries than a comparable change in trade policy.

[3] For instance, the econometric model developed by I. M. Hamdan-Livramento (2009) 'Examining how TRIPS Implementation Affects Access to Foreign Technologies for Developing Countries', Ph.D. thesis no. 4455, College of Management, EPFL, finds that stronger IPR protection via TRIPS implementation raises the cost of using new technology by entrepreneurs in developing countries.

[4] W. Keller (2004) 'International Technology Diffusion', *Journal of Economic Literature* 42: 752–82.

[5] Domestic absorptive capacity both conditions and attracts external flows. Both technological flows and technological adaptive capacity influence each other. See World Bank (2008) *Technology Diffusion in the Developing World*. Washington, DC: World Bank.

vectors for the transmission of knowledge embodied in people and in organizations. Finally, licence-trading allows firms behind the technology frontier to use foreign state-of-the-art technology.

As noted by Easterly,[6] poor countries are unlikely to be inventors of technology but they can advance their technological level by adopting inventions from rich countries. At times large technological gaps can even play in favour of developing countries. Lack of technological legacy and lack of vested interest to protect domestic technologies may allow countries to take advantage of new technologies through leapfrogging. In many parts of the world, the introduction of mobile telephony helped developing countries to bypass the (non-existing) fixed-line network and connect millions of people who would otherwise have had to wait several decades to access telephony.

The role of FDI

The relationship between trade, technology transfer and innovation cannot be fully understood without mention of FDI and the role of multinational corporations (MNCs). In fact, FDI acts as a key channel for international technology diffusion through interactions between foreign and domestic firms. Multinationals entering emerging markets are said to bring more advanced managerial practices, production methods, and other tacit and codified know-how. Technology then diffuses throughout the host economy as local incumbents imitate the new technology and hire workers trained by the multinationals.[7] MNCs are no longer the sole vectors as small and medium enterprises are increasingly linked to global markets.

Productivity and growth

Half a century ago Robert Solow showed that technological change – in this case the improvement in the instructions for mixing together raw materials – lies at the heart of economic growth. Technological

[6] W. R. Easterly (2001) *The Elusive Quest for Growth: Economists' Adventures and Misadventures in the Tropics*. Cambridge, MA: MIT Press.
[7] G. Blalock and P. J. Gertler (2009) 'How Firm Capabilities Affect Who Benefits from Foreign Technology', *Journal of Development Economics* 90(2): 192–9.

change was to provide the incentive for continued capital accumulation and, together, capital accumulation and technological change would account for much of the increase in output per hour worked.[8]

Theoretical models of productivity and economic growth now accept the importance of trade as a channel of technology diffusion. Contrary to wisdom, the major sources of technical change leading to productivity growth lie abroad.[9] Productivity benefits from foreign technology embodied in imported capital goods since they embody more technology than domestic machinery.

Akin to differences in absorptive capacity, the effects of technology transfer on the productivity of a recipient country vary. For example, the impact of US R&D on UK productivity is twice as large as the US effect in Germany or Spain, leading to highly asymmetric global patterns of technology transfer. Differences are also found at the firm level. A study in Indonesia has shown that firms with investments in R&D and firms with highly educated employees adopt more technology from foreign entrants than others. Firms that have a small technology gap – those closest to international best practices – benefit less than firms with weak prior technical competence. In other words, the marginal return to new knowledge is greater for firms that have more room to 'catch up' than it is for already competitive firms.[10]

Time has come for institutional change to catch up with technological change

Trade in the form of machinery, intermediate goods and services, patenting or licensing agreements gives access to foreign goods and, implicitly, technologies. Economic theory, backed up by mounting empirical evidence, shows that an environment conducive to trade facilitates technology transfer and, in the long run, productivity and economic growth. Openness to trade can help in breaking the path dependency which maintains certain countries on a historical pattern of technological (under-) development. East Asian countries, first

---

[8] Both new processes and new products play an important role in raising productivity and, in the long term, creating growth.

[9] A study shows that foreign research accounts for 87 per cent of productivity growth in France.

[10] See Blalock and Gertler (2009).

importers and imitators of high-tech goods have, over time, become
technological leaders in these same technologies. Last but not least,
the role of trade in the diffusion of innovation will be of particular
use in addressing global challenges such as climate change. More fluid
exchange of technologies, via reduced trade barriers, facilitated foreign
investment and adapted intellectual property regimes can in certain
cases help achieve significant economies of scale, making investments
in green technologies profitable. But learning from foreign technologies is highly dependent on a country's level of absorptive capacity.
Thus, while businesses are the main drivers for innovation, governments also have their role to play. In addition to funding fundamental research institutions, supporting private innovation and supplying
infrastructure including education, physical infrastructure and property rights, governments can encourage the transfer of technology by
ensuring both open and favourable trade and investment regimes.

D9 | *A frail reed: the geopolitics of climate change*

CHO-OON KHONG*

An awareness of climate change and of its potentially massive global effects is sharpening, just as the scientific consensus behind it has hardened and become more pessimistic. What is striking, however, about the response to this threat is the disconnect on the one hand between a growing awareness of its criticality, and on the other hand a blockage, both individual and collective, which results in a failure of policy to engage with the scale of the problem. Our growing awareness of the problem is then a frail reed on which to try to base a solution. What lies behind this disconnect?

The problem with climate change is that its consequences are high impact, but they are imprecise. They will occur at uncertain times and on uncertain timescales. There are also no parallels in our modern experience that we can draw on to make relevant comparisons. At an individual level, we are therefore slow to act because this looks like a complex nebulous problem, whose manifestations only play out some time in the future. And, as a general rule, the further into the future we look, the less detail we are able to pick out. So for many people, climate change becomes a problem where the most comfortable response (short of blaming others) is to ignore it, or to evade it. Knowledge by itself, as it turns out, is not enough.[1]

At a collective geopolitical level, a number of factors come into play. Climate change is fundamentally a global problem. But the political lenses through which we view it remain stubbornly national. We lack an established geopolitical process to tackle global problems. The Kyoto Protocol is an attempt to construct such a process,

---

* Cho-Oon Khong is Chief Political Analyst in the Global Business Environment team, Shell International. He wrote this article in a purely personal capacity.
[1] Thus Paul Krugman's comments on the Waxman-Markey climate change bill's passage through Congress, 'Betraying the Plant', *New York Times*, 29 June 2009.

227

to achieve better international coordination, specifically to tackle climate change. The problem, as the post-Kyoto process moves on beyond Copenhagen towards hammering out a successor treaty, and taking in the global economic crisis along the way, is that climate change demands an unprecedented level of global cooperation across a range of parameters. This is at a time when the international system is in a state of transition, heightening uncertainty, and making it especially difficult to reach a consensus.

The US National Intelligence Council released a report, at the end of 2008, on the emerging geopolitical landscape, which forecast that while the United States will remain pre-eminent, it will increasingly find itself as just one of a number of important actors, jostling with each other on the world stage.[2] As the report argues, there will be a host of new players – Brazil, Russia, India, China and others – coming to the international high table, each with its own agenda of what it wants to achieve. And while the international system is still working its way towards this new landscape, it is difficult to set rules of the game. In these inchoate circumstances, a range of uncertainties, including action on climate change, opens up. Indeed, climate change and resource competition receive particular attention in this report, as both move higher up the international agenda of concern.

Now throw in the 2008–2009 global economic crisis. It has underlined this shift in relative geopolitical and economic power. It has highlighted the need for the world's established powers to come to terms with accommodating the newcomers, and the need for the latter countries to take on new responsibilities to help manage the international system. And the global crisis may well end up catalyzing the beginning of a difficult process of adjustment, which could over time lead to the new geopolitical landscape picked out in the aforementioned National Intelligence Council report.

Major decisions on the world economy have begun to move to the larger G-20 forum, at the expense of the more narrow G-8, as the latter is seen as not representative of the current and emerging distribution of geopolitical power and hence no longer sufficient to meaningfully address such global concerns. As this has happened, non-G-8 members, and in particular the G-5 group of Brazil, China, India,

---

[2] National Intelligence Council, *Global Trends 2025: a Transformed World* (Washington, DC, National Intelligence Council, 2008).

Mexico and South Africa, are starting to participate more closely in other initiatives, including climate change. Indeed it is perfectly obvious that addressing climate change is a meaningless exercise unless all major greenhouse gas emitters are on board.

The deciding criterion on participation should surely be who is it that matters for the problem at hand, and what might work to get a solution in place. A larger grouping such as the G-20 (or the G-8 plus G-5, or other such combinations of countries that have been proposed) may be more representative of where global political and economic power lies. A larger grouping may also act as a salve to address the distrust with which those outside of the G-8 tend to view its motives (a distrust particularly keenly felt by Asian states after the 1997/8 Asian financial crisis).

But there is a price to be paid for inclusiveness. More members means that the larger group is more variegated, with less sense of shared values, than the established powers that comprise the G-8. And rather than inclusion building consensus, the larger forum exposes the divergent viewpoints of developed and developing worlds on critical global issues, including climate change. Hence it may well prove more difficult to make progress.

The national lenses through which we view climate change mean, of course, that what we see depends on where we stand. As *The Economist* puts it, there are two ways to emit less CO_2: by staying poor or through a miracle.[3] The rich countries opt for the second method to reach an 80 per cent reduction by 2050, a date so comfortably far into the future that it obviates the urgency of meaningful action now; while they recommend the first strategy to the developing countries. Not surprisingly, the latter group has a different view. The danger is that the diplomatic consensus that underpins the original Kyoto Protocol could begin to unravel.

So where do we go from here?

There are two possible futures, good or bad; a dichotomy which may appear clichéd, but which, in this context, captures an essential truth. A failure to cooperate unleashes a turbulent global future, defined by narrow national self-interest, as countries compete to secure access to energy and seek to avoid or to mitigate the harmful impacts of climate

---

[3] *The Economist*, 10 July 2009.

change. International tensions rise, raising the spectre of a new geopolitical cold war. Action on climate change is pushed into the future,
indeed to the point where it may require some early climate disasters
to drive home the need for change.

A positive future, by contrast, requires cooperation; but this will be
more difficult to achieve. Two things need to happen. One, as regards
the key governments that matter for climate change, each needs to
believe that the international system works, or can be made to work,
in its own individual national interest. Only then will there be sufficient faith in the system, for the major players that matter, to get
together in order to drive an agreed agenda for action. This removes
the blockage at the collective geopolitical level.

Two, the impulse driving cooperation has to be popular action,
from the bottom up, rather than government diktat, from top down.
Coercion, ultimately, does not work to produce real change. But a
shift in popular opinion requires overcoming that blockage at the
individual level, which enables people, in their minds, to avoid a
responsibility to act. This shift could happen when people start to
connect local environmental degradation and irregular local climate patterns with the larger climate change picture, and to make
the cost–benefit calculations that begin to drive effective policy at a
domestic level. Making this connection leads to political demands
which empower government leaders, and which then in turn open
up the political space for inter-governmental cooperation to become
possible. Progress today may look difficult, but it is just about feasible, and we need to move now.

Why does this matter for trade?

When the traveller-reporter Ryszard Kapuscinski first saw the
Great Wall of China, it struck him as 'proof of a kind of human weakness ... evidence of a historical inability of people in this part of the
planet to communicate, to confer and jointly determine how best to
deploy enormous reserves of human energy and intellect'.[4] Actually,
however, while the Great Wall was symbolic of an inward-looking
mental attitude, there was another mental attitude in Chinese history
that was its dialectical opposite, symbolized in the golden age of the
T'ang, when the nation turned outwards, new ideas and new products

[4] Ryszard Kapuscinski (2007), *Travels with Herodotus* (London: Allen Lane),
pp. 58–9.

flooded in, and the country grew rich on trade. This was a spirit open to outside influences, contemporaneous, seizing modernity.

We face this same dichotomy today. The international system provides a framework for conversations, negotiations and actions to be taken on a range of issues – economic, financial, security, environmental. Stresses that emerge in one area will impact on others as well. Should countries' positions harden on climate change, they will equally harden on trade and other issues as well.

A world of narrow energy competition is therefore also a more protectionist world, where governments seek to secure and to protect privileged relationships with energy suppliers, and where the goal of tackling climate change could ignite a trade war should governments impose tariffs or 'border adjustments' on environmental grounds. A world of cooperation on climate change, on the other hand, is also, in its ethos, a more open world of global markets. Reducing emissions will require disseminating technology and finance to help move towards more sustainable models of development and growth; it will require openness to make it work. Dealing with complex problems requires building trust.

The geopolitics around climate change is complex. And we may expect hard bargaining in the negotiations ahead. But acting on climate change requires openness and engagement, maintaining the integrity of global markets. Failure to act, by contrast, will likely be a factor moving the world towards a more insular closed international system. This is the choice that policy makers, indeed that all of us, face.

Global business responsibilities

Editorial introduction

Global business responsibilities

The concluding chapter draws on the previous analyses and flows from a simple question: how can the global business community instate faith in our collective abilities to confront the challenges faced by the global community? The 2008–2009 financial crisis exposed clear failures of responsibility and accountability. Many of the articles in this section lay emphasis on ethics and trust.

The first five articles scrutinize under a different lens the importance of leadership and education: a vision of the balance to be found between getting the right results and getting results the right way; the over-reliance of functional expertise at the expense of wisdom; a change in our educational systems to train a new generation of leaders with a better understanding of the respective roles of government and business to solve global problems; rewarding ethical behaviour throughout the chain of command to avoid ethical lapses; and encouraging human talent as the engine of innovation.

We then turn to supply-chain responsibility from a global and multi-sectoral perspective. This is followed by a proposition for global companies and governments to manage the new risks associated with trade and international capital flows. The next two articles underline in different ways the importance of building long-term coalitions under rules that align corporate objectives with those of government and society.

A survey of the extent to which human rights is dealt with in the world trading system is then put forth. And finally, the publication aptly concludes with an overview of the reasons for which the trends of the past decades translate into challenges for the rule of law embodied in the multilateral trading system.

E1 | Responsible leadership

JOHN WELLS[*]

The recent turmoil in financial markets is ascribed by many to be a failure of leadership and the calls for more responsible leadership continue to grow. But what is responsible leadership? There is a danger in taking too narrow a view and simply bowing to critics demanding more corporate social responsibility. Responsible leadership is more than this; it is a balance between getting the right results and getting results the right way.

Getting the right results

The goal of any enterprise is to deliver superior sustainable performance.

'Performance' is a measure of the value created per unit of resources consumed. For companies, we might look at return on investment; for a charity such as Operation Smile,[1] the number of cleft lip operations done for every dollar donated.

'Sustainable' means over the long term rather than to meet the next quarterly earnings targets. A firm might do well to remember that, unlike its employees, it *could* live forever and should encourage its managers to make decisions that reflect this long-term view.

'Superior' means better performance than others competing for the same resources. Success attracts more resources and therefore provides greater sustainability. It also generates a greater surplus to share among the many stakeholders who feel they are entitled to a return. Society benefits because it is the more profitable companies who can afford to be socially responsible; and, in a resource-constrained

---

[*] John Wells served as President of IMD. Previously, he was Professor of Management Practice at Harvard Business School. Carole Winkler contributed to this article.
[1] www.operationsmile.org/

world, is it not our moral responsibility to deliver greater value from limited resources?[2]

What does it take for an enterprise to deliver superior, sustainable performance? The foundation is always a good strategy – the integration of choices about where and how to compete. Successful enterprises focus on where they can create the most value and rely on outside suppliers for anything else. Second, it takes good execution, the integration of actions to deliver on the strategy. Both of these require good leadership to ensure that the right choices are made and the actions are taken.

But many enterprises with solid strategies and execution still fail eventually because, in a changing world, they fail to adapt. They are felled by inertia, a most fatal disease. As Jack Welch pointed out, 'I'm convinced that if the rate change inside the institution is less than the rate of change outside, the end is in sight. The only question is the timing of the end.' Responsible leadership demands agile strategy and an agile structure to support it. But the capacity of an organization to change is ultimately limited by the willingness and commitment of the people in the organization to change. Responsible leadership requires encouraging agile minds and attitudes.

Getting results the right way

Many enterprises, when evaluating their people, have come to the view that delivering results is not enough; how you deliver them has a profound effect on the long-term health of the enterprise. Companies must respect the simple principles of fairness and honesty, and encourage a long and broad view.

Be fair, build trust

The rather simplistic, traditional capitalist view of a firm is that its purpose is to maximize shareholder returns and minimize the cost of 'constraints' such as customers, employees, suppliers and regulators.

The danger of delivering the absolute minimum is clear. Customers will switch to another provider as soon as they find better value.

---

[2] Profitable firms have the luxury of being more socially responsible; social responsibility by itself does not automatically generate superior profits.

Instead, firms aim for a more loyal, stable customer base through 'delighting' customers by offering them more than they expected for their money. Regarding employees, paying them a pittance does not create loyalty and commitment; and with suppliers, aggressive purchasing techniques to drive prices down to a minimum are increasingly being discredited. Why should suppliers share their latest ideas on product design or cost reduction with customers who bully them?

Minimizing cost constraints may make economic sense in a one-off negotiation, but business, like life, is a multi-round game, where relationships of trust are crucial. If trust fails, transactions don't take place; just look at what has happened in the financial securities markets.

In practice, few companies really operate on this model. Most executives prefer to pay more than the minimum to the 'constraints' since this creates trust and loyalty, drives more innovation and creates more options for the future.

Be honest – don't steal assets from the balance sheet

A core value in delivering results the right way is honesty, but some firms discourage honesty by presenting their employees with moral hazards. Consider the plant manager who gets promoted for achieving greater profitability by deferring important equipment maintenance. This is tantamount to 'stealing' from the physical asset base. Firms must ensure that assets are handed to the next generation in the same excellent condition as they were originally.

The same holds for human assets. In professional service firms, there are those managers who exploit young professionals, working them to exhaustion and doing little to develop them. This is stealing from the asset base and from the firm's future.

Brand assets may be devalued by breaking the promise that the brand implies. One example is an insurance company that improved its profitability (for a time) by not paying claims.

There is also stealing from the financial balance sheet. CFOs have a great deal of discretion over how profit is defined, so they can hide profits in the balance sheet in good years and scrape profits from the balance sheet in the bad years. This is called earnings smoothing. It all starts to go wrong when earnings collapse and suddenly there are no assets left to scrape. Painful changes follow, which might have been avoided had executives practised more responsible reporting.

The challenge for firms is to create incentive systems which discourage members of the firm from stealing from the asset base. It is less of a problem in firms where executives spend entire careers, since they are more likely to be 'found out'. This is also true of family businesses where the stigma of 'stealing from family' is high. However, in a world where CEO and employee tenures have shortened dramatically, the moral hazard is clear. It is imperative that we instil these values and monitor them closely.

Take a broad, long view

The benefits of honesty and fairness become more apparent when taking a long, broad view of performance. We are part of a complex, dynamic system. We would do well to reflect on how our current decisions might affect performance, both today and tomorrow.

The reality is that firms have many stakeholders, and it is dangerous to consider any of them as costs to be minimized. We are in this for the long run.

Corporate social responsibility

Corporate social responsibility had just a brief mention at the beginning, but this is not to say that it is not an important part of responsible leadership. The concern for social responsibility is probably best channelled by enlightened self-interest – the pursuit of superior sustainable performance.

Firms can make high returns while showing concern for society. Whole Foods offers a wide range of sustainably produced products, a great shopping experience for its customers, and an excellent work environment for its employees while also providing high shareholder returns. Patagonia is equally successful in outdoor clothing. There are a myriad of companies generating profits from renewable energy and water purification. Other companies have discovered the benefits of serving the bottom of the pyramid while improving the lives of the poor. These are all examples of enlightened self-interest. Whenever there is value to be created from solving a problem, the efficiency of private enterprise is a fast and effective way of realizing that value.

Thus I would encourage firms to be concerned in profitable ways.

Responsible leadership at the national level

Nations, too, should strive for superior sustainable performance while being fair and honest with other nations, taking a broader, global, long-term view. A regulatory environment that encourages enterprises to seek superior, sustainable performance is a must. The nation state by itself cannot effectively regulate huge global corporations, which are larger than many small countries and reside in many corners of the world. Equally important is that nations provide the necessary infrastructure to support competitive enterprises. Superior national performance comes largely through superior enterprise performance.

Trade policy that focuses the nation on doing what it is best at and relying on other nations to focus on their comparative advantages is also key. Responsible nations should invest in competitiveness, not protectionism. By doing so, they will ensure a fairer distribution of global wealth, more inclusive growth, and less chance of conflict driven through inequity. And with the democratization of information via the Internet, populations are watching and increasingly demanding fairness.

Each nation cannot, alone, deal with the challenges this planet faces over the next fifty years. The sooner our species wakes up to this, the more we increase the chances we will survive into the next millennium.

E2 | *For great leadership*

Two lessons, among others, stand out from the experience of the 2008–2009 financial crisis. The crisis has shown that greed can lead to ruin, not only of persons but also of institutions. It has also shown that an uncritical faith in what is perceived as 'brightness' is no prescription for achieving the best results.

On the issue of greed, it is important to recall Max Weber (1864–1920), the noted German sociologist, who wrote *The Protestant Ethic and the Spirit of Capitalism*. In this celebrated book, Weber does not equate 'the spirit of (modern) capitalism' with the reign of unscrupulousness in the pursuit of material interests. He sees this 'spirit' instead in the ethos of industry, frugality, punctuality, and honest dealings in the pursuit of increasing one's capital. Weber traces this attitude of making money to the idea of a 'calling', an idea that defines a life-task in a given field of activity. Such an idea was, he argues, present predominantly in the Western world among the Protestant people. For the saints, so ran the belief in ascetic Protestantism, the everlasting rest belonged not to this world but to the next. On Earth, man must do the work of God who sent him here. In his own lifetime, Weber saw how the idea of duty in one's calling had been reduced to the ghost of dead religious beliefs. The pursuit of wealth, stripped of its religious and ethical meaning, had become an indulgence in 'mundane passions'. The full fury of these 'mundane passions' became visible recently as the Madoffs of the financial world indulged in frauds of staggering magnitude.

On the reliance on 'brightness', I tried to argue in the final panel discussion of the Responsible Leadership Summit held at IMD, Lausanne, in early 2009 that the 'brightest' do not necessarily offer the most desirable form of leadership. It is often forgotten, as Frank

---

[*] Professor Dr Surendra Munshi is a Fellow of the Bertelsmann Stiftung and retired Professor of Sociology at the Indian Institute of Management Calcutta, India.

Rich points out in his column in *The New York Times,* that David Halberstam's book *The Best and the Brightest* did not intend to suggest that the 'brightest' were the 'best'. On the contrary, Halberstam wanted to suggest in a tone of irony that the hubristic team of John F. Kennedy had mired the United States in Vietnam. It was unbelievable to see how some of the brightest persons to serve in government turned out to be the architects of the worst tragedy faced by the country since the Civil War.

Prescriptions against greed exist in all cultural traditions; greed is one of the deadly sins in Christian thought, which St Thomas Aquinas described as 'a sin against God'. In Hinduism, for instance, there is the famous exhortation in the *Bhagavad Gita* to work without the expectation of rewards (you have the right to work, not to the fruit thereof). As to the reliance on 'brightness', this arises out of the importance that is given at present to functional expertise which operates through multiple regressions. Mathematics or rather superficial mathematical models tend to replace economics, economics tends to replace political economy, political economy tends to replace philosophy, and so on. This reduces the scope for learning from the vast reservoir of human wisdom that is available from folklore to epics to philosophical reflections. The 'wisdom' of ages is thus lost in 'bright' choices. Actually, these 'bright' choices tend to be superficial choices. It has been pointed out, for instance, in *The Economist,* that we would have been less surprised at what happened in 2008 had we remembered that there had been many bank-centred crises around the world since 1970.[1]

How can we promote great leadership in different spheres of life? The answer that can be drawn from the reflections so far is by overcoming greed and our exclusive reliance on 'brightness'. There is a need for investing our work with a broader meaning, one based on cherished values. We also need to cultivate wisdom that tells us in all possible traditions that human beings must find ways of living together peacefully. This need is an urgent one, for we live in a world at present that is more interdependent than ever before. Great leadership happens when the leader can think beyond his or her narrow interests and help others to see beyond themselves as well. It has to do with vision and

[1] *The Economist,* 26 September 2009.

the ability to actualize it in practice. For our present world it involves the realization that all of us are in the same boat, and we float or sink together. For promoting great business leadership we need to understand that a moral sense is important so that we may live in cooperation with each other. The need at present, unlike in previous times, is not so much to protect ourselves from animals but to protect ourselves and indeed animals from the forces that we have ourselves unleashed.

It is here that Mahatma Gandhi is relevant to us today, a leader who President Barack Obama said recently he would like to have dinner with, given a free choice of having dinner with anyone, dead or alive. He chose Gandhi even though he was aware of Gandhi's frugal food habits! Obama pointed out that he found a lot of inspiration in Gandhi. Without him and the inspiration that he provided to Dr Martin Luther King there might not have been a non-violent civil rights movement in the United States. We need to remember that Gandhi was a transformational leader who challenged in India an entire nation to think in radically different ways for realizing an objective which he pursued with all the strength of 'a pragmatic dreamer'. He had a vision, and he communicated it across the nation in an effective manner. Above all, he was convinced about the necessity of morality for every human being and every society.

In a lecture that I delivered at the Bertelsmann Stiftung, Guetersloh, Germany, on 15 February 2008, I tried to argue that for drawing leadership lessons, even at the corporate level, we need to look at Gandhi's strategy, which should be considered in relation to his vision, which made the means as important as the end. It is this perspective that lifts his strategy to a higher level. Gandhi was the first human being ever to realize with the effectiveness that he brought to bear on this insight that adherence to *satya* – truth – for a worthy end was not only a moral choice but also a smart one, even in the field of politics. If one were to formulate a trendy slogan for this perspective, one could say for him *satya is smart*. Thus, he could counter ruthlessness with morality, selfishness with selflessness or service, hatred with love, force with legitimacy, unjust with just, and fear with courage. This worked well for his political purpose also. A mighty empire was forced to fold up on the strength of Gandhi's vision-inspired strategy. The world needs today in different spheres and at different levels a conscious application of this Gandhian insight.

E3 | A lesson on trade, regulation and competition policy?

ARTHUR E. APPLETON[*]

There are important lessons to be learned from the 2008–2009 global financial crisis – but there are equally important lessons to be taught. The public quickly blamed greedy business leaders, particularly those in the financial sector, as well as globalization for the financial crisis, but perhaps the blame lies elsewhere – first with our education system, and second with the political dogma that nourishes many students.

Some suggest that business and legal education, particularly in the United States, creates robber barons devoid of morality and ethics. Too often they point their finger at the present models of professional education, not realizing that business and law schools almost always integrate values and ethics into their curricula. While there is a need to strengthen business and legal training to assure that students have a better understanding of right and wrong, there are other serious problems waiting to be addressed – and almost certainly at an earlier stage in the educational process.

Frequently business leaders, lawyers, politicians and, importantly, other members of civil society, do not have much familiarity with basic economic principles, international economics and international economic institutions, and more specifically about the economic and political benefits of a sound international trade, investment and competition policies. Without this knowledge it is difficult to appreciate the economic benefits of open markets, international trade and sound competition laws. Without a good knowledge of economics, in particular the concepts of 'market failure' and 'externalities', it is difficult to assess when regulations, including prudential ones, are necessary

* Arthur E. Appleton, J.D., Ph.D. is a Partner in the Geneva office of Appleton Luff – International Lawyers. He has written, published and practised in the trade field for twenty years. He has appeared before the WTO's Appellate Body and teaches at the World Trade Institute (University of Bern) where he serves on the Board of Directors. He also serves as counsel and arbitrator in international arbitrations, including ICC arbitrations.

for economic growth and social wellbeing. Although it would be possible to better integrate the study of economics, international economic law and 'international economic institutions' (such as the WTO, IMF and IBRD) into business and legal education, ideally this training should come earlier and reach all members of society.

We live in a transition period that coincides with the collapse of the Soviet model. In recent years many developed countries, in particular the United States, were influenced by the laissez-fare economic views given voice by Reagan and Thatcher. The 'Thoreauian' ideal, 'That government is best which governs least', has pervaded our social thinking and resulted in suspicion of national governments and the work of international economic institutions. Now, however, as a result of the financial crisis, serious environmental problems and unequal patterns of economic development, the Hegelian pendulum is swinging back, and we are beginning to rethink our assumptions and to ask ourselves: what is the proper role of government in society and what must be done at the international level to resolve pressing problems? This is the question that future businesspeople and lawyers, as well as political leaders, must consider. But to do so, they need the right economic training and good analytical tools so that they can re-evaluate previous dogma and invent new tools. This calls for a change in our educational system.

Widespread agreement remains that economic incentives and free market principles have a tremendous role to play in economic development. They are part of the dynamo that powers prosperity and growth. However, there is also a growing realization that market forces, supported by a liberal trade policy, are not a panacea. In previous generations we learned how unregulated markets might lead to the emergence of monopolies that abuse their dominant position and stifle creativity and development. In response, national competition laws emerged in many developed countries and political leaders in the developed world have not abandoned efforts to incorporate principles of competition law into the multilateral framework.

The present generation is faced with analogous problems. The free market system alone cannot solve global problems such as climate change and environmental degradation, nor will it alone bring discipline to battered markets, nor bring about acceptance of the values and ethics that business leaders and legal professionals must adopt if we are to restore confidence in our financial institutions. Laissez-faire economic dogma is giving way to the realization that some degree of government intervention and collective international action is necessary to address the market failures that gave birth to these problems.

Viewed in this light, there is a positive side to the present financial, environmental and developmental crises. Voters are becoming increasingly leery of ideologically simplistic laissez-faire solutions. They are more willing to examine existing problems more deeply and to challenge existing thinking. This is a moment of opportunity for colleges and universities worldwide to begin training a new generation of leaders based on sound economic theories, and a better understanding of economics, and the role that government, as well as the business and legal community, must play at the national and international level to solve global problems. With a better understanding of economics should come a better appreciation of the economic values and business and legal ethics needed to restore economic confidence and address pressing international problems.

Most people have long accepted the need for a government hand in defence policy, anti-trust (competition) policy, education and healthcare. Now they are beginning to realize that government has a greater role to play in other sectors – in particular assuring adequate regulation of the financial industry. They are also beginning to appreciate the fact that some problems, such as climate change, require international solutions that capitalize on the creativity of the business, legal and scientific community. This means that there is a need to train a new generation of leaders who understand the economics behind our present environmental problems, comprehend the increasingly complex financial instruments that are so important for our economies, and who realize the need for open markets, tempered by value-based and ethical decision making. We need leaders, businesspeople and legal professionals who understand what government can do well, what government does poorly, what is better left to the private sector, and what must be addressed at the international level. We can achieve this goal by better training our students at an early age about economics, ethics and business values.

There is also a need to train future business leaders, lawyers and politicians about what can be done at the international level and which problems require international coordination and international solutions. This training cannot wait until business or law school. It should be commenced early in the educational process and should reach the largest audience possible. And it should have a moral and ethical component. Not everyone should be trained to be an international economist, but everyone should at least have a basic understanding of general economic principles, and of the international economic institutions that are so important for our economic system. With adequate understanding of economics, people would stop pointing their finger at the WTO, IBRD and IMF for our present problems. These institutions are wrongly maligned as the 'handmaidens of globalization' by those who do not realize the important role that trade, development and economic stability play in maintaining international peace and security and bringing about prosperity.

In recent years the mantra of the business community and the common man has echoed Deng Xiaoping's maxim that 'To get rich is glorious' – with the titans of industry, investment and the legal profession enjoying heroic (or at least cult) status in many countries. The role of government has received little positive attention. Reform of the education system has also not received ample attention. It is time to reverse this trend. The financial crisis has extinguished the bonfires of the vanities, as well as important parts of the domestic and international economy. As we go about rekindling the economic system, we need to explore how we can instil economic morality into our leaders and a basic economic understanding into the average person. The obvious answer is through our educational system. The world needs a profound cultural change to address the problems with which it is confronted. This can only come about by assessing the shortcomings of our educational system, by developing curricula that will meet our future needs, and by harnessing the strength of our young and future leaders and the creativity of our business and legal community to address these problems.

E4 | *International trade and business ethics*

STEWART HAMILTON*

In November 2006, 200 German policemen and prosecutors raided 30 offices and homes of Siemens managers to investigate allegations of embezzlement at Siemens' fixed-line phone unit. Six suspects were arrested, among them current and former high-ranking managers. In 2007 a German court fined Siemens €201 million in relation to illegal payments of €12 million made by its information and communication business unit to government officials in Nigeria, Russia and Libya. At the same time prosecutors in at least ten countries, including the USA, were investigating allegations that Europe's largest engineering company by sales had bribed officials to win big infrastructure contracts around the globe.[1]

Also in 2007, in the wake of internal investigations started at the end of 2006, Siemens finally admitted to having identified dubious payments amounting to €1.3 billion from the years 1999 to 2006. As a result, the 'trains-to-light bulbs' conglomerate replaced all but one of its managing board members.

On 15 December Siemens pleaded guilty to charges of bribery and corruption and agreed to pay US$350 million in disgorgement to the SEC. In related actions, Siemens paid a US$450 million criminal fine to the US Department of Justice and a fine of €395 million to the Office of the Prosecutor General in Munich, Germany, on top of the earlier €201 million.

The Siemens case was a compliance scandal of unprecedented scope. The SEC alleged that between 12 March 2001 and 30 September 2007, Siemens violated the Foreign Corrupt Practices Act (FCPA) by

---

* Stewart Hamilton has been Professor of Accounting and Finance at IMD since 1981, and Dean of Finance and Administration since 2008. His areas of special interest are corporate failure, governance, risk management and investor protection.
[1] Siemens: Legal Proceedings – Third Quarter Fiscal 2008, Munich, 29 July 2008.

249

engaging in a widespread and systematic practice of paying bribes to foreign government officials to obtain business. Siemens created elaborate payment schemes to conceal the nature of its corrupt payments, and the company's inadequate internal controls allowed the conduct to flourish. The misconduct involved employees at all levels, including former senior management, and revealed a corporate culture long at odds with the FCPA. At least 4,283 of those payments, totalling approximately US$1.4 billion, were used to bribe government officials in return for business to Siemens around the world.

As a result of this the confidence of the business world and the public in what was reputed to be a model company has been severely shaken. But in retrospect this can be seen as a positive example for deterring others. Of course one case will neither address nor change the systemic weaknesses in international anti-bribery efforts. Or to put it another way, the fact that one major company has been punished by two major economic powers will not stop other companies from being routinely corrupted, nor will it compel other governments to enforce their laws.

However, since the early 1990s fighting corruption has engendered an unusually high degree of international cooperation, leading to an armoury of international instruments, such as the OECD's Convention on Combating Bribery of Foreign Public Officials in International Business Transactions,[2] or indeed the Council of Europe's Criminal Law Convention on Corruption.[3]

The reason the international community has mobilized to fight the problem is simple: corruption respects no borders, knows no economic distinctions and infects all forms of government. In the long run, no country can afford the social, political or economic costs that corruption entails. As Lori Weinstein, the Justice Department prosecutor who oversaw the Siemens case pointed out: 'Crimes of official corruption threaten the integrity of the global marketplace and undermine the rule of law in the host countries'.[4]

---

[2] Convention on Combating Bribery of Foreign Public Officials in International Business Transactions, Adopted by the Negotiating Conference on 21 November 1997.
[3] Criminal Law Convention on Corruption, Strasbourg, 27 January 1999.
[4] Siri Schubert, T. Christian Miller, 'At Siemens, Bribery Was Just a Line Item', *The New York Times*, 20 December 2008.

Corruption erodes public confidence in political institutions, distorts the allocation of resources and undermines competition in the marketplace; it has a devastating effect on investment, growth and development. Furthermore, corruption exacts an inordinately high price from the poor by denying them access to vital basic services.

But the fundamental question for every international company remains: how can business remain both competitive and be morally and ethically responsible? The answer, it seems, may be found in part in initiatives on the micro-level. Major players in specific sectors or regions may simply decide to stop paying bribes or other forms of inducements. One recent example was provided by Ikea. In June 2009 Ikea declared that it was suspending further investment in Russia, because of pervasive corruption and demands for bribes. This announcement came after a statement by Ikea's 83-year-old founder Ingvar Kamprad on the Swedish radio station P1, that Ikea had decided not to solve problems by slipping money under the table.[5]

It is however remarkable how many leaders of business organizations seem content to operate with one set of principles in their homeland and another overseas if cultural differences can be used to gain competitive advantages. In business ethics we often use the metaphor 'when in Rome, do as the Romans do'.

But can such moral relativism be the appropriate way of approaching complex dilemmas? Can following a morality of the marketplace that is violating the morality of the homeplace be truly an acceptable answer? How can the creation of the same value have a different price depending on geographic coordinates? Are we really willing to accept that the values of the working place be more important here and less important there?

Having posed these questions in the classroom, we know that the responses regularly refer back to the aspects of different cultures. Yes, different cultures can have different value systems. What is condemned in the West, e.g. child labour, discrimination against women, may well be the rule, or at least be tolerated, in other cultural systems. But no matter what a cultural difference might be, it can never serve

---

[5] http://dailyreporter.com/blog/2009/06/15/ikea-expansion-in-russia-stalled/ (accessed 3 July 2009).

as an alibi for circumventing minimal ethical standards related to social life, to the environment or to human rights.

And then – and here we come back to the Siemens story – what is significant about ethical scandals (once they are revealed and addressed) is the damage they do to great organizations. If you were leading such an organization, would you risk permanently damaging your company in order to win a few overseas contracts? Regrettably, for some executives the answer is yes. Here the reality proves that applying 'situation ethics' in developing countries is the fastest way to destroy a global organization. To sustain their success, companies must follow the same standards of business conduct in New York, Shanghai, Mumbai or Kiev as in Munich.

It's easier said than done? Definitely! The challenge of creating and enforcing an ethical set of values within an organization remains the Holy Grail for many companies. Employees of all different backgrounds, education and religious beliefs need to indentify themselves with, and accept, these values, rather than allowing individual diversity within a multinational company, with often only very narrow and ill-defined corporate standards.

The tone has to be set from the very top. The Scottish expression that 'the fish rots from the head' applies also to companies (and indeed, to not-for-profits) and the board must set the boundaries. What is most important is that employees feel that their corporate leadership is practising the same principles that they require of them. Furthermore, if they are doing so, employees want to know what the policies are if ethical standards are broken. These standards must be clear, concise and ultimately enforced. As the profit margins often determine management remuneration, this can encourage greed and inappropriate behaviour. Businesses should reward top performers but within the ethical boundaries in the organization.

Until organizations start rewarding ethical behaviour throughout the chain of command, we will continue to see ethical lapses. The potential employee's ethical attitude needs to become part of the hiring criteria since an organization can only behave as ethically correctly as its employees. Incentives for the correct attitude and no tolerance for breach are steps in the right direction. It starts and remains in the hands of corporate leaders to maintain a culture of ethical behaviour.

E5 | Who's driving twenty-first century innovation? Who should?

BILL FISCHER*

Innovation will drive the future, but who's driving innovation? In modern, market-based societies this is a question of some import. We live in a time of impending crisis. Our planet's fragile ecological inheritance is being carelessly squandered and the 'seas of change' are literally rising as we dawdle. At the same time, the one resource that we do have that can offer us a chance at salvation – the creative power of the human intellect – is at risk of being wasted in complex organizations that all too often have become 'prisons of the soul'. This goes beyond mere frustrations over business as usual; this is vitally important to us all: who speaks for the species at a time such as this?

Popular imagination typically ascribes the innovative role to 'independent inventors' – contemporary 'Davids' struggling against massive industrial 'Goliaths', with nothing but goodwill on their balance sheets and only altruistic objectives on their minds. Ah, if only this were true! The reality is, in fact, quite different. The great bulk of twenty-first century innovation will be pursued in the private, non-governmental sector, led mostly by big and multinational firms, operating from a handful of favoured locations, mostly in the developed world. Is this good? Well, first of all, it's not a choice, but a reality, so the question might be moot; but then the real question becomes: is this what we want?

Despite Thomas Friedman's arguments to the contrary, the world of contemporary innovation is not flat and never has been, and while the promise of invention might be anywhere, it is within the modern multinational corporation (MNC) that our best hopes for delivering

* Bill Fischer is Professor of Technology and Management at IMD. Professor Fischer has been actively involved in technology-related activities for his entire professional career, including over fifteen years of short-term consulting assignments with the World Health Organization on strengthening research and development institutes in developing countries in Asia, Africa, the Middle East and Latin America.

innovation on a global scale are to be found. While we might wish otherwise, at its best, no other organizational format is as exquisitely sensitive to customer needs; nor as global in its reach; as efficient in global resource allocation; as potentially politically neutral in ensuring equitable treatment of its talent; as accomplished in its execution; and as effective in really weaving resources and needs together on a worldwide stage, as is the modern MNC. In addition, the MNC has become the true architect of the global economy, as it establishes supply chains and deploys talent, investments and assets around the planet. Governments have decidedly not done this. In fact, they are all too often the largest source of resistance to profound change, especially if it comes at some economic disadvantage to their own local interests.

'Delivery of innovation', however, is not the same as actually 'innovating', much less *inventing*, and it is within the creative sphere where the modern MNC is at greatest risk of losing its allure. To be fair, there are several characteristics of innovation that *do* argue in favour of the multinational: the first is resources – multinationals have more resources for risk-taking activity than do their smaller, or government-influenced, peers; second, everything that we know about the economics of innovation demonstrates the existence of economies of scale that are alive and well within the realm of R&D. Multinationals might actually also be considerably better at listening to market needs than are lone, obsessed, inventors.

However, the bigger concern is: are multinationals really the best place to unleash the abundant human talent that is the engine of invention (and here one might add 'the salvation of our species') on a broad scale? Here the evidence is at best quite variable, and in general truly discouraging. Contrary to it being a launching pad for dreams, there is ample reason to argue that the modern complex organization has become, all too often, a place where too many good ideas languish or die. Numerous, albeit unscientific, inquiries into talent utilization have convinced me that for the most part, modern, complex organizations are not even receiving 50 per cent of the useful talent that is offered to them by their employees. The reason: a paucity of enlightened leadership. It's hard to think of any position of similar power or responsibility where we know so little about the individuals who play the key roles affecting us all, or are so unable to accurately gauge the objectives or promise of the organizations that 'host' these innovative activities.

My IMD colleague, Professor Jean-Philippe Deschamps, in the joint IMD-MIT Driving Strategic Innovation programme classroom, elicited the following set of characteristics associated with successful innovation leadership from a group of experienced CTOs:

- A person who is dissatisfied with the status quo, who sees opportunities where others see nothing, and with the humility to ask for ideas, needs and assistance;
- A person who is not risk-averse, but self-confident in their own ideas and yet willing to accept failure in the pursuit of learning and is, in fact, supportive of mavericks and contrarians;
- A person who has the capacity to listen, be open-minded, and who is willing to set aside their own ego in the support of another's ideas, and is able to refocus;
- A person who has an insatiable passion for learning, who is curious and willing to reach out to people beyond the traditional boundaries of their everyday world, and who has the capacity to integrate these diverse ideas; and
- A person who has a high level of business acumen, across a wide swath of the value chain, and a mastery of the balance between creativity and discipline.

While such characteristics are not at all outside of the realm of what we've seen in our studies of teams of extraordinary talented (and mostly young) people, who have launched innovations that have revolutionized their industries,[1] we also find that it is far more common in corporate life for levels of hierarchy, centralized control and even *fear*, to characterize work situations, and lead to situations where talent is all too often trapped and diminished. As a case in point, one group of Asian high potentials, working for a large, well-known, global fast-moving consumer goods company, observed that 'our ideas are indiscriminately killed, railroaded, or corralled', and added that while 'we find ourselves in wrong roles, [we] are unwilling or unable to escape'. A much more senior group of European banking executives admitted that in their organizations 'we only allow certain people to think', as titles, turf and hierarchy all conspired to kill new ideas.

---

[1] Andy Boynton and Bill Fischer (2005) *Virtuoso Teams*, London: FT/Prentice Hall.

Is it then to our advantage for such organizations to be able to play such an important and independent role on the world economic stage, beyond providing high-quality goods and services at affordable prices? Do we trust them to also serve as impresarios who identify and nurture the world's innovative talent? And, if not, are there alternatives?

Let's begin with what we know about innovation today: there is nothing about it that is flatly distributed. For years, the overwhelming majority of industrial R&D has been funded and pursued in the most developed economies on the planet. Similarly, the great universities and inventive performances, either in total or on a per capita basis, have largely centred on the same developed countries; so, too, for Nobel prizes, and most prizes in the creative arts. This is not surprising, as there is a long history of research revealing profound economies of scale in R&D associated with creative activity, largely as a result of greater conversational possibilities. In addition, look at any map of creative activities and they are even further from being 'flat', being overwhelmingly centred on such 'spikes' as few, select, big-name urban, or urban-proximate, locations: New York, Milan, Shanghai, for example. And not just any urban area will do. Richard Florida has argued persuasively that innovation requires urban areas with an 'edge'; locations that have diverse and somewhat bohemian populations, where 'cultural' clashes occur and new combinations result. Ironically, 'edginess' appears to be related to wealth, with rich cities being more able to attract the bohemians needed to spark change and innovation. And, equally ironically, in most large corporations, the 'bohemian' is not welcome.

So, what then is the message? My feeling is that for the development and distribution of the innovative arts, big is better over the long run; and 'spikyness' wins over flatness. Does this mean that there is no role for smaller, emerging players? Not at all, but what it does mean is that the mortality rate of such competitors will be very high – a few will make it big: the Microsofts, Googles and even the Sonys, but they are few, and relatively far between, and tend to have the biggest opportunity at the birth of a new industry. In addition, the most ambitious will likely figure out ways to migrate from 'innovative plateaus' to edgy places along the spikes, which will give them the best chance for realization of their dream. In fact, far from the romance of 'flatness', 'spikes' remain as important as always, and this is probably a force for good, as is the global influence of the multinationals. What cries out for attention, however, is the leadership of these institutions. Let's not waste our energies decrying the structures themselves, but instead turn our attention to encouraging a new generation of innovation leaders who have a broader mission for the betterment of our species, and the self-confidence to pursue that mission.

E6 | Responsible sourcing

MARTIN WASSELL*

What is responsible sourcing?

Responsible sourcing, also referred to as supply chain responsibility, is a voluntary commitment by companies to take into account social and environmental considerations when managing their relationships with suppliers.

This strategy is now an integral part of effective supply chain management. Responsible sourcing practices contribute to efficiency and continuity of the supply chain in the long run.

As production chains expand, companies of all sizes and sectors are devoting more efforts to managing supply chain risks and building effective supplier relationships. Improving social and environmental performance in production chains is becoming a major element of this process.

As experience has shown, one bad incident with one supplier can lead to a disproportionate amount of adverse publicity, damaging a company's reputation and brand image. This has led a growing number of companies to develop and promote responsible sourcing practices.

Indeed, effective supply chain management is a way for businesses to build a competitive advantage, especially in sectors where production is largely outsourced, such as clothing, footwear, electronics, or food products.

For many companies, working towards improving social and environmental standards in the supply chain has become a natural

* Martin Wassell has been First Director of the International Chamber of Commerce since 1997. He previously served twelve years as Economic Director. Earlier in his career before joining ICC in 1985, Mr Wassell held London-based posts as: Coordinator of Policy to the President of the Confederation of British Industry; Editorial Director of the Institute of Economic Affairs, an independent economic research trust; and General Director of the Centre for Policy Studies.

extension of their commitment to corporate responsibility and, as such, forms part of their overall business model.

Getting involved

Many companies have literally thousands of suppliers across the globe. While a company cannot be held accountable for the actions of all its suppliers, its purchasing activities may create leverage to influence and monitor its suppliers' conduct in areas such as working conditions, respect for labour rights and environmental protection.

The ability of companies to influence their suppliers' business conduct will vary greatly depending on the commercial environment in which they operate and the nature of their supplier relationships. The great diversity that exists within business requires companies to consider a range of tools and approaches so that these can be tailored to their specific circumstances.

To help companies develop their own approaches to responsible sourcing, the International Chamber of Commerce (ICC) has produced a guide in the form of six practical steps from a global and multi-sectoral perspective. These steps are based on real-life experiences collected from ICC member companies around the world, and can be used by companies from all sizes, sectors and regions. The guide is a product of the ICC's Commission on Business in Society – the ICC's main working body on corporate responsibility issues.

Six steps to responsible sourcing

Step one: selecting a supplier

A careful selection of suppliers is one of the best ways to ensure continuity and long-term efficiency of the global supply chain as well as enduring brand support.

When choosing a supplier, in addition to making a final determination on cost, companies often need to evaluate a range of supply chain issues: product quality and safety, continuity of supply and speed of delivery, and intellectual property protection. Criteria such as working conditions, environmental practices, safety standards and human rights policies should also be factored into the selection process.

As a first step, companies should check basic facts about the social and environmental legislation and the level of enforcement in the country of production, to assess potential production risks.

Step two: set clear expectations on compliance with the law

When contracting with a supplier, companies should make it known that they expect their business partners to comply with all national laws and regulations – including labour and environmental laws – and, as appropriate, to take into account principles from relevant international instruments, which may sometimes go beyond local legislation.

These instruments include the International Labour Organization (ILO) Declaration on Fundamental Principles and Rights at Work, other ILO conventions and the Universal Declaration of Human Rights. Another useful reference is the Global Compact and its '10 principles' covering human rights, labour standards, the environment and anti-corruption.

A company can also adopt a supplier code of conduct. Before doing so, it should consider the possible difficulties for suppliers to comply with the proliferation of such codes and their requirements.

Step three: integrate responsible sourcing into buying practices

By integrating responsible sourcing into its own buying practices, a company should avoid undermining the capacity of suppliers to respect social and environmental standards. Inefficient practices, such as rush orders, last-minute changes or placing orders that surpass suppliers' capabilities, which often lead to excessive overtime work and other compliance violations, should be avoided.

Step four: support suppliers in setting their own business standards

A company should encourage suppliers to develop their own responsible practices rather than imposing requirements on them. In doing so, it is essential to stress the commercial benefits of responsible business practices on quality, productivity, contract renewals and lowering employee turnover.

To help them internalize change, suppliers should be directly involved in the shaping of performance objectives. This way, suppliers can integrate these objectives into their own business strategy, based on their individual capacity and needs. If useful, a company can provide training to its suppliers to help them improve their management practices and performance.

In sectors where labour or health and safety risks may be present further down the supply chain, a company can also work with its direct suppliers to ensure that social and environmental considerations in turn play a role in their relations with second- and third-tier suppliers.

Step five: track supplier compliance

Companies can ask their suppliers to provide comprehensive information about their social and environmental practices. On-site visits can also be organized to monitor suppliers' progress, or lack of it, in meeting social and environmental performance objectives. Evaluating this information may become part of a company's regular assessments of business requirements, such as quality control.

To make performance checks truly effective, companies should involve their suppliers' factory management and workers in monitoring, and give them the training and tools to develop their own compliance system and to raise problems should they occur.

Taking a risk-based approach can help with a large base of suppliers when monitoring social and environmental compliance. Companies should focus on high-risk suppliers rather than monitoring across the board, as well as on suppliers in charge of the main steps in the production process.

A company can save monitoring costs by collaborating with other companies from the same sector and developing common approaches for auditing suppliers.

To harmonize monitoring practices and ease the compliance burden of suppliers, several sector associations have brought together manufacturers of branded goods, suppliers, retailers and customers with a view to developing common tools and rationalizing supply chain requirements.

Initiatives which bring together non-governmental organizations, trade unions and companies can also help encourage dialogue and build overall confidence in the compliance process.

Step six: manage stakeholder expectations and reporting

To build customer trust, companies can collect information on supplier performance across markets, and publish it in an annual report or other publicly available format. Reporting efforts should be used to measure performance and flag areas for improvement.

Some companies also choose to validate their first- or second-party monitoring (audits conducted by the company or on behalf of a company by another organization) by third-party monitoring (conducted by independent bodies). A company's strategy in this area will often be shaped by the way it manages its broader stakeholder relationships – for example, its relations with consumers and local communities.

Conclusion

Through these six practical steps, companies can go a long way towards securing the efficiency and sustainability of their supply chains. Building effective supplier relationships, based on mutual trust and continuous improvement, is a central element in enabling businesses to manage the social and environmental impacts of their activities along their production chains.

Today, as consumers care more and more about how their purchases were made – not only how much they cost – responsible sourcing is increasingly seen as an integral component of companies' overall business model. Tomorrow, as global trade continues to expand and supply chains continue to extend, the ability of companies to manage their supplier relationships in a responsible way will play a key role in maintaining public support for globalization and open trade.

E7 | Trade, international capital flows and risk management

THIERRY MALLERET*

As with all good risk management, dealing successfully with the risks that stem from trade and international capital flows boils down to a set of simple, yet vital, rules: (1) recognition that risk thinking must be an integral part of the organization's culture; (2) adequate alignment of risk assessment, management and communication; (3) correct assessment of the vulnerabilities; (4) creation of partnerships – in today's interdependent world, no stakeholder is powerful enough to mitigate risks on their own; (5) cultivate and exploit knowledge and networks; (6) be aware of the many cognitive biases that affect human decisions in conditions of uncertainty; (7) puncture denial (which is our most common strategy for dealing with risk) by being prepared and acting fast; (8) display humility.[1] While the first four are merely organizational the last are more 'attitudinal' and thus their implementation is directly dependent on the traits of those who lead the business or govern the organization. Ultimately, good risk management – that is, the ability to strike the right balance between risk taking and risk mitigation – rests upon the capacity of the leadership to adapt to a world characterized by greater volatility and uncertainty in which new risks emerge continually and at a bewildering pace.

Contingent with the globalization of trade and capital flows, new 'global' risks have emerged. They can be defined as events with the potential to affect a range of industries in several countries or regions and which may inflict major economic and social damage in some or all of these. Many such risks have been repeatedly in the headlines

* Thierry Malleret is a Senior Partner and Head of Research and Networks at IJ Partners (IJ stands for Informed Judgement). It is an investment company based in Geneva that offers its clients the possibility to invest in liquid and direct investments.
[1] These eight 'key success factors' are derived from: Sean Cleary and Thierry Malleret (2007) *Global Risk – Business Success in Turbulent Times*, New York: Palgrave Macmillan, pp. 139–54.

since the turn of the millennium: pandemics such as swine flu, terrorism, natural disasters such as tsunamis, failed and failing states, oil-
price spikes and, of course, all the deleterious effects associated with
climate change. These risks reinforce one another through complex
interactions and 'ricochet' effects. They all share the commonality of
being capable of inflicting major damage on trade and capital investment by restricting their flows. How do companies and other institutions deal with them?

At the time of writing (mid-August 2009), international trade and
capital flows have retrenched significantly. Both are recovering at a
snail's pace from the collapse of the previous year – most countries are
experiencing slightly higher trade volumes and capital flows than in
2008, but levels remain far below those of 2007. When might the global economy get back to the levels last seen in 2007? We don't know.
In this short article, I explore a counterintuitive, if not outright provocative, idea: paradoxically, the best way for global companies and
governments to manage all the new risks associated with trade and
international capital flows may be to 'de-globalize', creating in turn
a negative feedback loop that will restrict the flows of international
trade and capital. In effect, the combination of a profound economic
downturn and the growing concerns about how best to mitigate the
impact of global risks may force global companies to restructure their
supply chains in their entirety by progressively abandoning global
supply chains in favour of regional ones – a move supported by governments which are starting to raise tariffs, to increase subsidies and,
more perniciously, to impose non-tariff barriers (protectionism by
stealth par excellence). Many states also actively engage in economic
nationalism, with the associated risk of a new mercantilist system
centred on credit availability as many banks are *de facto* nationalized
and unwilling to lend abroad.

'Going more local' may thus become a new risk mitigation strategy, blessed by various national governments, for all those companies
involved in international trade and capital flows. We see this phenomenon as a potentially significant new global trend.

To illustrate the point, take one of the most significant global
risks: climate change. Whether one agrees or not that the phenomenon is human-induced, companies have to adapt, no matter what (if
they do not, governments are likely to force them to do so through
regulation). Apart from the substantial reputational risks it poses for

companies that remain in denial and refuse to address the issue, global warming is now causing immediate concerns over energy supply.
As oil prices increase, companies are forced to reconsider the extent
to which they should globalize their supply chain. Gerard Kleisterlee,
the CEO of Philips, puts it bluntly: 'a future where energy is more
expensive and less plentifully available will lead to more regional supply chains'.[2] In a world with more expensive transport costs, Mexico,
for example, becomes competitive with China to supply the USA.
Equally, a world in which a pandemic could easily entail the closing of
some borders (it happened with SARS in 2003) requires companies to
consider sacrificing greater cost efficiencies for the benefit of securing
their supplies in a disruptive environment. In short, risk mitigation
associated with the vagaries of trade and capital flows will constitute
a tendency by global companies to substitute global supply chains
with regional ones. The reasons are twofold: (1) it's probably easier to
master the intricacies of your supply chain when it is relatively close
by, rather than at a distance (a reason why some multinationals now
favour Eastern Europe over China for supplying the EU); (2) it makes
a lot of sense for a company to reduce its carbon footprint (70 per cent
of it comes from transport and associated costs in the supply chain)
to go local.

Globally integrated supply chains may well follow the fate of complex financial products: they won't be condemned to oblivion, but their
influence will wane. Both were supposed to generate greater efficiencies and to disperse the risk, but in fact did just the opposite. As one
study conducted by the World Economic Forum concluded: 'supply
chains frequently appear to disperse risk between multiple parties but
they can also lead to an unrecognized aggregation of risk'.[3] As manufacturing becomes ever more dependent on cross-border systems of
production intended to make business more efficient by placing each
stage of production in the region where it can be most profitably per-
formed, risks become overly concentrated. Many manufacturers are
now realizing that dealing with a crisis is exponentially more difficult
when companies are scattered round the globe. This phenomenon –
known as 'risk squeezing' in the literature – means that the risk is not
properly mitigated, but simply displaced to new centres of production

[2] As quoted in the *Financial Times*, 10 August 2009.
[3] See World Economic Forum (2008) *Global Risk Report*.

where costs, standards and conditions are lower. The risk is therefore not eliminated, but transferred, which poses an ethical dilemma and strong reputational issues for the companies that engage in this 'risk squeezing' process. Taking again the example of the environment, it makes little sense for a Western company to improve air and water quality in its home country if it exports the problem to a factory in China. In so doing not only is little or nothing achieved towards a risk-adjusted sustainability of economic growth (a toxic spill in a Chinese river will pollute agriculture and might ultimately enter into the production of goods for global exports or threaten the water supply of a neighbouring country), but also and more significantly could entail reputational damage for the company.

As bankers and economists start to rethink many assumptions underpinning the functioning of globally integrated capital markets, business and political leaders may rethink their dependency on globally integrated supply chains: while they do provide important cost efficiencies, they also raise very substantial downside risks.

E8 | Trade, corporate strategies and development

MICHAEL GARRETT*

Globalization, a positive force for development

Despite the critics of globalization, an objective review of its achievements over the past two decades reveals it has been a positive force for progress and prosperity in the world. Expressed in simple terms, globalization has been responsible for raising productivity levels, revolutionizing communications, increasing competition and boosting global economic growth and interdependence through trade and foreign direct investment (FDI) flows. Most importantly, globalization has created additional employment opportunities which have helped lift millions of poor people out of poverty in the developing world.

The facilitators of globalization included the international integration of capital markets during the early to mid 1980s followed shortly by the globalization of the manufacturing industry ('companies trade, countries don't') during the late 1980s and early 1990s. In turn this was followed by the emergence of regionalization (North America and Mexico; Western Europe; and South/North East Asia including Oceania) that took place during the early to mid 1990s (Kenichi Ohmae's *The Borderless World* – published in June 1990), by which time intra-regional trade had grown to three times that of the total of world trade.

Globalization could not have taken place on the scale and speed at which it did without the political leadership and will to adopt open market principles in place of centrally planned/import substitution-based economics. Support for this new liberal economic thinking was expressed through GATT (the Global Agreement on Tariffs and

---

* Michael Garrett joined the Nestlé group in the UK in 1961. During his forty-four years with the company he held many positions including Market Head in Australia, Japan and ending his career an EVP responsible for Asia, Africa, Middle East and Oceania. He is also co-Chairman of the Evian Group.

268

Trade), which was founded with the objective of putting in place a multilateral rules-based framework for trade, and the conclusion of the Uruguay Round in 1994.

Asia's economic miracle

Never far behind the resurgence of Japan, Asia's economic 'miracle' actually coincided with the very period in which capital, technology and markets began to globalize. And faced with enormous social and economic challenges, the region's visionary leaders responded to developments taking place in the rest of the world with both speed and pragmatism ('It doesn't matter if a cat is black or white so long as it catches mice' – Deng Xiaoping).

In so doing the Association of Southeast Asian Nations (ASEAN) was established in August 1967 in Bangkok. The Founding Fathers included Indonesia, Malaysia, the Philippines, Singapore and Thailand. In addition to the goal of 'accelerating economic growth, social progress and cultural development' articulated in ASEAN's statement of purpose was the ambition 'to collaborate more effectively for the greater utilization of agriculture and industry, expansion of trade, study of the problems of international commodity trade, improvement of communication facilities and raising of people's living standards'.

Nestlé's commitment to Southeast Asia

At that time, as the Director responsible for the Nestlé business activities in Asia and Oceania, it was my responsibility to develop a long-term strategy for our company within the region. This vision not only had to understand the social and economic 'landscape' of the different markets but also be consistent with the development objectives of each of the member states. Finally, to be successful it should also achieve the business and financial goals of our company.

Given our long-term presence throughout the ASEAN region, first trading (early 1900s), later manufacturing (1950s onwards), Nestlé was not only familiar but also a highly respected company by both government and consumers alike. In fact in Malaysia, as well as being among the most highly capitalized companies on the stock market, Nestlé sales represented no less than 1 per cent of the country's total

GDP. This was probably unique in the world for a nutrition, food and beverage company.

Therefore with this 'insider' knowledge we came to develop a major strategic investment initiative under the ASEAN Industrial Joint Venture (AIJV) scheme. Within this framework, Nestlé put up a production plant with regional capacity in each of the five Asian countries. The idea was to become the regional production centre for a particular product to be distributed not only within ASEAN but also other Asian countries.

So Indonesia was picked to produce soya-based beverages; Malaysia, chocolate wafers (Kit Kat) and chocolate dragees (Smarties); Singapore, soy sauce powder and malt extract; Thailand, non-dairy creamer; and the Philippines, breakfast cereals. The products were selected so the benefits would accrue not only to ASEAN as a whole but also to each member country. The location of each of the plants was determined according to demand patterns, marketing and sales force capabilities, as well as closeness to raw and packaging material suppliers and, importantly, labour skills.

Some two decades since the first factory was commissioned, the AIJV project can be assessed as having achieved the following benefits:

• Consumers were provided with a wider choice for products at lower, more affordable prices;
• Substantial economies of scale were achieved as the whole of the ASEAN region became the marketplace;
• Pricing for ASEAN manufactured products was more competitive than those imported from outside the region;
• Long-term capital inflows and large savings in foreign exchange were achieved for both the host and participating countries;
• Greater use of local raw materials;
• Systematic transfer of technology, adding value to products made from indigenous raw materials; and
• Development of small and medium local enterprises.

Just one of the benefits of the AIJV project accruing to the Nestlé Group was the management of highly complex supply chains. Managing this level of complexity would have been impossible without:

• The advances made in modern logistics systems, in particular 'containerization', which provided for the smooth cross-border transfer of raw/packaging materials as well as finished goods between supplier, production centre and the market.

• Quantum leaps in information technology coupled with lower telecommunications costs were key enablers providing us with the means to handle vast amounts of data implicit in the process.

The outcome of this very ambitious project was a 'win' for the people of the ASEAN countries; a 'win' for Nestlé's business partners and stakeholders, including government; and a 'win' for Nestlé and our shareholders. Also the successful implementation was a powerful demonstration of how much of the development agenda of a country can be achieved when the objectives of the private sector are fully aligned with those of government and when the 'rules of the game' are clearly articulated in advance. Only then can corporations commit to long-term strategic investments to the benefit of all stakeholders, including civil society.

Enormous challenges ahead

One of the major challenges facing the world is food security. According to the Food and Agriculture Organization (FAO), in 2003 around 850 million people were critically hungry due to extreme poverty, while up to two billion people lacked food security intermittently due to varying degrees of poverty. As at the end of 2007, increased farming for use in biofuels, population growth, climate change, loss of agricultural land for residential and industrial development as well as growing demand in China and India, have all contributed to pushing up raw material prices to such an extent that food riots have broken out in many countries throughout the world.

Were this not enough, the world's population is set to reach 9 billion by mid-century. Scientists estimate we need to double food production by the year 2030.

To do this we need another 'green revolution' similar to that of the early 1960s when India was on the brink of mass famine. At that time, through what later became known as the 'green revolution', farm productivity was dramatically increased through a rigorous process of plant selection, use of fertilizers and irrigation. Supported by the Indian government, this application of science and technology saved millions of lives.

What will success look like?

Given the interrelated problems of global trade imbalances, poverty and population growth, not to mention food security, water shortage and climate change, the challenges are greater today than they were the 1960s. The scale and complexity of these problems are too big for governments or industry to solve alone. New coalitions will need to be formed between the public and private sectors and civil society to constructively address the issues. New business models will have to be found and innovations in science and technology will provide the platforms to deal with the problems of a world with finite resources.

Until present, growth has been achieved more or less 'at any cost'. In future our goals for development must be achieved through 'balanced', 'inclusive' and 'sustainable' growth. Any alternative is not an option.

E9 | *How can trade lead to inclusive growth?*

RAVI CHAUDHRY[*]

The global crisis of 2008–2009 gave firm credence to a commonly held perception that business objectives and society's needs tend to be like the two tracks of a railway line. Looking ahead from any point, they appear to converge in the distance; in reality, they never do.

One always expected that the regulatory framework created and monitored by the state was ostensibly meant to prevent such excesses – but it transpired that the elected representatives of the people were either willing collaborators or silent spectators; they merely watched and, through sheer lethargy or complicity, ended up in accelerating the downslide well beyond the financial sector. The question that continuously haunts us today is whether businesspeople and politicians have learnt any lessons. The well-entrenched conventional wisdom that it is perfectly legal to maximize profits, irrespective of the consequences on others, continues to be the driving force that prompts all actions and steers all policies.

The World Trade Organization (WTO) has the unique opportunity to revitalize and rechannellize its approach and put together a new dialogue framework – one that transcends the erstwhile system of one nation disagreeing with another, lobbyists with contrarian narrow interests arguing with each other, and businesspeople solely focused on how they can continue to keep emerging competitors at bay.

Fundamentally, the new dialogue calls for a paradigm shift, with the spotlight radically shifting from 'what a nation needs' to 'what humanity needs'.

---

[*] Ravi Chaudhry, the Founder Chairman of CeNext Consulting Group, is based in New Delhi, India. Prior to that, he was CEO/Chairman of five companies in the Tata Group. He has served on the boards of several corporations and organizations. He is a Member of the Evian Group Brains Trust on Fair Global Trade; and Convener, Future500 India – a global initiative to generate social consciousness in business. He is passionately committed to improving the state of corporate governance.

I put forth four thoughts to take this concept forward and call upon all to deliberate upon these and help generate a movement to give a decisive push forward.

1. G-20 leadership alone can provide the new vision

Interlocutors and negotiators engaged in the Doha Round discussions need new instructions and guidelines from their national leaders. G-20 leaders hold the key. More than anyone else in the world, they are acutely conscious that the destiny of humanity is more intertwined than ever before and the sustained growth of their citizens is henceforth contingent only on collective growth. No nation can grow in isolation any more. Together, they have this unique historic moment today to re-invent the role of state leadership. Can they rise above the din of the lobbyists and the constricted vision of business leaders and genuinely pursue the UN Millennium Goals? Even from nationalistic perspectives, an unbiased analysis would clearly show that such actions are in the interest of an overwhelming majority of their citizens.

I invite the G-20 leaders to embrace a new way of leadership, one that looks upon all dialogue as a dialogue among humans, of humans, for humans.

Not humans that belong to a particular country, firm or organization, but humans that comprise the entirety of humanity. Even if a few of the G-20 leaders take this stance, the rest will find it hard to disagree. Jointly, they hold the power to irrevocably upgrade the level of dialogue among themselves and with others. Their 'new vision' will generate a Jurassic spark to create a new set of global leaders in every domain – leaders who are genuinely more conscious of the needs and perspectives of the 'silent majorities', the underprivileged and the marginalized people all over the globe. Merely doing more of what we have been doing will not help us escape from the trappings of prevalent logic and the tyranny of analytical thinking.

The clarion call is: 'Leaders of the G-20: unite and lead.'

2. The WTO creates an alternate group to
propose Doha Round Draft Agreement

It is proposed that the WTO creates an Alternate Standing Group representing the non-state viewpoints from across the world, comprising people who have the maturity to understand both the humane ethos to bring about equity through fair trade as well as the complex issues relating to the Agreement being acceptable in countries whose stated position is ostensibly different. The Group is envisaged to include realistic thought-leaders and collators of collective wisdom from all regions and cultures, and creators of practical planet-encompassing programmes for transforming our world.

The 'neo-colonial' economic thought that still manages to transfer wealth from 'those at subsistence to those in affluence' must be dispensed with. The central yardstick in their recommendations must necessarily be based on the following premise.

The deprived three billion people of the world, who are not a part of the growth story, will no longer accept poverty as destiny.

Quite rightly so, as it cannot be a divine plan that they are to be consigned to the realm of permanent destitution. Their condition is a consequence of humankind's deliberate actions, and the leaders of humankind must set the imbalance right. 'Poverty is not merely a shortage of incomes. We have to see it as unfreedom of various sorts … These gross asymmetries do not correct themselves. Whether your actions contributed to inequality or whether you see and tolerate this, both are equally to blame.'[1]

The Group must ensure that the livelihoods of 1.4 billion people in the developing world living in 'poverty that kills' (earning less than US$1.25 a day) and another 1.5 billion people living in moderate poverty (earning US$1.25 to US$2 a day) are not compromised.[2] It is likely that the interests of a few large transnational corporations may be affected by such decisions, but it is time they willingly accept these changes. They have unprecedented global reach and power; they need to re-calibrate their business and profit objectives and start using their energies and clout in the larger interests of human society. They should do this because they will soon discover that these policies are compatible with their long-term, sustainable interest.

---

[1] Quoted from Amartya Sen's Foreword in *From Poverty to Power – How Active Citizens and Effective States can Change the World* by Duncan Green (2008). New Delhi: Academic Foundation.
[2] The data on poverty is based on World Bank Report: August 2008.

The Alternate Group must ensure that it does not evolve into a networking event. It must take cognizance of all divergent views, and evolve a practical, convergent viewpoint. Its recommendation of a *Draft Doha Round Agreement will focus not merely on greater global trade volumes – but more on global trade that is equitable and does not call upon the underprivileged 3 billion people to make any sacrifices or wait until the next round of trade talks.* Their 'development' is the prime motivator of the Doha Round and the proposed Agreement must reflect that as transparently and as effectively as possible.

How should such an alternate group be constituted? I propose that the WTO Director-General should appoint a five-member Selection Panel of genuinely respected, non-controversial, unbiased distinguished leaders, who in turn would choose a twenty-one-member panel comprising different viewpoints and nationalities – but all of them committed to seeking an accord in a short time frame, within the framework of the parameters outlined above.

3. Independent NGOs to create Domestic Enabling Trade Index

The Global Enabling Trade Report[3] has created a thoughtfully designed Enabling Trade Index (ETI) for each nation. The ETI measures the institutions, policies and services facilitating the free flow of goods over borders and to final destinations. It was developed within the context of the World Economic Forum's Industry Partnership Programme for the Logistics and Transport Sector. The index mirrors the main enablers of trade, breaking them into four overall domains: market access, border administration, transport and communications infrastructure, and business environment.

It is proposed that a group of NGOs should evolve a similar Domestic Enabling Trade Index for all emerging economies with a population above 30 million. It could well be that certain countries have such inhibiting trade provisions within their own countries that the real benefits of liberalized global trade structure cannot be realized. The

---

[3] *The Global Enabling Trade Report* 2009 © 2009, World Economic Forum.

purpose would be to force the pace of reform in such countries against benchmarked practices elsewhere that have made 'domestic trade as an aid to equity'.

4. WTO 'aid for trade' initiative to be rechristened 'aid and trade for development'

It has been increasingly felt that the 'aid for trade' programme, a worthy initiative launched in 2005, is somehow getting geared to donors' interests – rather than towards development and poverty reduction. Results are measured by trade facilitation and trade creation, instead of creating long-term indigenous trading strengths based on improving the skills and quality of added value products that would create employment among the poorest of the poor.

While the initiative should continue, there is a case for sensitizing the donors to take a more holistic and generous view. A selfless view, if possible. A name change is proposed to focus on *'inclusive development'* rather than merely trade, and realign the plans and priorities accordingly.

Humankind has unlimited capacity to form bonds and cooperate. It is for us to remove the fear of domination through trade and rekindle hope among the masses by clearly demonstrating that those who are better off are ready to lend a helping hand to make the lives of the less well off better.

We, the privileged ones in this generation, have the opportunity to reverse the tide of history, provided we succeed in emulating the inherent nobility of the masses and align ourselves with their most basic aspirations.

Let those who have wealth try to create more wealth for others than for themselves. Let those who have power wield it in such a way that they empower others so that together they use that power to achieve shared goals.

This is the challenge – the challenge of transition from today's rule-bound dialogue to a new humane era of dialogue where business objectives and society's needs are in sync with each other and with nature. This transition hinges on *exercising our right to make the right choices*. In an inter-dependent world, making the right choice on key issues is not just a commercial or philosophical exercise; it is

a matter of the quality of life of the human race. More than that, it
is a matter of survival for the human race, including our own.

> You've heard it said there's a window
> That opens from one mind to another,
> But if there's no wall, there's no need
> For fitting the window, or the latch.
>   Rumi

E10 | Trade and human rights: friends or foes?

CÉLINE CHARVÉRIAT AND
ROMAIN BENICCHIO*

Nearly all the member countries of the WTO have signed the 1948 Universal Declaration on Human Rights. To the extent that trade boosts or hinders these rights, WTO members have a collective responsibility to ensure that world trade rules are consistent with human rights obligations. Yet the phrase 'human rights' continues to raise eyebrows at the WTO, as if the fulfilment of political, economic, social and cultural rights were foreign to, or inherently contradictory with, the pursuit of increased world trade flows and a rules-based trading system.

The reticence of many governments to take into account human rights in trade negotiations is probably linked with the long-standing use of unilateral trade sanctions to pursue a variety of public policy goals including international security or the respect for human rights. Indeed, trade sanctions have been used for centuries: in 432 BC Pericles enacted a decree banning trade with Megara in order to protest against the kidnapping of Aspasian women.[1] Since World War I, there have been more than 170 cases of economic sanctions including trade, investment, or travel restrictions. Most of them have been applied unilaterally.[2] Most recently, a number of developed countries have decided to withdraw trade preferences or offer increased market access based on the respect of human rights by exporting countries. Even with the best of intentions, these initiatives have convinced many developing country governments that rich country governments want to use human rights as a tool to threaten their sovereignty or to shut them out of their markets.

---

* Céline Charvériat is Deputy Advocacy and Campaigns Director of Oxfam International. Romain Benicchio works for Oxfam International as a policy and media advisor working on trade, access to medicines and climate change.
[1] Gary Clyde Hufbauer, Jeffrey J. Schott, Kimberly Ann Elliott and Barbara Oegg (2007) *Economic Sanctions Reconsidered*. The Peterson Institute.
[2] *Ibid.*

279

In spite of this, freer trade and the respect for human rights should not be seen as antithetic. In fact, the ultimate goal of both trade and human rights is to improve the wellbeing of individuals and communities. The preamble of the 1994 WTO agreement states that the objectives of this agreement are to 'raise standards of living, ensure full employment and a large and steadily growing volume of real income and effective demand, and expand the production of and trade in goods and services, while allowing for the optimal use of the world's resources in accordance with the objective of sustainable development ...'[3]

Indeed, under the right conditions, increased trade flows can be a powerful tool towards greater prosperity. Greater market access for developing country products, whether at the local, national, regional or international level, can provide new livelihood opportunities and contribute to lifting millions of people out of poverty, allowing them to fulfil their right to development. Asian countries such as China, whose trade with the rest of the world has boomed over the past two decades, have made great progress towards poverty reduction. Across China, there are over 400 million fewer people living in extreme poverty than two decades ago. Trade expansion has undoubtedly played an important role in such an achievement. Similarly, cases abound where the lifting of protectionist measures would provide a conducive environment for poverty reduction and human rights. US cotton subsidies, which artificially lower world prices, hurt small farmers' livelihoods in West Africa.[4] In Palestine, trade restrictions imposed by Israel are impeding on the right to food and development.[5]

Moreover, the respect for basic human rights can be an important step to stimulate the growth of markets and international trade, creating a virtuous circle between trade and human rights. An educated, healthy and informed workforce, with more sustainable means of existence, leads to greater demand for both domestic and imported goods.

---

[3] Agreement Establishing the WTO (1994).
[4] Realizing Rights and 3D (2004) *US and EU Production and Export Policies and their Impact on West and Central Africa: Coming to Grips with International Human Rights Obligations.*
[5] Oxfam (2007) *Breaking the Impasse. Ending the Humanitarian Stranglehold on Palestine.*

Is trade sufficient to ensure the fulfilment of human rights?

There is ample evidence that trade – on its own – is not sufficient to ensure the fulfilment of human rights. In some specific cases, trade can actually hurt human rights. For instance, unregulated trade can contribute to the depletion of natural resources, endanger public health, or fuel wars. This is why rules are so essential.

This was clearly recognized by the 1947 GATT agreement, which provided for exemptions to protect human, animal or plant life or health; to prevent exports of goods made by prisoners; to promote the conservation of exhaustible natural resources; and to maintain international peace and security.

In fact, these exemptions have successfully been used to regulate trade and fulfil the human rights obligations of WTO member countries on several occasions. For instance, WTO rules were waived in 2003 to approve the outcomes of the Kimberley Process, an international agreement regulating the diamond trade in an effort to stop war in Sierra Leone, Angola and the DRC. Similarly, the WTO Dispute Settlement body ruled in 2001 against Canada's claim regarding a French ban on imports of asbestos on the grounds that the WTO agreements authorize trade restrictions if their objective is to protect human health.[6]

Within the Doha Round, members have also directly or indirectly referred to human rights in the negotiations. For instance, the 2001 Declaration on Intellectual Property and Public Health clearly established the primacy of public health over IPR rules, and clarified rules contained in the TRIPS agreement so that patents would no longer be an impediment to access to generic medicines in the developing world. In the agricultural negotiations, there has also been a recognition that developing countries might need to maintain tariffs on *special products* in order to protect small farmers' livelihoods and promote food security.[7]

---

[6] 3D (2004) *Righting Trade, Avenues for Action in: Practical Guide to the WTO.*

[7] WTO (2001) Doha Declaration on TRIPS and Public Health; WTO (2005) Hong Kong Ministerial Declaration.

Practice versus theory – a yawning gap

One might prematurely conclude from the evidence presented above that the issue of human rights is adequately dealt with in the world trading system through an adequate balancing of the goals of freer trade and human rights requirements. Unfortunately this is not the case: while theoretically signing on to the principles above, most countries ignore human rights principles in the course of defining trade policies or positions within trade negotiations. As a result, taking into account human rights implications remains an exception rather than the norm both at the national and international levels.

At the domestic level, serious assessments of human rights implications of trade policies and rules are still too rare. For instance, most developing countries fail to assess the impact of trade policies on the most vulnerable populations and therefore fail to protect vital sectors or, at the very least, provide for training, investment policies or social protection measures that might be necessary in the case of job or business displacement linked with an increase in import competition.

In the Doha Round of trade negotiations, member countries have too often ignored that trade negotiations should be conducted under the 'presumption of good faith', which means that all countries should act consistently with their existing human rights obligations, and should not seek rules that would lead other countries to violate their human rights obligations. For instance, in the agricultural negotiations, both the EU and the USA, alongside some net exporting developing countries, have pushed for limiting the ability of developing countries to keep high tariffs on *special products*, thereby making this crucial provision, meant to help poorer countries protect small farmers' livelihoods, almost meaningless. This has sparked concerns by many stakeholders, including NGOs such as Oxfam and the UN Special Rapporteur on Food.[8]

In the case of essential medicines, even though all WTO members have signed on to the Doha Declaration, and there is ample evidence that the increased availability of generics was saving lives, most rich countries have done very little to implement the Declaration in practice

---

[8] Report of the Special Rapporteur on the Right to Food, Addendum, Mission to the World Trade Organization, 25 June 2008.

and have, in some cases, created new barriers to the trade of generic medicines. The United States imposed restrictive IPR rules on other countries within FTA agreements, or threatened with trade sanctions and withdrawal of trade preferences countries that were trying in good faith to implement public health safeguards included under the Declaration.[9] Countries in the European Union have recently blocked generic medicines transiting over their territory under the spurious argument that these might be counterfeit goods.[10]

What role for the business community?

While governments hold the primary responsibility of ensuring respect for human rights in trade policies and negotiations, the business community has a very important role to play.

At the moment, the loudest voices within the business community on trade issues are often those defending narrow protectionist measures in an effort to thwart import competition or seek market access at all costs, even if it leads to violations of human rights. These special interests are too rarely counterbalanced by the voices of the silent majority that would benefit from more balanced, mutually beneficial trade agreements and rules.

As a result, some might argue that there is too much lobbying by the International Chamber of Commerce (ICC) and other business groups. Actually there is probably not enough. But businesses, like governments, should lobby under the presumption of good faith. They should argue for the kind of policies and rules that would make the world trading system fairer and more transparent so that it can lead to full employment and raised living standards for all, better health and education standards, and a preserved environment.

---

[9] Oxfam (2005) *Patents vs. Patients Five Years After the Doha Declaration.*
[10] 'Dutch Seizure of HIV Drugs Highlights Patent Friction', *Financial Times,* 5 March 2009.

E11 | *Trade: the spirit and rule of law*

VALÉRIE ENGAMMARE*

Often referred to but seldom defined, the rule of law is much more than a mere legal concept. As developed by the Enlightenment thinkers, it sets certain requirements regarding the organization of the state, in particular the separation of powers. Today, in addition to its political and institutional meaning, the economic dimension of the rule of law is widely acknowledged, and it is considered to be a key component of a sound business environment. The rule of law calls for the existence of transparent, predictable, general and enforceable laws. It also implies that laws be applied in a fair and coherent manner by governmental bodies, whose actions can be challenged before the courts. Under the rule of law, the enforcement of rights and obligations is guaranteed by an independent, well-functioning and accessible judiciary. These elements provide safeguards against arbitrary decisions, contribute to deter corruption and ensure that contracts can be enforced. They are part of a good investment climate and may – in a long-term perspective – contribute to growth and economic development. The rule of law is indeed only one factor among others for prosperity – many countries have developed despite a weak rule of law; however, in the long run, a deficient legal framework and weak institutions can only have a negative impact on an economy.

While traditionally considered primarily as a matter of domestic governance, the rule of law has gained relevance in the international context as well since the second half of the twentieth century, when an unprecedented expansion of international law took place and the

* Valérie Engammare has been advisor at the international economic law section of the Swiss State Secretariat for Economic Affairs since 2007. In 2004, she obtained her Ph.D. in international investment law from the University of Zurich. Between 2002 and 2007, she was Research Fellow and then Associate Fellow at the Evian Group.

The views expressed in this article are those of the author and do not necessarily reflect those of the State Secretariat for Economic Affairs.

major multilateral institutions were created. This expansion has been most significant in the trade field. The first treaties of commerce date back from the Roman Empire and the most-favoured nation principle was already enshrined in the bilateral commerce and navigation treaties concluded at the end of the nineteenth century. International trade law, however, experienced its most drastic developments after World War II, with the adoption of the GATT and the multilateralization of trade law, which led to the establishment of the WTO. The multilateral trading system is probably the most complete example of concretization of the rule of law existing at the global level: it includes a comprehensive body of rules, a high degree of institutionalization and, most of all, a sophisticated dispute settlement mechanism. A rules-based multilateral system is very valuable as such for the development of peaceful trade relations, but it also has a positive impact on the rule of law at the domestic level: the prospect of joining the WTO does provide acceding countries with a strong incentive for undertaking legal and institutional reforms. The WTO and its functioning as they stand today are indeed far from perfect. However, to date, the multilateral trading system remains the most consummate example of a multilateral regime.

The system and its institutions are bound to continuously evolve and adapt to the changes happening in the global economic environment. The developments that took place over the last few decades – growing economic interdependence; technological change; the emergence of new non-state actors on the global stage, such as multinationals or non-governmental organizations; global challenges such as climate change, pandemics, the imperatives of and development – require constant adaptations of the system and of the body of rules on which it rests. In addition, these trends translate into a number of challenges for the rule of law embodied in the multilateral trading system.

First, since the creation of the WTO in 1995, there has been a considerable *quantitative* expansion of world trade law: 271 regional trade agreements have been notified to the WTO up to February 2010 and are currently in force; taking into account agreements that have been notified and that are not yet in force, this brings the number to a total of 462 trade agreements. Never before has the nexus of trade instruments been so large and complex. One can indeed argue that such a development should both strengthen the rule of law in international trade and foster trade liberalization. However, it also creates an environment that is increasingly complex to deal with for business as well as for members of the WTO. Ensuring coherence between the different sets of rules as well as a legal environment that is practicable for its stakeholders – in particular business – and, above all, maintaining a system that is open and inclusive should be a priority for members of the WTO.

Second, international trade law has also experienced a significant *qualitative* development over the last two decades. In a globalized environment, the linkages between trade and other issues must be taken into account. Today, trade no longer amounts to trade in goods, as was the case in the old treaties of commerce. It goes well beyond. Disciplines on intellectual property protection, trade-related investment measures, electronic commerce, movement of natural persons or government procurement are now part of the WTO corpus of rules. Discussions are taking place on whether and how trade disciplines should take into account issues such as environmental concerns, human rights or health. In addition, trade relations do involve a great variety of trading partners having different interests, needs and levels of economic development. These developments make both the international debate and the policy-making process more complex. They also highlight the need for greater coherence between the different sets of rules and international institutions dealing with these topics. In the perspective of the rule of law, the opening of the trade debate to other issues also implies a reflection on what kind of values trade rules should convey. The idea that the rule of law should not only have a formal meaning, but should also embody some moral values, has been defended for instance by Nobel Prize winner Friedrich Hayek, who referred to the rule of law not only as a safeguard, but also as the 'legal embodiment of freedom'. Looking for common moral values should thus also be part of the international trade policy-making process.

Third, the current international legal order is largely inherited from the Westphalian system that emerged in the seventeenth century, based on sovereign nation-states. However, today, state sovereignty can no longer be as absolute as it was in the past. Many issues go well beyond the boundaries of nation-states, making international cooperation indispensable. This is the case, for instance, for the regulation of global markets, environmental and energy issues or poverty reduction. At the same time, states are no longer the sole international actors.

Many players, such as non-governmental organizations, multinational enterprises and citizens now interact globally. These players often do challenge the legitimacy of rules made by nation-states. They also give birth to new types of rules, such as codes of conducts elaborated by private companies or associations. These developments call for new forms of governance, able to better take into account the various stakeholders.

Fourth, the rules-based international trading system, despite its high level of sophistication, is very often called into question. Over the past couple of years, unilateral action, not only in economic policy, but also in the political and security fields, has put multilateralism under threat. In the trade field, in particular in times of economic downturn, many states are tempted to take protectionist measures. These measures do not necessarily constitute formal breaches of international obligations. However, they clearly contradict the spirit of an open and non-discriminatory trading system and the core values on which it relies, let alone the long-term interests of all members of the global economic community. To tackle these risks, coalitions defending an open and fair global trading system and committed to its strengthening and improvement are necessary. Business – as a key beneficiary of the system – should play a central role in building such coalitions.

The rule of law is one of the major achievements of the Enlightenment and has not lost relevance over the centuries. The concept has evolved and adapted to the changes happening in the global environment. It is certainly of great relevance to the global trading environment. However, in addressing the challenges that the multilateral trading system faces, a narrow approach should be avoided. The focus of all players should not only be to enforce the rights and obligations that derive from the system, but also, more broadly, to defend its spirit and values, and to engage constructively in continuously strengthening and improving it.

Conclusion: the imperative of inclusive global growth

VICTOR FUNG

As the world enters the second decade of the twenty-first century and approaches the hundredth anniversary of the founding of the ICC, in 2019, there are good reasons why one should feel optimistic. In citing just a few, one would highlight the tremendous impact that information and communication technologies have had on society. The mobile phone has become ubiquitous in all parts of the world and has succeeded in reaching millions of people at the bottom of the pyramid, thereby improving productivity, connectivity and opportunities. Without by any means seeking to minimize the considerable geopolitical threats, comparatively speaking the world is at peace; there are fewer wars currently than at any time since the end of World War II. In particular, there can be hope that the imploding states that seemed endemic to Africa in the 1990s and early 2000s have stabilized and that the continent could be on the verge of sustained growth. China's trade and investments in Africa have contributed considerably to its greater integration in the global economy. Throughout the global South there is the emergence of a new 'middle class', which *The Economist* has estimated at some 1.2 billion people. And without doubt one very important reason for optimism is that the world economy seems to have withstood the greatest shock it has experienced since 1929. The global economic system, therefore, would appear to be resilient.

Realism, however, would also dictate that we should look at the future with considerable caution – even if not, at least not yet, alarm.

The world economy has withstood the global economic crisis of 2008–2009, yes, but it has emerged badly shaken. In the aftermath of the crisis, an estimated additional 200 million people are suffering from chronic malnourishment, bringing the total to 1 billion. While the global economic engine was kept moving as a result of stimulus packages widely applied, it remains to be seen what will happen once they are removed. A major transformation has clearly occurred in the American economy. In the short term it is highly unlikely that American patterns of consumption will resume – thereby distilling its role as consumer market of last resort – and in the medium and longer term it will have to face a colossal debt. And the banking industry, in the USA especially, but also elsewhere, shows no sign that it has learned its lessons or that it will mend its ways.

A grave matter of concern must also be with respect to global governance. The establishment of the G-20 as the locus of global economic management is without doubt a positive and progressive step, yet it remains too early to determine how effective this body will be. Two key issues of the global agenda, trade and climate change, remain in a state of suspense. This is somewhat unnerving especially as a number of thorny issues will without doubt fester, notably that of 'global imbalances'. The spirit of mistrust that appears to permeate the global community's leadership will be an impediment to seeking to solve such really complex issues.

But probably the greatest element of concern is employment, hence social stability and development. Even the more optimistic forecasters of renewed post-crisis economic growth concede that it will be largely jobless. The International Labour Organization (ILO) has estimated that in the course of 2009 unemployment rose between 30 and 50 million. That figure, as the ILO admits, conceals widespread hidden unemployment and pervasive underemployment.

As I noted in the Preface, the ICC vision is that of championing an open global economy as a force for economic growth, job creation and prosperity. In light of current circumstances, there is a strong risk that even in an 'optimistic' scenario, the world economy may experience growth, but without job creation and hence limiting prosperity to a smaller privileged proportion of humanity and expanding the already quite sizeable numbers of excluded. The divisions and inequalities the world suffers from at the moment – with an estimated 50 per cent of the world's population owning less than 1 per cent of its wealth – could become notably worse.

While jobless growth would be a calamity at any time, in fact it would be occurring at the worst possible time. Much of the poverty in the poor and emerging world economies is to be found in the rural areas. India and China combined, notwithstanding their impressive growth records, have about 1.5 billion people living in conditions ranging from dire to relative poverty in the rural areas. For poverty reduction to occur in the developing world there has to be in the course of this decade mass migration from the rural to the urban areas. However, if this migration occurs without job creation – as indeed is happening already to a very considerable extent, resulting in huge sprawling lawless urban slums – it is bound to lead to massive social instability.

Furthermore, this jobless growth will occur at a time when the developing world will be witnessing its biggest ever 'youth dividend'. An estimated 1.2 billion persons will be entering the global labour force this decade. Already in many parts of the world, notably in the volatile Greater Middle East, youth unemployment rates range from 30–70 per cent. This is obviously socially unhealthy and dangerous.

While there may be good reasons, therefore, to see the coming decade through an optimistic lens, there is also good reason to fear that we may be heading for global calamity. Needless to say, rising levels of unemployment whether in the industrialized world or in the developing countries will put pressure on politicians to resort to protectionism.

It would seem therefore that in this coming decade, with a view to realizing the ICC vision of world peace and prosperity through world trade, there is need for adjustment: while still championing an open world economy as a force for economic growth, job creation and prosperity, it is equally incumbent on all *to champion job creation and prosperity as a force for maintaining an open world economy.* Job creation and prosperity will not take place on autopilot. Hence the imperative of inclusive growth.

Whereas the previous decade witnessed the rise in momentum of centripetal forces both between states and to some extent within states, it is clear that in order for inclusive growth to be generated, these centripetal forces will have to be reversed and the world must move to a much more collaborative mode.

Critical in this respect would be to conclude the Doha Development Agenda and in so doing that the global trading powers should commit to a level playing field and that trade, as far as possible, should be a means for economic development, prosperity and job creation.

For that to be achieved, however, policy will not be enough. The next decade should be one where business, public authorities and civil society actively collaborate and engage in fostering inclusive growth. As is implied in the term 'inclusive', the intention must be to provide the poor and currently excluded with the means and opportunities to play constructive roles in economic life. In so doing public authorities must provide proper infrastructure, investment in human capital formation and an administrative regime that fosters rather than impedes enterprise creation, enterprise development, and hence job creation. Businesses must develop new models of inclusive capitalism. The main impetus for this comes not from altering the nature of capitalism or from seeking to diminish the importance of profit generation – in fact, not at all – but rather that profit generation and enterprise development should be promoted on a more long-term perspective. A great bane of the last couple of decades has been the prevailing short-termism. Short-termism ultimately will undermine the long-term prospects of both society and enterprises. Civil society institutions that bring specific experience and expertise should also be actively engaged in this triangular – government–state–NGO – process of employment generation and inclusive growth. The transfer and diffusion of appropriate technologies must clearly play a primary role.

The vision outlined in the previous paragraph is not Utopian. It is well within the bounds of reasonable realism. As I pointed out in the first paragraph, there are good reasons to be optimistic about the coming decade; and I listed a few, all of which provide favourable conditions for generating inclusive growth. Furthermore, there is no need to reinvent the wheel. There are fortunately many examples of enterprises participating with local governments and NGOs in generating inclusive growth. What is needed is to see a multiplication of these initiatives.

It is already clear that this coming decade will pose a number of daunting challenges. To address them successfully and thereby ensure peace and prosperity, there are two absolute imperatives: 1) the world economy must remain open – we must continue to eschew protectionism; 2) growth must be inclusive – jobs must be generated. In 2019, celebrating the hundredth anniversary of the ICC, we must aim to be able to look back on a decade of inclusive globalization.

Index

Abdel-Malek, Talaat, xii, 175
Abdel-Motaal, Doaa, xiii, 191
adjustment costs, 134
Africa
  agricultural productivity, 66, 67, 212, 216–17
  global trade, 62–3, 64–7, 96, 187–8, 289
  infrastructure, xxx–xxxi, 153–7
  pharmaceutical counterfeiting, 166–7
  subsidies, effects of, 280
  water scarcity, 211
  women, 160–1
Africa Growth and Opportunity Act (AGOA), 136, 155
agriculture
  Africa, 66, 67, 212, 216–17
  Brazil, 55–6
  food security, 134–5, 216–17, 271–2, 281
  human rights, 281, 282
  India, 25
  liberalization of trade, 29–30, 31, 207–10
  migration of labour, 15, 122
  subsidies, 42, 115–16, 145, 151, 156, 188–9, 208
  tariffs, 208–9
  water scarcity, 192, 211–15
Ahmad, Manzoor, xiii, 207
aid, 144–8, 151–2, 154, 209, 277–8
Aid for Trade, 146–8, 277–8
Al Kaylani, Haifa Fahoum, xiii, 158
Algeria, 64
Angell, Norman, xxvii
Angola, 64, 281
Anti-Counterfeiting Trade Agreement (ACTA), 110
anti-dumping, 10

apparel, 150–1, 152, 155–6
Appleton, Arthur E., xiii, 245
Arab region, 59–63
Arendt, Hannah, 76
Argentina, 52–3
Asia, xxx, xxxi, 5–8, 30–1, 62, 86, 187
Association of Southeast Asian Nations (ASEAN), xxix, 33, 97–8, 269–71
Australia, 33, 213

Bacchus, James, xiii, 9
Baldwin, Richard, 94, 95
Bangladesh, xxviii–xxix, 150–1, 152, 155
Belgium, xxi
Benicchio, Romain, xiii, 279
Benin, 155
bilateral food aid, 209
bilateral labour agreements, 122
bilateral trade, 32–5, 74–5, 214
Botswana, 64
Braga, Carlos A. Primo, xiii, 127
Brazil, xxix, 52–3, 55–8, 214, 228–9
Burkina Faso, 64, 155
Burma, 214
business
  ethics, 249–52
  global business responsibilities, 235
  innovation, 253–7
  and politics, xviii
  responsible leadership, 178–9, 237–41, 242–4
  responsible sourcing, 259–63
  risk management, 264–7

Cadot, Olivier, 93
Cambodia, xxviii–xxix, 214

293

Cameroon, 96
Canada, 33, 281
capital flows, 264–7
carbon capture, 61–2
carbon emissions, 205, 206
carbon footprint, 191, 192
carbon leakage, 191, 192–4
Carrere, Céline, 96–7
Celli, Umberto, xiii, 55
Central America Free Trade
    Agreement (CAFTA), 86
Chad, 155
Charvériat, Céline, xiii, 279
Chaudhry, Ravi, xiii, 273
Chile, xxix, 32, 52–3, 213
China
    and Africa, 65, 289
    apparel exports, 155
    carbon emissions, 206
    employment, 140–1
    energy consumption, 205
    exchange rate imbalances, 105–8
    export-driven growth, 280
    financial crisis, 203
    food security, 135
    geopolitical cooperation, 228–9,
        230–1
    growth of trade, xxix, 6–7, 13–16
    history of trade, xxvii–xxviii
    instinct for trade, xxx
    and Korea, 33
    poverty in, 280, 290
    preferential trade agreements
        (PTAs), 95, 97–8
    rebalancing trade, 101–4
    and Taiwan, xxxi
    and the United States (USA), xxiv,
        17–20, 150–1, 203
    water scarcity, 211, 214
Clémentel, Etienne, xxi
climate change
    geopolitical cooperation, xxiii,
        227–31
    regional networks, use of, 265–6,
        267
    subsidies, 115–16
    and trade, 191–4
    WTO role, 81–2, 191, 192–4, 198
clothing, 150–1, 152, 155–6
Cold War, xxii, 18, 45–9

Collier, Paul, 186
Colombia, 33, 96, 97
colonial rule, 22–3
Common Market for Eastern and
    Southern Africa (COMESA), 156
competition, 191, 192–4
Congo, Democratic Republic of the,
    281
consensus rule, 85–6
consumption, 195–9
cooperation, international, xxiii,
    227–31, 273–8, 286–7
corporate social responsibility, 240–1,
    249–52
corruption, 56, 239–40, 249–52
cotton, 155, 280
Cudjoe, Franklin, xiii, 153
cumulation, 95–9
currencies, exchange rate regime
    reform, 105–8

Dadush, Uri, xiii, 83
De Melo, Jaime, 93, 96–7
Deere-Birkbeck, Carolyn, xiii, 109
Deng Xiaoping, 248, 269
Deschamps, Jean-Philippe, 255
developing countries
    aid to, 144–8, 151–2, 154, 209,
        277–8
    food security, 135
    global imbalances, 101–4, 105–8,
        125, 273–8
    intellectual property (IP) rules,
        111–13
    remittances from migrants, 120–1
    social justice through trade, 136–7
    subsidies, 115, 116–17
    and the United States (USA),
        149–52
development
    and aid, 144–8, 154
    global cooperation, 273–8
    and globalization, 268–72
    inclusive growth, need for, 289–92
    sustainability, 185–90, 195–9,
        201–6
    and trade, 185–90
Diebold, William, 189
Doha Development Agenda
    agricultural trade, 29–30, 208–9

Alternate Standing Group proposal,
274–6
and climate change, 191, 194, 198
development role, 145, 146–7,
291
human rights, 281, 282–3
liberalization of trade, 130
paralysis of, xxiii, xxix
and security, 178
subsidies, effect of, 114–15, 188–9
WTO reform, 78–82, 84, 85
dollar (US), 105–8
domestic enabling trade index, 276–7
dual-opening development model,
14–15

East African Community (EAC), 96
East Asia, xxxi, 32–5, 136, 150
Easterly, W. R., 224
Economic Community of West
African States (ECOWAS),
154–5, 156
economic growth, 39, 202–3, 224–5,
273–8, 289–92
education, 38–39, 160–1, 168–73,
245–8
Egypt, 64, 152, 214
employment, 122, 138–42, 290–2
energy, 115–16, 201–6
Engammare, Valérie, xiv, 284
Enterprises, *see* business
entrepreneurship education,
168–73
environmental sustainability, 39, 48,
61–2, 115–16, 186–7, 195–9,
201–6, 227–31
equal opportunities, 158–63
Erixon, Fredrik, xiv, 41
ethics, 249–52, 286
Ethiopia, 214
euro, 107–8
Europe, structural reform for growth,
41–4
European Free Trade Association
(EFTA), 33
European Union (EU)
agricultural subsidies, 42, 145
Doha Development Agenda, 189
European Partnership Agreements
(EPA), 154

preferential trade agreements
(PTAs), 93, 95–6
trade agreements, 33, 61, 86
trade barriers, xxii, 144, 283
Evenett, Simon J., xiv, 89
Evian Group, xxxiii
exchange rates, 105–8
exports, 13–16, 28

Fan, Gang, xiv, 13
financial crisis
education of leaders, 245–6
geopolitical cooperation, 228
global effects, xvii–xix, 56, 65–6,
138–39, 203, 289–90
governance of global trade, 73–77,
273
greed, role of, 242
liberalization consequences, 131
non-reciprocal trade, 101–4
risk management, 265, 266
systemic transformations, 3
Fischer, Bill, xiv, 253
fisheries, 115, 196
Florida, Richard, 256
food aid, 209
food security, 134–5, 216–17, 271–2,
281
food subsidies, 42, 115–16, 145, 151,
156, 188–9, 208
foreign direct investment (FDI),
14–15, 36–7, 224
foreign exchange, 14–15, 105–8
France, xxi, xxviii–xxix, 42, 281
free trade agreements (FTAs), 30–1,
32–5
Fung, Victor K., xii

G-5, 228–9
G-8, 84, 207, 228–9
G-20, 76, 103–4, 105–8, 228–9, 274,
290
Gamberoni, Elisa, xiv, 93
Gandhi, Mahatma, 244
Gandhi, Rajiv, 23
Garrett, Michael, xiv, 268
gender equality, 158–63
General Agreement on Tariffs and
Trade (GATT), xxi–xxii, xxix, 5,
102, 144–5, 208, 268–9, 281

General Agreement on Trade in
Services (GATS), 121–2
Generalized System of Preferences
(GSP), 136
geopolitical cooperation, xxiii,
227–31, 273–8, 286–7
Germany, 5–6, 101–4, 225, 249–50
Ghana, 96, 154, 156, 166
global business responsibilities, 235
global governance, 71, 73–7, 178,
273, 290
global imbalances, 101–4, 105–8,
125, 273–8
global recession, xvii–xix, 65–6,
101–4, 138–9, 203, 265
global trade
  and agriculture, 29–30, 31, 207–10
  and climate change, 191–4
  and development, 185–90
  enabling trade index, 276–7
  and energy, 201–6
  financial crisis, xvii–xix
  future of, xxiv–xxv, xxxi–xxxii
  and human rights, 279–83
  infrastructure, xxx–xxxi
  instinct for, xxx
  openness, 29–30, 59, 90–1, 149–52
  patterns since 1919, xxi–xxiv
  and peace, xxvii–xxix, 5–8,
    129–30, 175–9, 186–7
  and poverty, 125, 127–32, 201–2,
    280
  rebalancing, 101–4, 149–52
  vs. regional trade, 156–7, 264–7
  and resource constraints, 195–9,
    201–6
  and security, 175–9
  technology diffusion, 222–4
  volume, 197
  water scarcity, 211–15
globalization, 129–32, 177–9, 183,
  201–2, 264–7, 268–72,
  289–92
goods, trade negotiations in, 79–80
governance, global, 71, 73–7, 178,
  273, 290
government, role of, 177–8, 241,
  246–47
Gresser, Edward, xiv, xxviii, 17
Grevi, Giovanni, 203–4

Growth, *see* development; economic
  growth
Guebuza, Armando, 65–6
Gulf Cooperation Council (GCC), 33,
  61–3, 86

Haiti, 188
Halberstam, David, 243
Halle, Mark, xiv, 114
Hamilton, Stewart, xiv, 249
Hanshaw, Natasha, xiv, 36
Hayek, Friedrich, 286
health and safety standards, 90–1,
  164–7
healthcare, 43, 164–7
Henderson, David, 42
Higgott, Richard, xiv, 73
Hong Kong, xxix
Hull, Cordell, xxviii, xxix
human rights, 279–83

Ikea, 251
inclusive growth, 289–92
India
  and Africa, 65
  and China, 7
  energy consumption, 205, 206
  financial crisis, 203
  food security, 135, 271
  geopolitical cooperation,
    228–9
  and Korea, 33
  pharmaceutical counterfeiting,
    166–7
  poverty in, 15, 290
  and trade, xxx, 7, 22–6
  water scarcity, 211, 213
Indonesia, 139, 269, 270
Inequality, *see* global imbalances
infrastructure, xxx–xxxi, 38, 56,
  60, 66–7, 153–4
innovation, 222–6, 253–7
institutions, 46, 66–7, 153–7, 177–8,
  185–90, 225–6
integration, 24–5, 30–1, 156–7,
  264–7
intellectual property (IP) rules,
  109–13, 145, 164–7, 223, 281,
  283
interlocking crises, 183

International Chamber of Commerce (ICC)
history of, xxi–xxiv
mission of, xvii–xix, xxi, xxiv–xxv, xxvii, xxxii
responsible sourcing, 260–3
role of, 132, 179, 283
International Labour Organization (ILO), 261, 290
International Monetary Fund (IMF), 106, 248
Ismail, Faizel, xiv, 144
Israel, 33, 280
Italy, xxi
Ivory Coast, 96

Jansen, Marion, xiv, 138
Japan
and China, 7
Doha Development Agenda, 189
and Korea, 33
and trade, 5–6, 27–31, 59, 101–4, 144
Voluntary Export Restraints (VERs), xxii
water scarcity, 214
Jefferson, Thomas, 149–52
Jha, Veena, xiv, 133

Kanoria, Raju, xv, 22
Kapuscinski, Ryszard, 230
Kennedy, John F., 152
Kenya, 165–6
Khaldun, Ibn, xxxiii
Khong, Cho-Oon, xv, 227
Kleisterlee, Gerard, 266
Korea, Republic of (South Korea), xxix, 7, 32–5, 96, 97, 214
Krugman, Paul, 42, 186–7
Kuan Yew, Lee, 24
Kyoto Protocol, 227–8, 229

labour markets, 42–3, 119–22
Lamy, Pascal, 76, 153–4
land, access to, 214
Laos, 214
Laperrouza, Marc, xv, 222
Latin America, 51–4, 187, 212
leadership, 237–41, 242–4, 245–8, 253–7, 274

legitimacy, 73–7
Lehmann, Fabrice, xii, 45
Lehmann, Jean-Pierre, xii
liberalization of trade, 5–8, 29–30, 31, 127–32, 207–10
Liberia, 64, 139
Libya, 214, 249
Low, Patrick, 94

Maddison, Angus, 23
Mahbubani, Kishore, xv, 5
Malaysia, 139, 269–70
Mali, 155
Malleret, Thierry, xv, 264
Manchin, Miriam, 97–8
medicines, 164–7, 281, 282–3
Medvedev, Dmitry, 48, 106
Mehta, Pradeep S., xv, 119
Meléndez-Ortiz, Ricardo, xv, 185
Mercosur (Southern Common Market), 33, 54, 57–8
Messerlin, Patrick S, xv, 42, 78
Mexico, xxix, 33, 52–3, 213, 228–9
Middle East, 206, 211, 216–20, 291
Middle East and North Africa region (MENA), 160–1, 216–17
migration, 15, 25, 119–22, 290–1
moral values, 249–52, 286
Morocco, 61
Mozambique, 64, 214
multilateral agreements, 86–7, 121–2
multilateral trade, 32–5, 110, 284–7
multinational corporations (MNCs), 249–50, 253–7
Munshi, Surendra, xv, 242
murky protectionism, 89–92

Nair, Chandran, xv, 195
nations, role of, 241, 273–8, 286–7
natural resource constraints, 195–9, 201–6
negotiation, 79–80
Nestlé, 269–71
New Zealand, 33, 151
Newfarmer, Richard, xv, 93
Niger, 64
Nigeria, 156, 166, 249
Ninkovic, Nina, xv, 216
non-governmental organizations (NGOs), 276–7

non-tariff barriers, 209
non-reciprocal trade, 101–4
North American Free Trade
  Agreement (NAFTA), 86, 93, 150

Obama, Barack, 11–12, 176, 244
Oberhänsli, Herbert, xv, 211
Oman, 213–14
openness, 29–30, 59, 90–1

Pakistan, xxviii–xxix, 152, 213, 214
Palestine, 280
Pan Arab Free Trade Area, 86
Panama, 96, 97
peace
  and environmental sustainability,
    186–7
  and leadership, 243–4
  and trade, xxvii–xxix, 5–8,
    129–30, 175–9, 186–7
  and water management, 219
Peña, Félix, xvi, 51
Peru, 33
Pettis, Michael, 103
pharmaceuticals, 164–7, 281, 282–3
Philippines, 269, 270
politics, role of, xviii, 10–11, 24,
  37–8, 64, 76, 78–9
population, 196
poverty
  and economic growth, 39, 290–2
  financial crisis effects, 289
  geopolitical cooperation, 273–8
  and trade, 125, 127–32, 201–2, 280
  World Trade Organization (WTO)
    role, 275–6
preference schemes, 136–7
preferential trade agreements (PTAs),
  xxiv, 74–5, 80–1, 93–9
privatization, 212–14
protectionism, 89–92

Quadir, Iqbal Z., xvi, 149

recession, xvii–xix, 65–6, 101–4,
  138–9, 203, 265
reciprocal trade, 101–4
regional integration, 24–5, 156–7,
  264–7

regional trade agreements (RTAs), 86
regulation
  as barrier to trade, 38, 90–91
  pharmaceutical products, 164–7
    and quality, 28
  role of, xxix, 76, 79
  safety of products, 19
resource constraints, 195–9,
  201–6
responsible leadership, 178–9,
  237–41, 242–4
responsible sourcing, 259–63
Ricardo, David, 11, 41, 149, 222
Rich, Frank, 242–3
Rijsberman, Frank, 211
risk management, 264–7
Rodrik, Dani, 139, 188
Rongji, Zhu, 6–7
rule of law, 284–7
rules, xxix, 76, 79
rules of origin, 95–9
Russia, 6, 33, 45–9, 206, 214, 228,
  249, 251
Rwanda, 64

Sager, Abdulaziz, xvi, 59
Salim, Nidal, xvi, 216
Sarkozy, Nicolas, 105
Saudi Arabia, 192, 212
security
  and development, 186–7
  food security, 134–5, 216–17,
    271–2, 281
  and trade, 175–9
  and water, 216–20
Sen, Amartya, 145–6, 178
Senegal, 64
service sector, 79–80, 121–2
Siemens, 249–50
Sierra Leone, 64, 281
Simons, Bright B., xvi, 164
Singapore, 33, 269, 270
Singh, Manmohan, 24
Single Undertaking principle, 79,
  80–1
Smith, Adam, 11, 41, 127, 149
social justice, 133–7
social protection, 138–42
Soko, Mills, xvi, 64

Solow, Robert, 224–5
South Africa, 33, 65, 228–9
South Asia, xxx, xxxi
South Asia Free Trade Agreement
    (SAFTA), 86
South Korea, xxix, 7, 32–5, 96, 97,
    214
Spain, 211, 225
Special and Differential Treatment
    (S&D), 144–5
standards, 90–1, 164–7, 209, 261–2
state, role of the, 177–8, 241, 246–7
Stokes, Bruce, xvi, 101
structural change, 36–40, 41–4
Subacchi, Paola, xvi, 105
subsidies
    agriculture, 42, 115–16, 145, 151,
        156, 188–9, 208
    effects of, 114–17, 209, 280
Sudan, 59
suppliers, relationships with, 259–63
sustainable development, 185–90,
    195–9, 201–6
Sutherland, Peter D., xii, xvii
Sweden, 187
Switzerland, 107, 213–14
systemic transformations, 3

Taiwan, xxix, xxxi
Tanaka, Nobuo, 205
Tanzania, 64, 65, 165–6
tariffs, 135–6, 208–9
technology, 139–40, 205, 222–6
Thailand, 139, 269, 270
Thucydides, 18
Tia-Sugri, Alfred, 156
Tocqueville, Alexis de, 22
Trade, *see* global trade
Trade-Related Aspects of Intellectual
    Property Rights (TRIPS), 110,
    112, 145, 165, 223, 281
Trade-Related Investment Measures
    (TRIMs), 144–5
transparency, 90–1
Trichet, Jean-Claude, 102
Turkey, xxix, 33

Uganda, 65, 165–6, 214
United Arab Emirates (UAE), 59

United Kingdom (UK), xxi,
    xxviii–xxix, 160, 225
United Nations (UN), 210, 261
United States (USA)
    agricultural subsidies, 145, 151
    and China, xxiv, 17–20, 150–1, 203
    Doha Development Agenda, 189
    exchange rate imbalances, 105–8
    financial crisis, 139, 289–90
    geopolitical cooperation, 228
    International Chamber of
        Commerce (ICC), xxi
    openness to trade, 59, 149–52
    politics, and trade negotiations, 78
    rebalancing trade, 101–4
    Siemens bribery case, 249–50
    subsidies, 280
    sustainable development, 205, 206
    tariffs, xxviii–xxix
    technology transfer, 225
    trade agreements, 33, 61, 95,
        96–97, 155
    trade barriers, xxii, 144, 283
    trade policy, 9–12
    water scarcity, 211, 213
    women as business leaders,
        160
Universal Declaration of Human
    Rights, 279
Urata, Shujiro, xvi, 27
Uruguay, 52–53
Uruguay Round, 144–5, 188, 208

Van de Putte, Alexander, xvi, 201
Vietnam, xxxi, 36–40, 188
virtual water, 218

Wassell, Martin, xvi, 259
water, 81–82, 115–16, 192, 211–15,
    216–20
Weber, Max, 242
Weinstein, Lori, 250
Welch, Jack, 238
Wells, John, xvi, 237
Wilson, Karen, xvi, 168
women, 158–63
World Intellectual Property
    Organization (WIPO), 110, 112
world trade, *see* global trade

World Trade Organization (WTO)
  agricultural productivity, 212
  Aid for Trade, 146–8, 277–8
  Alternate Standing Group proposal,
    274–6
  Brazil's role, 56, 57
  China's accession, 6–7
  and climate change, 81–2, 191,
    192–4, 198
  development role, 144–8, 188,
    273–4
  governance of global trade, xxii,
    71, 73–7, 248
  human rights, 279, 280, 281
  intellectual property (IP) rules, 110,
    112
  and Latin America, 54
  migration agreements, 121–2
  problems of, xxii–xxiv, xxv
  reform of, 78–82, 83–8
  resource constraints and trade, 198
  rule of law, 284–7
  and Russia, 6, 47–8
  subsidies, 116
  transparency, promotion of,
    90–1
  Vietnam's accession, 36, 37
World War II, xxi

Xiaochuan, Zhou, 106, 108

Young, Soogil, xvi, 32